Bartholomew City Guides

York

D1227087

*The Publishers and Authors gratefully acknowledge a grant
towards the publication costs of this book made by*
THE SHELDON MEMORIAL TRUST

Bartholomew City Guides

York

JOHN HUTCHINSON
& D.M. PALLISER

Photographs by A.F. Kersting, F.R.P.S.

John Bartholomew & Son Limited
Edinburgh

British Library Cataloguing in Publication Data

Hutchinson, John
  York. – (Bartholomew city guides).
  1. York, Eng. – Description – Guide-books
  I. Title   II. Palliser, David Michael
  914.28′43′04857   DA690.Y6

First published in Great Britain 1980 by
JOHN BARTHOLOMEW & SON LIMITED
12 Duncan Street, Edinburgh EH9 1TA
© John Hutchinson and D.M. Palliser, 1980
All maps © Bartholomew, 1980

ISBN 0 7028 8060 4 (cased)
ISBN 0 7028 8050 7 (paperback)

Book and jacket design: Frances Dobson
Maps prepared by Kirkham Studios and Pica Design
9/11pt Linotron Baskerville
Printed in Great Britain:

To the Staff of
York Minster Library

Contents

Contents

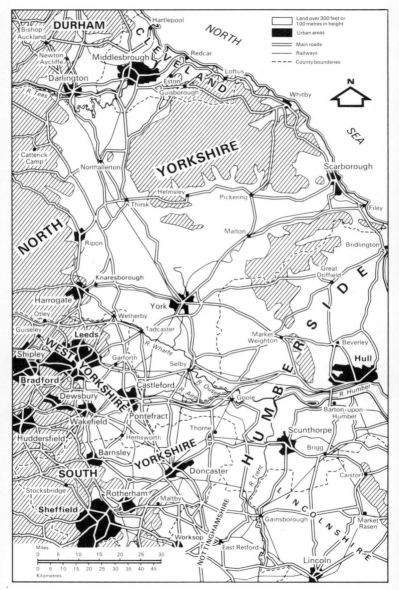

Preface

York is embarrassingly well provided with works on its history and architecture, but the great classics are almost unobtainable, and only Pevsner, invaluable for the surrounding countryside, fills the gap for the general visitor between the sensible *Official Guide* and such monumental and inconvenient works as the *Victoria County History of York* and Royal Commission volumes. We hope that this book may do something to remedy this. It has been planned with both the inquisitive resident and the visitor in mind. David Palliser wrote the Historical Introduction, John Hutchinson the Walks, both reading and commenting voluminously on the other's contributions.

The prospect of encompassing the city's history, architecture, and art in one convenient volume was daunting, and selection has necessarily been very personal. Residents especially may be aggravated by our omissions and puzzled by our conclusions. However, we hope it may prove to be a sufficiently thorough, detailed, and catholic guidebook for most tastes. We shall be pleased to be informed of the doubtless numerous omissions and inaccuracies.

☆

We should like to acknowledge the assistance we have received from many sources in writing this book.

The Yorkshire Architectural and York Archaeological Society has been generous in providing the means for some extra illustrations.

David Black and the late J.E. Williams of the Royal Commission on Historical Monuments have been most generous in allowing access to information so far unpublished. Bernard Barr at the Minster Library and Maurice Smith at the Reference Library have patiently answered niggling questions. Mr Harry Galpin kindly allowed access to his records in the City Engineer's and Surveyor's Office. Dr Eric Gee and Dr John Harvey have been sources of encouragement and recondite information over many years. The many friends who have helped with particular points will forgive us if we mention David O'Connor, J.T. Lang, Elizabeth Hartley, Barrie Dobson, Richard Hall, John Ingamells, and Peter Brears. Many citizens, led by the Archbishop and the Lord Mayor, have been kind enough to let us visit their houses, to the majority of which there is no public access but whose private treasures are an essential part of the city.

Finally, Brian Nelson, Alan Bottomley, Kenneth and Barbara Hutton, Christopher Wilson, and John McMullen have read all or part of the manuscript and corrected numerous points of history and punctuation, and Shirley Swann and Christine Robinson have done wonders of elucidation with our handwriting.

Christopher Wheeler, of John Bartholomew and Son, has edited the book with skill and exemplary patience. Most of the photographs that illustrate it have been taken by Mr A.F. Kersting, F.R.P.S., who coped calmly with weather, crowds, and the impossible demands of one of the authors.

John Hutchinson
David Palliser
May 1979

Editorial Note

References in the text to the book's black-and-white photographs, which form a section between pages 148 and 149 are given as numbers within square brackets.

The City and its Origins

York lies in a flat, fertile, unromantic countryside, from which the historic core is thickly insulated by suburbs of many times its own area. Along the riverside narrow rural fingers reach into the city centre, and the Rivers Ouse and Foss were essential to the origin of the city, which grew up at their junction. The Vale of York is an outlier of the Trent–Humber basin, thrust northwards between the Pennines, the North York Moors, and the much gentler Wolds (Fig. 1). The Pennines are mountains of Carboniferous limestone, coal measures, and Millstone Grit, the Moors a plateau of oolitic limestone, and the Wolds hills of Cretaceous chalk. On the E fringe of the Vale is a low range of Jurassic limestone and sandstone hills, while the W fringe is a belt of magnesian limestone. The magnesian stone recurs constantly in the city's history as the best local building stone: pale and soft when quarried, hardening on exposure to an attractive creamy or yellowy white. The Vale itself is of New Red Sandstone, overlaid in the Ice Ages by a thick blanket of glacial clays and gravels. It was until medieval times heavily wooded, and provided plentiful supplies of building timber.

This geological setting accounts for the physical fabric of the city. Major Roman and medieval buildings were of magnesian limestone, quarried near Tadcaster and then floated to York along the Wharfe and Ouse. The Romans also used gritstone, which survives re-used but unmistakable in many medieval buildings. Imported stone was, of course, costly, so lesser buildings were of beaten earth, timber, or brick baked from the glacial clays; from the late 17th century brick predominated. The historic city is therefore built of local materials. Georgian and Victorian brick is interspersed with earlier timber-framing, dotted with limestone towers, ringed by limestone walls, and dominated by the massive bulk of the limestone Minster.

There is a narrow gap between Wolds and Moors, and a broader one (the Vale of Mowbray) between Moors and Pennines, but only to the s is the Vale really open. Consequently almost the entire Yorkshire river-system drains E, S, and w into the Vale, and the Ouse, flowing through York, collects the waters from a vast catchment area. Water transport was of crucial importance until the 19th century, and the Vale had in one direction access to the Pennines, on the other to the sea via the Humber. Before 1757 the Ouse was tidal to Nether Poppleton, four miles upstream from York, and small boats plied as far as Boroughbridge. Furthermore, the main land communications between southern England and Scotland have always lain along the Pennine edge of the Vales of York and Mowbray (the Great North Road, the London to Edinburgh railway, and now the M1), which provides an easier corridor than the narrower, hillier Lancashire route.

The Vale has thus always been a useful district from which to dominate the North. York has, however, never had an ideally central site within the Vale, since though it commands the river system it has stood apart from the main road system since Roman times (Fig. 1). The city lay between two long-distance Roman routes and was served only by transverse linking roads. The central Vale was low-lying, boggy in parts, heavily wooded in others, and liable to flood, legacies of the Ice Ages, which had carpeted the Vale with ill-drained clays. However, they had also provided natural causeways in the form of two E–W moraines (ridges of debris deposited by the glaciers as they melted), one crossing the Ouse through York, and the other a little further s, near Escrick. The Romans used the N moraine, along the ridge between Tadcaster and York, as their main approach to the city, and their line is still largely followed by the A64. The natural crossing-point was therefore just s of the Ouse–Foss confluence, but the Romans diverged from this natural route to plant their city in the more easily defended angle between the two rivers, thus establishing permanently the site of

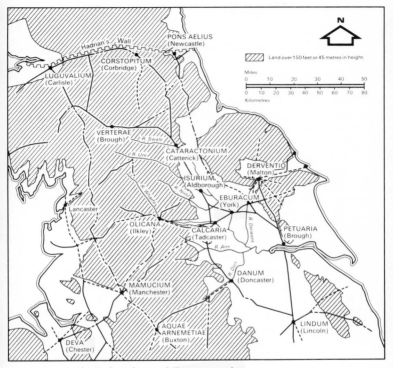

Fig. 1: Physical setting and Roman roads

York's historic core. This decision proved crucial to York's aesthetic impact as well as its historical development, since it was set on level ground only just above the river-level. Even its major monuments lack the resonance that a slight hill could have given them, as at Ely. Moreover, lying below the moraine, the city has almost no impact from the level countryside to S and E. Only from the N does the Minster really dominate the surrounding countryside. If the Romans had fortified the moraine, the city could have been one of the sights of Europe.

The moraine has also left the city subject to flooding. Thaws and thunderstorms on the Pennines can cause a rapid rise in the level of the Ouse, which is unable to drain quickly enough through the narrow gap at York. Some of the floodwater spills harmlessly on to the natural 'washland' of Clifton Ings, but a moderate or severe flood still invades the low-lying streets. Flooding may have destroyed Roman York, and it was melting Pennine snow that destroyed the only bridge over the Ouse in 1565 and brought chaos to the city. Citizens old enough to remember the winter of 1947 have vivid recollections of York as a series of islands, with the Ouse 16 ft 6 in. above normal.

In Stone Age and Bronze Age times the Vale was apparently unattractive to man, who preferred the higher ground to E and W. Much of the area was heavily wooded and boggy, and a vivid impression of the prevailing conditions can be glimpsed at Askham Bog, just outside the city boundary, where the Yorkshire Naturalists' Trust has preserved a rare fragment of the prehistoric landscape. Recent archaeological work, however, has suggested that by the later Iron Age – the last two centuries B.C. – the Vale was more heavily settled by man than was once thought. The Brigantes, a powerful confederation of Celtic tribes, occupied the region, and one of their central strongholds was at Aldborough, upriver from York.

As to the origins of York itself, however, no clear answer has yet emerged, though a 1,900th anniversary was confidently celebrated by the Corporation in 1971. It is not certain whether 71 was the year the Romans established their first fort, and still less certain whether they found an existing Iron Age settlement. Early historians made much of a pre-Roman origin for York, a tradition they took from Geoffrey of Monmouth's *History of the Kings of Britain*, written *c.* 1136. Geoffrey told of a British King Ebraucus, who founded York about the time that David reigned in Jerusalem, and called it Kaerebrauc after himself. There is, however, no evidence that this is any more than a piece of medieval romance to explain York's name, until recently the only evidence for a pre-Roman origin. The Roman invaders called it *Eboracum* or *Eburacum*, apparently an adaptation of a Celtic name meaning either 'the place of yew trees' or 'the estate of Eburos', a masculine personal name that occurs in Gaul at the same time. Either way, the implication is that a settlement with a name already existed when the Romans arrived, and recent archaeological research is bearing it out. It seems probable that there was an Iron Age settlement at York in the years following the Roman invasion of Kent in A.D. 43, perhaps near the present railway station, substantial enough to be trading with the Roman-occupied areas further south.* During that generation the Roman border lay along the Trent and Humber, and the invaders had no need to stretch their resources by trying to conquer the Brigantes, who under Queen Cartimandua formed a friendly client-state.

Having said that, York as an *urban* settlement owes its creation to the Romans. It was they who introduced Greco-Roman ideas of town life to Britain; Iron Age Britons had not produced anything one could firmly call a town. The Brigantes deposed Cartimandua and made her anti-Roman husband King in her place, and in A.D. 71 the Roman Ninth Legion advanced from Lincoln to invade Brigantia. The campaign is described very briefly by Tacitus, who does not mention York, but it seems probable that the Roman commander, Q. Petilius Cerialis, picked on the site of York with a strategist's eye for a good military strongpoint; and that soon afterwards York became the legion's new head-quarters. The Romans added to the natural defensive position of York by throwing up an earth-and-timber fortress between Ouse and Foss, and they added to its accessibility by building new metalled roads linking the fortress to the existing main roads to E and W. By this choice of site, as Sir Ian Richmond remarked, 'Roman initiative once and for all determined the position of the Northern Command in England'.

At some date between 108 and 122, for reasons not clear, the Ninth Legion (Legio IX Hispana) was replaced at York

* H.G. Ramm, 'The origins of York', *Yorkshire Philosophical Society Annual Report* for 1976 (1977), pp. 59–63.

by the Sixth (Legio VI Victrix). Historians and novelists have speculated that the Ninth was annihilated in battle, or defeated with disgrace and disbanded by the Emperor Hadrian (117–38). New evidence, however, suggests that it was transferred overseas soon after Hadrian brought the Sixth Legion to Britain, moving first to Nijmegen and then to Palestine, finally perhaps being destroyed by the Parthians in 161.* Under both legions the York fortress was developed in standard Roman military fashion, leaving its mark on the topography of the city to the present day, to the confusion of visitors, for the fortress was aligned at 45° to the compass points, so that its plan, which survives largely unaltered at the city's core, does not relate at all to the rigidly E–W alignment of the Minster (Fig. 2).

The camp had four gates giving access to the four main roads, a pattern little changed over 1,900 years: the SW and NW gates led to access roads to the Great North Road (the modern A64 and A19), the NE gate to Malton and the E coast (A64), and the SE gate to the Humber crossing at Brough (A1079). Its original earth-and-timber defences were replaced in stone soon after A.D. 100, a date confirmed by the magnificent inscription found under King's Square, showing that the fortress's SE gate was built by the Ninth Legion in the year 107–8. The defences were rebuilt about A.D. 200, perhaps after a sack by rebellious natives, and again about 300 after another rebellion. The fortress walls enclosed 50 acres and housed a legion of some 6,000 soldiers. The SW and SE walls have long vanished, but most of the NE and NW walls still survive above ground or buried within the mound of the medieval city walls. Bootham Bar stands exactly on the site of its Roman predecessor, the gate towards Hadrian's Wall and the North, and Petergate still follows approximately the main road of the fortress (*via principalis*) from Bootham Bar to King's Square. The other main road (*via praetoria*) ran from the SW gateway under St Helen's Square, exactly on the line of the modern Stonegate. Where the two roads met, at Minster Gates, was the entrance to the *principia*

* E.B. Birley, 'The Fate of the Ninth Legion', in *Soldier and Civilian in Roman Yorkshire*, ed. R.M. Butler (1971), pp. 71–80.

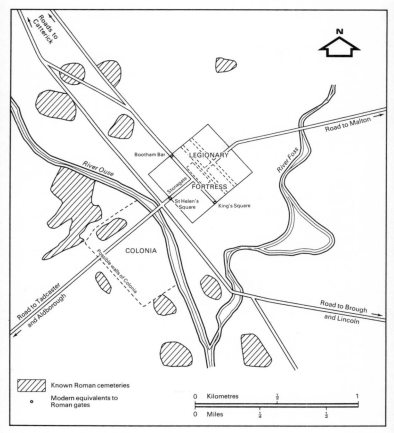

Fig. 2: Roman York

or headquarters building, roughly on the site of the Minster. Part of it, excavated during the strengthening of the Minster foundations in 1967–72, can be seen *in situ* in the Undercroft Museum. Most of the fortress was naturally occupied by barracks; the traders who served the legionaries lived in straggling suburbs outside its walls. Across the Ouse,

7

however, there grew up gradually a civilian town (*colonia*), probably also walled, which occupied roughly the area within the city walls on both sides of Micklegate. Indeed there are reasons for thinking that the Micklegate city walls, like those between Museum Gardens and Jewbury, stand on Roman foundations.

The Roman period is fundamental to an understanding of York. It was the Romans who chose its site for a major settlement, and they who gave the city centre much of its present shape. They ruled York for a period equivalent to that from the battle of Marston Moor (1644) to the present, and gave it a prominent place in world history. The Emperor Severus designated it the capital of Lower Britain when he divided the province of Britain in two, and made York the home of the imperial court for the last three years of his life, dying there in 211. A century later Constantius I also died at York, and his son Constantine I the Great (306–37) was almost certainly proclaimed Emperor by the army there. It was the start of a momentous reign that reunited a divided empire, made Christianity its official religion, and moved the imperial capital from Rome to Constantinople ('city of Constantine'). Appropriately, when Constantine summoned a council of western bishops to Arles in 314, one of the three British representatives was a bishop of York. It is little wonder that medieval Yorkers had a special devotion to St Helen (Constantine's mother, and the traditional discoverer of the True Cross), creating the patriotic myth that she was a Briton and that Constantine had been *born* in York.

In another sense, however, the Roman period is of less significance for a modern visitor than almost any later age. Very little remains above ground of Roman construction save for the Multangular Tower (Walk 2) [5] and some sections of fortress wall (Walk 8). That is scarcely surprising after so long a lapse of time; but even the street-plan reflects little of its Roman origins except in Petergate, Stonegate, and Chapter House Street. Roman York has to be reconstructed mainly by archaeology, and the superb quality of the Roman collections in the Yorkshire Museum confirms the city's Roman importance. However, the heart of medieval and modern York is built on top of Roman York, so preventing systematic excavation of large central areas, and we know surprisingly little about the layout of either the fortress or the *colonia.* The fortress, in particular, is almost a closed book except for its defences. The only large structures excavated and accessible to visitors have been a bath house under the Roman Bath Inn (Walk 4), parts of the *principia* beneath the Minster, and a large sewer system beneath Swinegate. The *colonia* is a little less of a blank, for public baths are known to have stood beneath the old railway station on Toft Green, and a large colonnaded building was found beneath the Co-operative Society's buildings in George Hudson Street. Most major buildings of Roman York – imperial palace, amphitheatre, forum, temples – have not even been located, still less excavated. It has recently been suggested that large-scale flooding devastated York some time after the end of the Roman period, perhaps *c.* 550, and thus obliterated much of the Roman street-pattern and destroyed or damaged many buildings. However, no archaeological evidence has yet been found to corroborate the idea.

Angles and Vikings
c. 400–1066

The end of Roman Britain used to be treated as a sudden catastrophe. The legions left to defend Rome, allowing pagan and illiterate barbarians from across the North Sea to massacre, drive out, or enslave the leaderless natives, and let roads, towns, and all vestiges of civilization go to ruin. Evidence from York and many other places now shows that this picture is a distortion of the truth. Romans and Celts were of mixed culture and stock by the 5th century and are best described as Romano-Britons; and cremation urns from local cemeteries (now in the Yorkshire Museum) suggest that Germanic troops were already in the York area by 400, acting as 'federates' or barbarian allies of the Romans. In 407 the last imperial soldiers left Britain, and there are hints that in 410 the Romano-Britons – attacked by invaders from Scotland and the Continent, and receiving no further help from Rome – made what we might now call a unilateral declaration of independence, and started to organize their own defence.

That defence was more successful than has usually been thought. Though the Germanic invaders ('Anglo-Saxons') finally conquered what is now England and gave their name to it, the process was a long one, long enough for the two peoples to mingle and for the invaders to become literate and Christian. A series of war-leaders and local kings, of whom the shadowy Arthur became the most famous, held back the invaders here and there for long periods. Geoffrey of Monmouth picked up a tradition that Arthur's uncle recaptured York from the Saxon invaders and installed St Samson as Archbishop, but that the Saxons captured it again and were later driven out by Arthur himself. There may be shreds of truth behind these romances, and it is possible that the rare dedication of St Sampson for one of York's churches may refer to the same man. Certainly there are Welsh traditions that York survived as a functioning Celtic city in the 5th century, under the name Cair Ebrauc. Eventually the Britons in the North were conquered piecemeal after they had been weakened by internal divisions and perhaps by a severe plague in 549. Two petty tribal states of invaders on the east coast joined forces to create the kingdom of Northumbria, and their forces captured York some time in the late 6th century. Another early tradition records that Peredur, the last king of York (the original Sir Percival of Arthurian romance), was killed in battle about 580. Even then a British kingdom of Elmet survived within sight of York for another generation. Its name survives in Sherburn-in-Elmet and Barwick-in-Elmet to indicate how near the independent Britons still were; and the Anglian Tower behind the City Library may well represent a patching-up of York's walls by the invaders to guard themselves against a British reconquest. Eventually the conquered Britons were assimilated by the Angles; but two York districts (Jubbergate and Navigation Road) retained separate groups of natives long enough to be called Bretgate ('street of the Britons') by the invading Vikings three centuries later.

Northumbria was an independent kingdom from *c.* 592 to 876. At its peak it included all of England north of the Humber as well as much of lowland Scotland, and insofar as it had a 'capital' in the modern sense, that capital was York. Its greatest warrior kings – Edwin (616–32), Oswald (633–41), Oswiu (641–70) – were also recognized as over-lords of the rest of England, or 'Southumbria' as northern writers occasionally called it. Had their successors been able to maintain and build on their supremacy, Northumbria might have become the kernel of a united England, with York the capital of a state stretching from the Forth to the English Channel. As it was, supremacy passed to the kings of Mercia (the modern Midlands) and later to Wessex, and it was the kings of Wessex who united 'England' in the 10th century.

King Edwin is best remembered for his conversion to

Christianity, which had been re-introduced to southern England by a papal mission in 597. In 625 he married a Christian princess from Kent who brought with her a bishop called Paulinus. Paulinus became first bishop of York and converted Edwin, baptizing him on Easter Day 627 in a timber church specially built for the occasion. So began the first cathedral of St Peter at York, or the Minster as it has always been known, from the Saxon word for a community of clergy or monks. Traditionally the Saxon Minsters were thought to lie beneath the crypt of the present Minster; but the results of the 1967–72 excavations were quite unexpected. No trace was found of any pre-Norman cathedral, but instead the massive buildings of the Roman *principia* were found to have remained in use until about the 9th century. Obviously the Saxon Minster could not have stood on the traditional position unless it had been simply adapted out of rooms in the *principia*, which may have been used by Edwin as his palace. This puzzle leads to another – not only where was the Saxon Minster, but where was the Saxon city? The capital of Northumbria is known to have been important from literary sources, including Bede (*c.* 730) and Alcuin (*c.* 780). It had a cathedral, an important school, and a great deal of trade, and it kept up the Roman fortress defences: the Anglian Tower is proof of that. Yet the archaeological evidence does not bear this out at all, and Mr P.V. Addyman has recently commented that 'all the middle Saxon pottery from York could readily be accommodated in one bag'. This becomes even more puzzling when one considers the quantity of 8th-century pottery recently excavated at Wharram Percy near Malton. Only more archaeological investigation can provide a full answer; but possibly the Roman fortress was kept up purely as a royal fortified enclosure, while ordinary folk lived outside, beyond the areas still subject to river flooding.

Many of his subjects took Edwin's conversion to Christianity as an example. Bede tells us that his chief priest was one of the first converts, arguing that though second to none in his devotion to the gods, he had not prospered, and that if the new religion were 'better and more efficacious' it should be adopted. All the nobles and many commoners are said to have been christened with Edwin, others in mass baptisms shortly afterwards. Although Paulinus fled from York during a pagan reaction after Edwin's death, his work was continued by James the Deacon, and worship was maintained. Since 664 there has always been a bishop in York, and from 735 an archbishop, the present Archbishop being 93rd in direct line from Paulinus. So York became the mother-church of all Northern England from the 8th century to the 16th, and so it still remains for members of the Church of England. Pope Gregory's original scheme of 604 allowed for two equal and independent archbishops at London and York. In the event the sees were established at Canterbury and York, with Canterbury having much the larger territory, striving to make York subordinate. This led to undignified disputes, the worst occurring at a synod in 1175. Archbishop Richard of Canterbury took the place of honour on the right hand of the papal legate, and Roger of York, rather than lose face, sat down in his lap, and was pulled off and beaten by Canterbury retainers. Eventually, after centuries of squabbles, Archbishop John de Thoresby of York made a very English compromise, giving York effective independence but allowing a meaningless precedence to Canterbury: the Southern archbishop was designated Primate of All England and his Northern colleague Primate of England.

The conversion of Northumbria in the 7th century reintroduced learning as well as Christianity, and St Peter's School at York even claims its foundation from 627, on the ground that James the Deacon introduced Roman church music to the North, therefore that a song school existed from his arrival, and therefore a grammar school also. That goes far beyond the evidence, but there is no doubt that the Church fostered learning to a point where Northumbria – on the edge of the Roman Christian world – became one of the intellectual centres of Europe. The double monastery of Monkwearmouth and Jarrow produced in Bede (d. 735) one of the greatest European scholars of the entire Middle Ages, while York itself was the early home if not the birthplace of Alcuin (d. 804), who introduced the Northumbrian scholarship he had learned at York to the court of Charlemagne, the greatest ruler in western Europe. The 'Northumbrian renaissance' flickered out under Viking attacks while Alcuin was on the Continent, but he had ensured its enduring influence in what is now France, Belgium, and Germany. European civilization owes him an immense debt, and it is entirely appropriate that one of the colleges of the new University has been named in his honour. He retained an exile's affection for the city that 'cherished the tender years of my infancy', and one of his elegant Latin poems provides the earliest surviving description of York:

> It was a Roman army built it first,
> High-walled and towered . . .
> To be a merchant-town of land and sea . . .
> A haven for the ships from distant ports
> Across the ocean, where the sailor hastes
> To cast his rope ashore and stay to rest.
> The city is watered by the fish-rich Ouse
> Which flows past flowery plains on every side;
> And hills and forests beautify the earth
> And make a lovely dwelling-place, whose health
> And richness soon will fill it full of men.*

One should be grateful to have any description of an 8th-century town, but it hardly presents a detailed picture. The only firm facts it establishes are the already important overseas trade by way of the Ouse, and the survival into Alcuin's own time of Roman stone buildings. Alcuin's citizens, like the men of medieval Rome, lived among ruins and patched-up buildings. It is frustrating, but scarcely surprising, that nothing remains above ground of the buildings of his day; most would have been built of timber, vulnerable to accidental fires as well as to later sackings. There are terse records of major fires in 741 and 764, and the city was fought over and sacked in 866–7 and again in 1069.

The Roman fortress walls remained in use as defences, but

---

* Reprinted from Stephen Allott's translation in his *Alcuin of York, c. 732 to 804 A.D. – his Life and Letters* (Ebor Press, 1974), by kind permission of Mr Allott and William Sessions Ltd, The Ebor Press, York.

otherwise the whole alignment of York had changed. The severe flooding of the 6th century had, it is suggested, not only submerged much of the city, but had also broken down the Roman bridge, which had spanned the Ouse opposite the present Guildhall. In its place, the Angles used a ford on the site of the present Ouse Bridge, thus distorting the Roman street-pattern. The Roman road from Tadcaster, which had run to the river roughly on the line of Toft Green, was diverted to the ford, producing the rightward curve of Micklegate as a happy accident. Once over the ford, the new route bypassed the old fortress, continuing on the line Ousegate–Pavement–St Saviourgate–Peaseholm Green. This became and remained until recently the main SW–NE route through York, though in the other direction Petergate remained the NW–SE route. To link the new road with the old fortress, the Roman road running in front of the fortress developed into Coney Street ('King's Street'), one of the very few city routes to have retained the Anglo-Saxon 'street' rather than the Danish 'gate'. As to the buildings of Anglian York, apart from the Minster and the fortifications, nothing whatever is known. Alcuin mentions a second major church of the Holy Wisdom, otherwise totally unrecorded; and archaeology will probably establish eventually that some of the many medieval churches began life in Anglian times. A strong candidate would be St Michael-le-Belfrey, only a stone's throw from the Minster but aligned NW–SE on the Roman street pattern. There are also hints of very early churches on Toft Green and beneath Parliament Street; the latter may have been dedicated to St Swithin, a favourite Saxon saint. Anglian York may have formed a twin town on both banks of the Ouse much like Buda and Pest in Hungary. The names Micklegate, Littlegate, and North Street – and the existence of one, or two, early St Mary churches on Bishophill – make most sense if one envisages a town on the right bank entirely separated from the fortress area by the wide, floodable, and unbridged river. The usual Anglo-Saxon name for York was Eferwic or Eoforwic. This has been derived from a corruption of the Roman name, or from the Saxon word for 'boar', but it may well mean the commercial or harbour settlement (*wic*) on the River Ure (Ouse), and may even be a double name for two settlements on opposite banks.

Alcuin's York, though intellectually important, was a political backwater. Eighth-century Northumbria was a minor state with an uncertain royal succession, subject to assassinations and coups d'état. England south of the Humber was dominated by the powerful kings of Mercia, who ignored Northumbria; while to the north expansion had been checked at the battle of Nechtansmere (685), when King Ecgfrith had died fighting the Picts and the English retreated to the Firth of Forth. York was still the capital of a substantial kingdom, covering roughly the middle third of Britain, but it was not one that could offer serious resistance to a determined invader. At that time Scandinavian adventurers, the so-called Danes, Northmen, or Vikings, were spreading by sea and river all over Europe from Paris to Novgorod; and the declining Northumbria, easily reached over the North Sea, made a soft target. In 793 the Northmen sacked Lindisfarne – the island monastery, which had been a Christian cathedral before York – a disaster said to have been signalled by a miraculous shower of blood on York Minster. Alcuin saw the sack as the beginning of God's judgements about to fall on his native country because of the violence and sinfulness of the Northumbrians and their kings. Then there was a pause in the decline; the Viking raids ceased or were checked, largely through the power of Charlemagne and his son, who thus repaid (consciously or unconsciously) some of their debt to the School of York. From 796 to 840 Northumbria again enjoyed a strong and stable monarchy, and the scholars at York apparently continued their work in peace. But in the middle of the century the throne once more became unstable, just as Viking raiding was renewed. In 844 one of the kings was killed by a heathen army, and in 865 all the English kingdoms were threatened by a great Danish host under Ivar the Boneless and his brother, which landed prepared to settle and conquer. Northumbria was in the grip of civil war when on 1 November 866 the invaders captured York, and on 21 March 867 they defeated and killed the two rival kings who had joined forces to try to retake the city. Accounts of the battle show that the Roman fortress walls were still standing and made good defences, but that there were breaches through which a determined enemy could penetrate. Scandinavian sagas made the struggle for York an affair of honour; Ivar and his brother attacked Northumbria because King Aella had captured their father and thrown him into a pit of snakes in York. The story is colourful fiction, for Aella had only seized the throne just before the brothers' army arrived, and he could not have been their father's murderer. Probably the Danes simply took advantage of a civil war to seize a prosperous kingdom ripe for plunder and conquest.

Did the Scandinavian conquest involve a genuine mass migration of settlers? Or was it only a political change, with a small group of warrior nobles seizing power and land, as happened at the Norman Conquest? The Anglo-Saxon Chronicle records that in 875–6 Halfdan 'shared out the lands of Northumbria', and that his men turned to settlement and agriculture instead of plunder. Halfdan founded a Danish kingdom with its capital at York; so that when the city was captured in 919 by a Norse Viking from Ireland, that meant only a change of masters. Under Danish and Norse rulers the Scandinavian kingdom of York lasted, with some interruptions, for nearly 80 years. Little is known of its kings, but their names can be recovered from the numerous coins that they struck, proof that prosperity and stability had returned after the initial shock of the conquest. Finally in 954, King Edred of Wessex drove out Eric Bloodaxe, the last Viking ruler of York, and united Northumbria and South-umbria in a single realm.

The period of Scandinavian rule, though short, was crucial to the development of York. By 954 the Northum-brians were so intermixed with the Danish invaders that many had adopted their language, laws, and customs – a strong argument for a mass settlement – and until the Norman Conquest the North continued to be ruled by earls best described as Anglo-Scandinavians, under Danish law respected by the distant kings at Winchester. The greatest of the earls – immortalized by Shakespeare – was Siward, who defended the North against the Scots, then invaded Scotland and defeated King Macbeth (1054), and was buried in the church of St Olaf that he had founded at York (1055). There is reason to believe that the palace of the earls stood in what are now the Museum Gardens, so that the church would have acted as the palace chapel. St Olaf was the first Christian king of Norway, and his church is another reminder of the close contacts between York and Scandinavia. It is anachronistic to think of 'English' people in the 10th and 11th centuries; they were a mixture of different ethnic backgrounds, and many Northerners, including some Archbishops of York, plainly preferred rule by men of Scandinavian descent to rule from Winchester. This became clear in the 1060s, when the city was at the heart of a confused international power struggle. The local Danes and English broke into York in 1065, driving out Siward's successor, the half-Danish Earl Tostig, who had been imposed by the king in the south, and hunting down his supporters. Tostig went into exile, and joined forces with the King of Norway. They invaded Northumbria, where he still enjoyed some support, sailing up the Ouse in a large flotilla of boats as far as Riccall. They disembarked and marched on York, defeating with great slaughter a Northumbrian army at Fulford just outside the city (20 September 1066). King Harold II, Tostig's brother, rushed to the North, passed through the city, and in turn defeated the invaders at Stamford Bridge, where both Tostig and the Norwegian king fell in battle (25 September). Almost at once, however, Harold learned at York that Duke William of Normandy (another ruler of Scandinavian descent) had landed in Sussex to claim the English Crown. He returned rapidly south to meet the new threat, only to be defeated and killed near Hastings (14 October).

For exactly two centuries (866–1066) York was under Scandinavian or Anglo-Scandinavian rule. Its old names of *Caer Ebrauc* and *Eoforwic* gave place to the Danish *Jorvik*, which may mean 'the trading port on the Ure'. Certainly the city was a great river port on the network of Viking trading routes, which stretched from Dublin to Novgorod. A monk, writing about the year 1000, called York a city 'crammed with the merchandise . . . of traders who come from all parts, but especially Danes'. As if to prove his point, three-quarters of the English coins minted before 975 and found in Scandinavia were minted at York or Chester. The Viking rulers of York issued large quantities of coin to lubricate trade, and by the early 10th century there were also York coins (the 'St Peter' issues) without any kings' names, which may even have been issued by the citizens themselves. There was also a thriving trade over the Pennines with the Viking kingdom of Dublin, and a little quayside (appropriately near the new Viking Hotel) was called 'Dublin Stones' from this trade. The walled area was greatly enlarged in Viking times, the Roman fortress walls being extended down to the Foss, where the main Danish harbour was apparently sited (Fig. 3). Extensive suburbs grew up beyond the Ouse and Foss, and a whole chain of satellite villages became dependent on the city – Layerthorpe, Clementhorpe, Bustardthorpe, Middlethorpe, Bishopthorpe, and Copmanthorpe. 'Thorpe' means 'outlying settlement', and since the 'thorpes' were situated on the rivers or off the Tadcaster road they suggest commercial settlements. Copmanthorpe actually means 'the merchants' settlement', yet it is four miles by road from the city centre. After the Norman Conquest it dwindled to a small agricultural settlement, and only in the past 20 years has it become a satellite of York again with the creation of new dormitory estates. Nothing illustrates more clearly the powerful pull of Viking York at its height.

Jorvik remains, like Eoforwic, a difficult place to recapture, because so little of it is left. The Danes covered the Roman wall with an earthen bank, which they topped with timber defences; the bank can be seen today exposed behind the City Library. It is necessary to travel 10 miles out to Kirk Hammerton to see a complete building – a parish church – of the Anglo-Scandinavian period, though in York itself there remains the sturdy tower of St Mary, Bishophill Junior (Walk 7) [7], of 10th- and 11th-century date. The men and women of Jorvik are even more shadowy, other than the

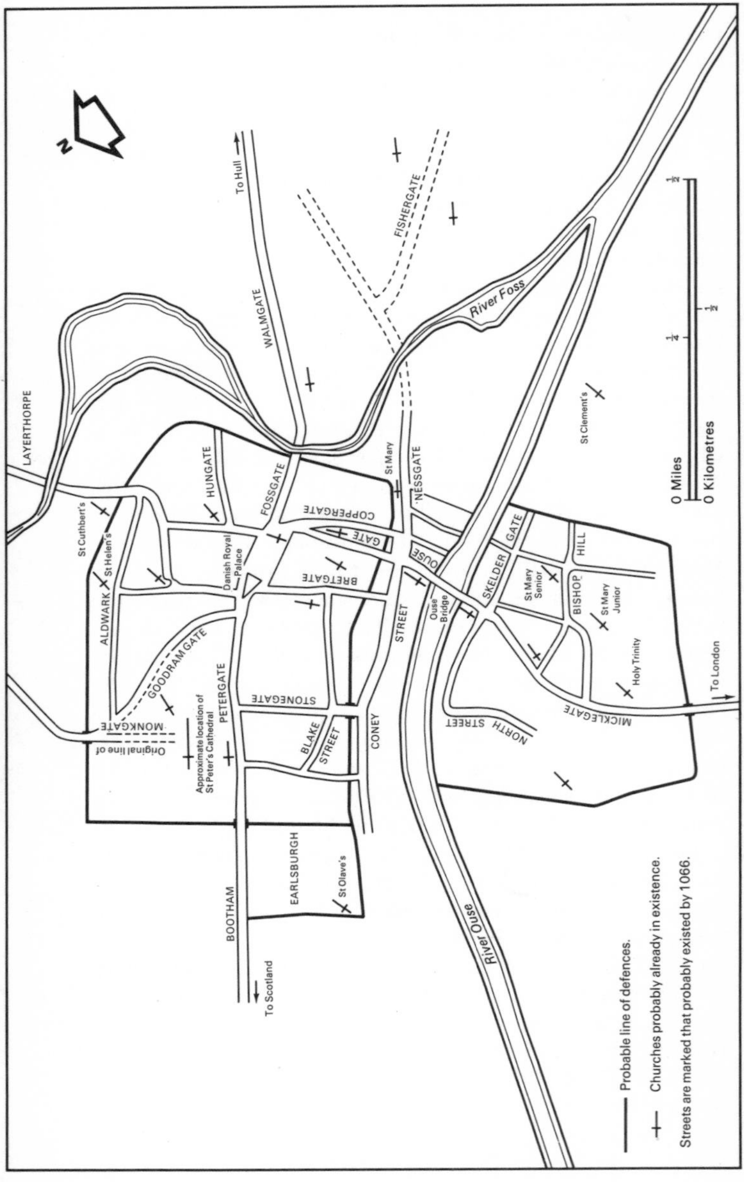

Fig. 3. Viking York 866–1066

kings and earls. The names of some, the moneyers, survive on their coins; three others are recorded on a dedication stone in St Mary's, Castlegate; and a local nobleman called Ulf has achieved immortality. Medieval tradition says that he was so vexed by quarrels between his sons over his inheritance that he decided to give his estates to the Minster instead. He drank from his drinking-horn before the high altar, and left it there as a title-deed. The story may well have a kernel of truth; the Minster did possess 'lands of Ulf', and his horn, a splendid ivory piece imported from Persia, is preserved among the Minster treasures.

But what was daily life like under Halfdan and Eric Bloodaxe and Siward, in 'York town, the dank demesne', as one of the Norse sagas calls it? The answers, once more, are being patiently teased out of the ground by archaeology. There have been particularly important discoveries in the Pavement–Ousegate–Coppergate area (Walk 6), where the commercial heart of Jorvik lay between the Roman fortress and the harbour on the Foss. It was probably a market district from earliest times, and it was surrounded by workshops making leather goods (other parts of Jorvik specialized in working bone, bronze, amber, and glass). The crowded houses and workshops were of timber, and they have partly survived in the waterlogged deposits. The Viking merchants were wealthy – they possessed gold and silver ornaments, and jet chessmen – but their workshops were damp and squalid. A leather workshop beneath Lloyds Bank, Pavement, was found to be carpeted by animal waste crawling with houseflies, stableflies, and beetles. An equally insanitary site has been found in the churchyard of St Mary, Bishophill Junior, where a herring-processing workshop of the 10th century was betrayed by a thick deposit of fish-scales. Another surprising pointer to the environment has been the discovery of over 40 bone skates from various sites, usually worn and highly polished. When the low-lying districts flooded, they must have frozen often enough to make the use of skates common.

Excavations have also shown that the street-lines of Ousegate, Pavement, Coppergate, and Skeldergate existed by the 10th century, and – more remarkable still – that the property divisions between houses have remained stable through the thousand years since, even though the houses themselves have been repeatedly rebuilt. Furthermore, most central streets have names formed from the Old Norse *gata*, 'street'. Ousegate, for example, is simply 'the street leading to the River Ouse', a crucial route that led from the commercial centre of Jorvik to the ford over the river where Ouse Bridge now is. Almost all the streets must have existed by 1066 under more or less their present names. It is still possible to walk round the centre visualizing the location of the Vikings' main streets and buildings – their royal palace (King's Square), their ways to the cathedral (Monkgate), to the rivers and harbours (Ousegate, Fossgate), and the main road south towards London (Micklegate, 'the great street'). In the centre were the commercial quarters of the butchers (Shambles) and of the coopers or coppersmiths (Coppergate). Outside the walled area lay the quarters of the fishermen (Fishergate) and ploughmen (Blossom Street, a corruption of Ploxwangate), and a suburb of pedlars' stalls (Bootham). So the street-names of Jorvik have survived, even though the citizens no longer speak of a street as a 'gate' as other Yorkshiremen still do. Long after the fall of the Viking kings the citizens must have spoken a dialect heavily laced with Old Norse, and William of Malmesbury, writing in *c.* 1125, said that 'almost everything about the language of the North, and particularly of the people of York, is so crude and discordant that we southerners cannot understand it'. Southumbrian jokes about Northern barbarians in caves have a long pedigree.

The Early Middle Ages
1066–1350

Viking York came to a sudden and frightful end at the orders of Duke William of Normandy. The Norman Conquest is often dated to 1066 as if the fate of England was decided by a single battle; but it took years for William to impose his authority in the outlying regions, especially in Northumbria. At first he was cautious and conciliatory, leaving local office-holders and landowners alone. York had an English archbishop until 1069, and Northumbria an English earl until 1076. The first trouble came with a rebellion in 1068: William easily suppressed it, and built a castle at York, which he garrisoned with Normans. Early in 1069 he had to return to suppress a more serious rising, and this time he pillaged the city and built a second castle. York, however, remained unreconciled to the new régime. When a Danish fleet sailed up the Ouse in September 1069 the citizens rose in support, and a joint Anglo-Scandinavian army besieged the castles. The garrisons tried to clear away houses near by by firing them, but the flames spread and engulfed much of the city. Despite this defence the castles were taken and many of the defenders massacred. This time William showed no mercy. He rushed to York with an army, repaired the castles, and systematically ravaged the whole district before returning to spend Christmas in the ruined city.

About 1086 Domesday Book was compiled on William's orders, a marvellous and detailed record thanks to which we have a clearer picture of early Norman York than of any earlier time in the city's history. Half of the city was returned as belonging to the King, and the other major property-owners in York were by then all Normans – the Archbishop, the Count of Mortain, William de Percy, and others – many of whom had been granted land taken from the defeated English. The city was still in a poor state 17 years after the events of 1069. Of its seven 'shires' (wards) one had been completely depopulated to make way for the castles, and of 1,600 houses in the other six shires, less than 1,000 seem to have been inhabited. However, there were already some signs of recovery, for over 200 new houses had been built. Gradually, York recovered some of the natural wealth and prosperity that came from its position. By 1130 it was able to pay more tax to the King than any town except London, Winchester, and Lincoln. Another sign of recovering prosperity in the city and Vale was the rebuilding of the Minster on a vast scale, begun by Archbishop Thomas of Bayeux about 1080, on a new E–W alignment cutting right across the old direction of the street-pattern.

York's reviving prosperity was helped by its position as the county town of the largest English shire. Even the modern county, familiar until the reorganization of 1974, was larger than the next two in size (Lincolnshire and Devon) put together, but Norman Yorkshire was larger still, including also Lancashire north of the Ribble and parts of southern Cumbria. Most of Cumbria was held by Scotland, intermittently, until 1157, the national boundary being marked by the Rere Cross on Stainmore, and the Scots Kings did not accept the present frontier until the Treaty of York in 1237. They could easily strike south into Yorkshire. In 1138 King David I took advantage of the troubled state of England to invade it. Fortunately the vigorous Archbishop Thurstan of York rallied an army and decisively defeated the Scots near Northallerton. The English army rallied round a ship's mast on a wagon, bearing the banners of St Peter of York, St John of Beverley, and St Wilfred of Ripon, giving rise to the name of the Battle of the Standard. Yet many Scots must already have begun settling in York, if we can trust the comment of a French Jew a little later – 'York is full of Scotsmen, filthy and treacherous creatures, scarcely human'.

Houses and probably even some churches were built of timber, thatch, and beaten earth, and remained very vulnerable. York's last major fire occurred on 4 June 1137 when, according to a contemporary, 'there were . . . conflagrations of many churches, of St Peter's of York . . . together with the hospital of the same city . . . and with 39 other churches'. This implies the destruction of the whole city, explaining why only a few stone buildings, and the earthen defences, have survived from before 1137.

There had been communal defences since Roman times – the walls of the fortress and of the Roman civil town, taken over and enlarged by Angles and Danes. The Norman innovation was the castle, a private fortress intended as a strongpoint and residence for King, royal official, or nobleman. William I built one in nearly every county town, for a garrison and as headquarters for his new official in charge of county administration, the 'shire-reeve' or sheriff. Only at York and London, however, did he build two castles. Those at York stood on either side of the Ouse, evidently to guard against further invasions upriver. Both were of the normal type of early Norman castle, the 'motte and bailey', with space for the garrison and supplies surrounded by an earthen bank and ditch, and a strongpoint (motte) consisting of a moated and artificial mound, the banks and mound encircled by pallisades of sharpened stakes; stone was a luxury reserved for major fortresses like the Tower of London.

The west bank castle at York quickly fell out of use, though its tree-covered motte survives (Walk 8), and the site retains the significant name of the Old Baile ('bailey'). The other castle (Walk 6) proved more defensible, being sited in the angle of the two rivers, with its moats supplied from a channel of the Foss. The motte remains as a tribute to the enduring work of William's forced labour, though the stone keep (Clifford's Tower) is 13th-century. The Norman Kings also dammed the Foss to create a huge fishpond and to protect the city on the E; they heightened the earthen banks of the Danish city defences; and by about 1150 they added an earthen bank round the Walmgate suburb, thus completing in earth and timber the line of the present city walls.

But the greatest legacy of the Normans was their religious foundations. By 1066 York already had numerous churches, chapels, and hospitals, but the Normans rebuilt them on a grander scale and added greatly to their number. They rebuilt the Minster – badly damaged in 1137 – and Archbishop Roger, the rival and colleague of Archbishop Thomas Becket, added a splendid new choir; part of his beautiful crypt can be seen in the undercroft [11]. By 1200 the citizens had founded most of York's huge total of 45 medieval parish churches, and the Kings and Northern landowners had founded or sponsored four monasteries, a nunnery, and several hospitals or religious almshouses. The two greatest foundations lay W of the Minster, and what survives of them can be seen in the Museum Gardens (Walk 2). The Hospital of St Leonard was the largest in the North, and at its zenith accommodated some 500 poor; and next to it stood the Abbey of St Mary, the richest Northern house of the Benedictines, founded in the 1080s as part of a Northern monastic revival.

St Mary's Abbey started with great zeal, yet within 50 years some of the monks felt it had become too comfortable and worldly. Fired by the teachings of St Bernard, and supported by Archbishop Thùrstan of York, the stricter monks left St Mary's and founded instead the Cistercian abbey of Fountains near Ripon in 1132. Fountains quickly acquired such a reputation for austere and holy living that when Thurstan died, St Bernard persuaded the Pope to make Abbot Henry Murdac of Fountains the next Archbishop, overruling an earlier election of the King's nephew, William Fitzherbert. When Murdac died, Fitzherbert was finally accepted as Archbishop, and entered York in triumph (1153). He was welcomed by so vast a crowd that Ouse Bridge – a wooden structure – collapsed under the weight, and many bystanders fell into the river. The Archbishop, however, prayed that none might drown, and it is recorded that none did. When in the following year he died in doubtful circumstances, though his life was said by his enemies to have been far from holy, popular opinion demanded his canonization, so in 1226 he became St William of York. His tomb became a centre of pilgrimage, and the St William window in the Minster depicts many of his miracles, including the Ouse

Bridge incident, as well as some more properly ascribed to other saints.

However, the loyalties of most citizens were centred not on the Minster, nor on the monasteries, but on their local churches and chapels. Many of the 40 churches of Norman York survive, a few still possessing Norman features – notably the three superb carved doorways of St Margaret [10], St Denys, and St Lawrence (Walks 5 and 13) with their little figures, beasts, and signs of the Zodiac. Most have been completely rebuilt since the 12th century, but even so they serve as a reminder of how 'well churched' York was throughout the Middle Ages. They were, of course, places of worship for the whole population except the Jews, but, as almost the only stone buildings, they served many other purposes – fire-proof storage; facilities for public meetings, courts, and schools; and premises for the many parish gilds (clubs or friendly societies for the parishioners, with religious, charitable, and convivial activities).

By the end of the Norman period, private citizens were coming into greater prominence. The recorded story of York had previously been one of Kings, nobles, and great churchmen, but during the 12th century leading merchants and craftsmen were prospering sufficiently to take steps towards local self-government. By 1130 these men had a trading association or gild with its own meeting-hall (hansehouse), and in the 1150s they received a charter from Henry II confirming all their trading rights in England and Normandy. The charter, the earliest document among the city archives, was attested by Henry's friend and chancellor Thomas Becket. Soon the leading citizens became impatient for more power, and in 1173 one of their number, Thomas of Beyond Ouse (who presumably lived in Micklegate), tried to organize a 'commune' of the Continental type, a sworn association of citizens forming an independent corporation. Henry II would no more brook insubordinate townsmen than turbulent priests, and Thomas was promptly fined and the commune dissolved. But the pressure for chartered privileges increased as leading citizens grew richer and more self-assertive; and their chance came during the reigns of

Richard I and John. Both fought expensive wars, suffered financial embarrassment, and were glad to sell chartered rights to the larger boroughs. In 1189 the new King Richard, scraping together all the money he could for a crusade, granted York valuable trading privileges by charter, in return for the large sum of £133 6s. 8d.

Richard's accession also triggered off tragic events highlighting the growing trading wealth of York as well as the presence of racial prejudice. In Henry II's reign a small colony of Jews had settled in York, and two of them, Josce and Benedict, had become wealthy by lending money at interest to Northern landowners. This did not happen, as modern legend has it, because Christians could not lend money; there were rich Christian money-lenders, but the Jews gradually displaced them; probably they were more efficient. But greater efficiency by foreigners can lead to xenophobia, and at Richard's coronation in London there was a serious anti-Jewish riot; Benedict and Josce were attending it, and Benedict was mortally wounded. Josce returned safely to York, but in March 1190 there were anti-Jewish riots in the provincial towns too. Some Yorkshire barons indebted to the Jews whipped up hatred in York and began by slaughtering Benedict's widow and children. The Jews, led by Josce, were given protection by the Sheriff in York Castle, but through a misunderstanding they then found themselves under siege by the barons with an armed mob. Their spiritual leader, Rabbi Yomtob, urged mass suicide after the example of the Jews at Masada. Most followed his example, and the rest were massacred as they surrendered after promises of safety in return for Christian baptism. The baronial conspirators then hastened to the Minster, burned the Jewish bonds deposited there, and dispersed; they were never punished.* The horrifying drama was unusually well reported, and it was undoubtedly the worst anti-Jewish pogrom in English history. Yet, without mitigating the horror, it must be soberly pointed out

* The scene of the massacre was Clifford's Tower, or rather a wooden keep on the mound that preceded the present tower. The best survey of the medieval Jews of York is now R.B. Dobson, *The Jews of Medieval York and the Massacre of March 1190* (Borthwick Papers, 45, 1974).

that the figure of 500 Jews alleged to have died is a gross exaggeration, and that the true total was probably more like 150. Paradoxically, the massacre did not spell the death-blow to the city's Jewry, which was small and newly-established in 1190. It attained its peak between 1220 and 1260, when it was one of the largest and wealthiest Jewries in the realm. The great Aaron of York (d. 1268) was the wealthiest Jew in England until crippled by royal taxation in the 1250s. Finally, the Crown, which had relied on Jewish creditors, taxed them beyond the point where they could be of use, and the impoverished Jewish community was expelled from England in 1290.

One should not exaggerate the number or the wealth of York's Jews even at their peak; they were always a small minority in a city of wealthy traders. In 1190 the government fined the 59 leading citizens for allowing the massacre, the wealthiest having to pay the huge sum of £66 13s. 4d., and the list of fines is an index of Gentile prosperity. The belief that early stone houses must have belonged to Jews is a fallacy, for they merely indicated wealth. Parts of two 12th-century stone houses still exist – one off Stonegate (Walk 4) and one embedded in Gray's Court (Walk 1) – and niether can be convincingly identified with a Jewish owner, any more than can the two so-called Jews' Houses at Lincoln. The leading Jews lived, and had their synagogue, in the Coney Street area; and Aaron's own house was next door but one to St Martin's church, on the site of Leak and Thorp's department store. It is appropriate that one of the adjacent streets was named after them – Jubbergate, or 'Jew's Bretgate', though it has been colourlessly re-christened Market Street. Near Layerthorpe Bridge the street of Jewbury still commemorates the cemetery in which all the Jews of medieval Yorkshire and Lincolnshire were buried.

The rich merchants in their stone houses were not long in achieving local self-government. King John (1199–1216) was an efficient and conscientious administrator, far from the bad king of later legend, but wars abroad and troubles with the barons at home made him continue his brother's policy of selling rights and privileges to the towns. Somewhere around the year 1200 the leading citizens began to form a 'commune', presumably with the King's permission; for a charter of that period, preserved in the British Museum, was issued by 'the citizens of York' and authenticated by a common seal with a three-towered castle. In 1213 the leading citizens paid John what was then the huge sum of £200 and three palfreys for the right to pay their taxes direct to the Exchequer (so keeping the county Sheriff out of their affairs), and to be represented by one of their own number under the French title of 'mayor'. From 1213 to 1974 York was a self-governing city under its own Mayors,* who were gradually joined by a bevy of other officers as local government became more complex. During the 13th century the Corporation (as we can now begin to call the leading inner ring of citizens) acquired more and more privileges from the King. Perhaps the most cherished was the grant of the Ainsty, a tract of land covering 20 villages between Ouse, Wharfe, and Nidd, over which the citizens exercised authority from 1212 until 1836. This generous royal grant explains a curious feature of royal visits to York in later centuries; the city Sheriffs used to meet their sovereign, not at Micklegate Bar or even at the city boundary near Dringhouses, but nine miles out on Tadcaster Bridge, which was the limit of their jurisdiction. The drive from Tadcaster to York is still an eloquent testimony to the importance of 13th-century York.

Who were the leading citizens who made York independent in the 13th century, and how did they acquire the necessary wealth? What little we know of them suggests a small, tightly-knit group of families who made their fortunes partly from trading overseas, partly from investing profits in local property. The family of Selby, father, son, and grandson, imported French wine and exported English wool, and between them held the office of Mayor at least 17 times in 70 years. The greater merchants traded in all kinds of goods, sending ships overseas through the port of Hull,

* Since early Tudor times the Mayor has been known as 'Lord Mayor', a title often but wrongly attributed to a grant of Richard II in 1396. It is simply a shorter version of a Tudor courtesy title 'my lord the Mayor'.

from which a shuttle service of smaller boats plied upriver to York and beyond. But these greater men could only prosper because they led a large and prosperous city with a wide range of small crafts and trades, weavers, dyers, butchers, bakers, tanners, girdlers, and so on. We can also tell from their names that York grew by attracting villagers from a wide area to try their fortune in the city; surnames were not yet fixed, and a man named from a village was likely to have been born there. Just as the Selby family must have come from nearby Selby, so many of the 13th-century citizens came from villages over a 30-mile radius – the earliest register of citizens, starting in 1272, opens with the names of Thomas of Fulford, Peter of Foxholes, and James of Pickering. Neither did York adopt any exclusive policy towards foreigners. Trade links encouraged early immigrants from what is now Belgium to settle in York, and James the Fleming was Mayor in 1298, and Nicholas the Fleming Mayor several times between 1311 and 1319.

The houses even of the richest citizens have almost totally disappeared; but the men of 13th-century York have left an enduring mark on the city in their churches and walls. Private houses were mostly built of flimsy timber or even beaten earth, but for important buildings magnesian limestone from the Tadcaster area was used. The greatest monuments surviving to testify to this building boom are the city walls (Walk 8) and the present Minster, both begun in the 13th century. The classic picture-postcard view – the Minster from the walls by the railway station – combines the two most striking elements conceived and begun by the men of the reign of Henry III.

Earth-and-timber defences were becoming out of date; stone walls and towers were needed to withstand the developing power of siege warfare. In 1244 Henry III visited York and decided to rebuild York Castle in stone (Walk 6). This was carried out over 20 years at a cost of £2,500, under plans drawn up by the same royal master mason, Henry of Reyns, who rebuilt Westminster Abbey for Henry. Later alterations have removed most of Master Henry's work, and only the keep [29] and short stretches of the bailey wall still stand. This rebuilding may have provoked the city fathers to emulate the King; at any rate, rebuilding of the city walls in stone seems to have begun about 1250 and to have been completed (except for the Walmgate sector) by 1315. This was a costly operation, and the Corporation raised much of the money by a tax called murage, levied on goods entering the city gates. The original height of the walls to the battlement seems to have been about 12 ft, and on the inner side there was no broad footpath but only a narrow ledge for archers: a section with this original wall-walk can still be seen at Tower Place (Walk 6).

While King and citizens were raising money to improve the defences, Archbishop Walter de Gray (1216–55) was proceeding with rebuilding the Minster. Thomas's nave and Roger's choir already provided a church on the grandest scale, but the transepts were probably insignificant in comparison. Walter's work remedied any deficiencies in this respect: he himself built the S transept, while the N transept [13] and central tower were the work of his treasurer, John le Romeyn. Work probably started about 1220 and was finished by the time Walter died in 1255. Next to be built was the chapter house [16], completed by *c.* 1285, and the linking vestibule [17], probably finished by 1291, when work started on the nave. The nave [19] was not to be completed until the 1360s, but from the start it established the enormous scale of the rest of the rebuilding. This vast undertaking was of course a charge on the whole North, for pious men throughout the archdiocese were asked to contribute; but the building and rebuilding of other churches and chapels in York continued unabated. By 1300 York had about 45 parish churches serving a population that is likely to have been in the range 10,000–15,000 – that is, one for every 200 or 300 citizens. Admittedly they were often small and unimpressive, and it is easy to forget that the survivors – like All Saints Pavement (Walk 6) and St Michael-le-Belfrey (Walk 1) – were often the larger and more prosperous ones, and in any case were rebuilt on a grander scale in the later Middle Ages. Many of the vanished 13th-century churches were probably simple little structures with nave and chancel, but no aisle or tower, like the former church of St Andrew (Walk 5), which still survives, but so inconspicuously that it can be passed without realizing that it was ever a parish church.

Meanwhile numerous houses of the religious – monks, nuns, canons, and later friars – were being rebuilt, enlarged, or newly established. Holy Trinity Priory in Micklegate was largely rebuilt in the late 12th and early 13th centuries, and St Leonard's Hospital completely rebuilt in the early 13th century. Only 100 yards from St Leonard's, the surviving ruins of St Mary's Abbey represent a magnificent new building started in 1271 [18]. Just outside the walls stood St Clement's Priory (Benedictine nuns) and St Andrew's Priory (Gilbertine canons). These older religious orders were joined in the 13th century by a completely new group of orders, the friars (literally *fratres*, 'brothers'), men who like the monks lived under the vows of poverty, chastity, and obedience, but who unlike them were expected to work in the secular world and especially in the towns. The two greatest orders of friars originated in Italy with St Francis of Assisi and St Dominic, and they quickly became popular in England and throughout the Christian West. They appealed particularly to urban laymen for whom the traditional practices of the monks and nuns meant little; they preached in a popular style, and may even have done social work in the urban slums much as the Salvation Army has done in recent times. Where friary churches have survived, as at Norwich, they are found to have been large halls of simple plan designed for preaching to large congregations. Unfortunately the York friaries were so thoroughly demolished at the Reformation that they have not left the same traces as the monasteries; but at their height, in the late 13th century, York had no less than six friaries, a number reduced to the four main orders in the later Middle Ages. The Franciscans or Greyfriars settled between the castle and the Ouse, and part of their precinct wall still exists along the river-front (Walk 6). The Dominicans or Blackfriars lived where Hudson House stands off Tanner Row, the Carmelites or

Fig. 4: Medieval York c. 1066–1500

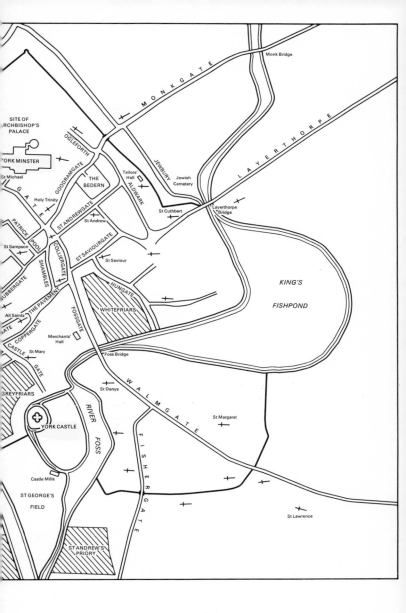

Whitefriars off Fossgate, and the Augustinian or Austin friars where the Post Office now stands in Lendal. It takes an effort of the imagination to picture the important part that they played in York's life for three centuries, preaching, hearing confessions, arbitrating disputes, providing hospitality. Edward II and Edward III both stayed at the Greyfriars, rather than suffer cramped accommodation at the castle next door, while Richard III lodged with the Augustinians.

Royal visits – colourful and well-recorded occasions – are a staple feature of the older histories of York, and they have perhaps been overwritten. From the 13th century, however, royal visits to York were connected with important issues of peace or war with the Scots, as well as bringing, since courts and armies had to be housed and fed, a measure of prosperity to the citizens. In 1221 and 1251 there were royal Anglo-Scottish weddings in the Minster, as Henry III sought for peaceful relations between the two countries. For a while all was quiet, but in 1290 the death of the girl-queen of Scotland produced a succession struggle to the Scottish crown and provoked bitter wars with England. Under the reigns of the first three Edwards fighting and raiding occurred over the whole area between York and the Scottish Highlands, and engendered a bitter hatred of Scotsmen in York that lasted until Tudor times. The worst moment for the city came in 1319, when the Scots reached the walls. The English government was paralysed and on the brink of civil war, so the Archbishop and the Mayor of York, Nicholas the Fleming, raised a scratch army in the city and neighbourhood, and pursued the retreating Scots. The York army was disastrously defeated upriver at Myton-on-Swale, about 15 miles from the city, and many citizens were killed, including the Mayor.

However, these conflicts were not without their compensations. Between 1296 and 1337 the three Edwards not only made York a campaigning base, but actually moved the departments of state there as well as the royal court. Edward I, for example, kept the Exchequer, Chancery, and royal law courts in York for seven years, besides summoning various national assemblies to meet in the city, and York was spasmodically a capital once again. During the first half of the 14th century men working at a wide range of crafts took up the freedom of the city, and the presence of the court and the armies was good for business. Cloth, shoes, bows and arrows were supplied by York, and the textile industry revived with growing demand. When the government became preoccupied with the French wars after 1337 and the court no longer came, business slumped again, although an astute group of York merchants under John Goldbeter remained wealthy enough to lend large sums to Edward III in the 1340s, helping the war effort at the time of the battle of Crécy.

What was York like in its days as an occasional capital for the Edwards? There is a danger that the splendour of the walls and the Minster, and the repeated presence of the court, may lead to a romantic picture of a chivalrous, white and castellated city, like a miniature in an illuminated manuscript – 'small, and white, and clean'. Nothing could be further from the truth. When Edward III summoned parliament to York in 1332, he ordered the Mayor and bailiffs to clean all the streets and lanes, complaining of 'the abominable smell abounding in the said city more than in any other city of the realm from dung and manure, and other filth and dirt wherewith the streets and lanes are filled and obstructed'. The city's own records admit the point by constant criticisms about dunghills and pigs scavenging in the streets, and the Greyfriars had to complain about butchers throwing offal into the river outside their priory. Lord Esher scarcely exaggerates in describing medieval York as 'a city of exquisite architecture rising out of a midden'.*

Despite the squalor, York remained a tempting magnet for local countryfolk, and it grew and prospered in the 13th and 14th centuries. There is evidence that the old walled city was becoming more densely built-up, while suburbs straggled a long way beyond the gates along Bootham, Blossom Street, Fishergate, and Hull Road. Many houses were

* Viscount Esher, *York: a Study in Conservation* (1968), p. 2.

squeezed in between the main streets, often forming little colonies of craftsmen – Glovergail (glovers' alley), Cook Row – while Newgate (New Street) was built about 1320. Most of the housing was too flimsy to have survived, but some richer citizens built substantial houses with stone ground floors, and part of one such house remains at the corner of Patrick Pool. More remarkable are several survivals of early-14th-century speculative building. A growing cult of the Virgin Mary called for new altars in her honour at just the time that a growing population needed housing; several York parishes met both needs by building rows of cottages in their churchyards, and using the rents to maintain an altar. Part of one such row survives in Newgate, and another off Coney Street; but the best is Lady Row in Goodramgate (Walk 4). This timber-framed row stands substantially as it was built about 1320, forming the earliest private housing in the present city.

Growing population was checked, as everywhere else in the country, by sudden disaster. Bubonic plague, a disease carried by rat fleas, entered England in 1348, and spread inexorably. It wiped out something like one-third of the population, and well earned its name of the Great Pestilence (the 'Black Death' is a modern invention). It raged in York throughout the summer of 1349, and although there are no figures for the city's mortality it must have been high. The number of newly-enfranchized citizens in 1350 was almost four times the usual annual figure; many dead men's shoes were being filled. Bubonic plague, once established in England, was to recur for three centuries, but never quite so lethally. This tragedy had a much greater impact on York – and on England – than the headline events of contemporary chroniclers like the battles of Crécy (1346) and Poitiers (1356), and it marks an appropriate end to the capital-city phase of York's history. And yet, as will be seen, the disaster proved to be only a temporary setback. Whereas some other communities never recovered completely from the de-populating plague, York was within two generations larger and wealthier than ever before.

Splendour and Decay
1350–1560

The 14th and 15th centuries are still seen by many as an age of gloom, civil strife, and the cult of death, when trade, prosperity, and population decayed. Support for this traditional view might seem to be provided by the fate of York's parish churches: their number shrank for the first time, and five out of 45 were closed in the 14th century. However, there were already too many small churches, not always in the right places, for population shifted and created problems of redundancy as it still does today. Three of the five churches lay in the Walmgate–Fishergate area, which was becoming poverty-stricken; but the central parts of the city flourished.

Recent research has made it clear that York's population and economic prosperity both reached a new peak in the late 14th century, and although recession set in in the early 15th century, the city did not seriously decline until after 1450. The evidence for this golden century is not confined to the archives, but lies all around in stone and timber. The completion of the Minster, the rebuilding of many churches, and the building of the great gildhalls and of many timber-framed houses in the Shambles and elsewhere, all took place between about 1350 and 1475. A building boom often follows prosperity with a time-lag, an interval between getting and spending; and it is significant that major building work came to an end about 1475, a generation after economic decay set in.

Bubonic plague, after its first terrible onslaught in 1349, returned to York in 1361, 1369, 1375, 1378, 1390, and on later occasions. The citizens must have been literally decimated several times; 1,100 are said to have died in 1390, but there was no shortage of immigrants to fill the gaps. Men from all over the North, as well as Flemish weavers and German merchants, flocked into York, and the total population rose despite the plagues. On Good Friday 1396 Richard II, who was staying in York, distributed alms to the enormous number of 12,040 paupers, implying, according to Dr Harvey, that 'greater York' had at least 15,000 people. This would make it easily the largest provincial city, though less than half the size of London. Many of the newcomers to York were probably rural poor looking for a better life in the city, and perhaps often disappointed; but York was no Calcutta, swarming with poor. It was not only the second largest city but also the second richest – or at least, it consistently paid more tax than any other except London. The immigrants were drawn to York by its commercial prosperity. Over 100 different crafts were practised there, many of them bread-and-butter occupations like milling, baking, and brewing, but some of regional and even international importance.

Wool was the staple English export in the Middle Ages – hence the symbolic woolsack on which the Lord Chancellor still sits in Parliament. Yorkshire wool had long been exported to the Low Countries to be worked into cloth, but now towns like York and Beverley were tapping this source of wealth more directly by working the wool themselves and exporting it as cloth. York became a medieval industrial city, its numerous weaving and dyeing workshops supplying cloth, which its merchants then shipped through Hull to the Netherlands, France, and the Baltic, and even Italy. Alderman Robert Colynson (d. 1458) owned what must have been a rudimentary clothworking factory in North Street, since he left 'a good breakfast' and 12d. each 'to the dyers, fullers, cutters and weavers working with me'. And cloth was only the most valuable among many products that were sold widely at home and abroad. York workshops supplied silverwork, pewter, bells, church woodwork, and stained glass to most of Northern England. Yet York never became a wholly industrial city, for its age of medieval prosperity depended also on its merchants and shipmen, who traded in commodities other than those made in the city. Its mariners fished as far afield as Iceland; its merchants exported cloth and Yorkshire lead, and imported wine from Gascony and skins and furs from Prussia and the Baltic. Its proud title of 'second city of the realm' was accurate and not yet an empty historical survival. It was entirely appropriate that when Richard II quarrelled with the Londoners in 1392 and moved the offices of state, he took them again to York, which enjoyed six months as temporary capital.

It is a curious fact that several of England's unluckiest monarchs – Richard II, Richard III, Mary I, and Charles I – at one time or another favoured York at the expense of London, more or less consciously cultivating a Northern power base to counterbalance opposition in the South. Richard II (1377–99) visited York at least nine times, and although he abandoned the idea of making York his capital after 1392, he returned again and again and showered the citizens with gifts and privileges. In 1393 and 1396 he granted charters that completed the structure of civic self-government begun under King John. The inner council of 13 who ran the city – a mayor and 12 aldermen – now formed a bench of justices as well as a town council, and were completely independent of the county of York in every respect. York became a 'county corporate', an independent island at the junction of the three ridings of Yorkshire but not forming part of any of them. The Mayor was given two new assistants called Sheriffs – to show that York was now independent of the Sheriff of Yorkshire – and both Mayor and Sheriffs were granted extra dignities. Richard gave a sword of his own to the Mayor, with the envied privilege of having it carried point upright before him in the presence of any but the King himself.* Richard was supplanted by Henry IV in 1399, and many of his policies were reversed, but his benefactions to York lasted. Indeed, until the municipal reforms of 1835 the city continued to enjoy the same structure of government and the same privileges.

Richard's generosity was repaid by gratitude from the leading citizens and churchmen. In return for his gifts to the

---

* Richard's sword has been lost, but the city still possesses a ceremonial sword made for his contemporary the Emperor Sigismund, and given to York in 1439.

completion of the Minster, the cathedral clergy set his portrait and his badge of the chained hart on the SE pier of the crossing, where they can still be seen. The Corporation, grateful for Richard's 1396 charter, offered lavish hospitality on the King's second visit that year. A civic deputation escorted him all the way from Nottingham, and the total cost of his entertainment was about £250, more than a normal year's civic income. It is true that his autocratic policy also involved forced loans from the leading citizens, and there seems to have been some relief among them when Henry deposed Richard. Many citizens, however, seem to have treasured the memory of King Richard, refusing to believe in his death, and in 1405 they rose in rebellion at the instigation of their Archbishop, Richard le Scrope. The revolt was crushed by treachery, and the Archbishop executed outside the walls, in a field between Bishopthorpe Road and the present Nunmill Street; but the offerings that were made at Scrope's tomb in the Minster for many years afterwards testified to the citizens' attachment to him. When the Minster choir screen was built, the face of Henry IV's statue was defaced and blackened; traces of the daubing can be seen even today.

One of the highlights of Richard's visits to York in 1396 had been a performance of the Corpus Christi plays, which the King had watched from a special box in Micklegate opposite the gate of Holy Trinity Priory.* These plays, performed every summer on the Thursday after Trinity Sunday, were one of the special glories of later medieval York, a tribute to the citizens' piety and prosperity. By the 14th century many English towns performed religious dramas in English, telling the Biblical story from Creation to Last Judgement, and the original York Corpus Christi cycle may date from about 1350. It was nationally famous by 1387,

---

* Richard's visit is dated 1398 in the *Victoria County History* and other sources, but Dr J.H. Harvey has shown that he must have watched the plays on 1 June 1396: *The Reign of Richard II*, ed. F.R.H. du Boulay and C.M. Barron (1971), pp. 211, 216–17. I have used the normal medieval English term of 'miracle' plays to cover such cycles. The revived York cycle since 1951 has unfortunately popularized the expression 'mystery plays', which puzzles many visitors. Much ink has been spilled over whether the expression derives from religious mysteries or from the use of 'mistery' for a medieval craft gild. However, no English play was called a 'mystery' before 1744, and the term is an anachronism.

and it continued to be staged until the 1570s. Fortunately a single copy of almost the whole cycle (48 plays out of about 55) was preserved by the Fairfax family. As a result it was possible to stage a modern adaptation of selected plays as part of the 1951 Festival of Britain celebrations, and ever since they have remained the popular centrepiece for the York Festival. The original cycle was not performed on a fixed stage, but on movable wagons or 'pageants', each play being the responsibility of a different gild or association of traders and craftsmen. The traditional route for the wagons began at Holy Trinity gateway and led through the heart of the city to Pavement. The Creation would be performed at the first 'station' perhaps about 4.30 a.m., and would then move down Micklegate to the second station, while its place was taken by the second Pageant, and so on, until, late in the evening, the wealthy mercers' gild performed the Last Judgement.

The mercers (or merchants) formed the largest and most powerful trading association in York. They organized their business from their great hall off Fossgate (Walk 5) [31], begun in 1356, conveniently close to their private quay, for water transport mattered more than roads. The second largest association, the tailors and drapers (now the Merchant Taylors) were driven to emulate the mercers, building their own great hall off Aldwark about 1400 (Walk 5). Then, in the 1440s, two major halls of a different character were begun. The Gild of St Anthony rebuilt their hall in Peasholm (Walk 5), and the Corporation collaborated with another religious fraternity to build the present 'Guildhall' off Coney Street (Walk 3). No other English city can boast so many large medieval gildhalls, and they provide visual evidence for the prosperity and self-confidence of the richer citizens in the 14th and 15th centuries.

The halls were only a part of the building achievement of the age. The imposing appearance of the city bars (gates) is due to late-14th-century extensions and improvements. The Minster was completed to the ambitious plan laid down by Master Simon in 1291. The eastern arm [24], the massive central tower, and finally the western towers, were all built between 1361 and 1472, and the Minster stood complete in more or less its present form, the largest surviving medieval church in England and indeed in Northern Europe. Most of the larger parish churches were rebuilt or enlarged in the same Perpendicular style, like St Martin's Coney Street (Walk 4), and All Saints' Pavement (Walk 6) with its graceful lantern tower. Northern magnates built themselves town houses for their visits to the city, and the Percies and the Nevilles each possessed a great mansion in Walmgate. The richer citizens were meantime building substantial timber-framed houses with tiled roofs: tile was gradually replacing thatch to reduce the risk of fires. The city centre was becoming congested, so the larger houses were often built upwards instead of outwards, some 15th-century houses having three or even four storeys. Normally each floor was built wider than the one below, to give extra floor space and to produce a more stable structure, so producing the characteristic jetties or overhangs. More examples survive than a hurried visitor will realize, for timber-framing was unfashionable in the 18th century, and medieval houses in Micklegate and Petergate are often hidden behind façades of Georgian brick. There are still recognizable 15th-century houses here and there, and a particularly attractive group, Church Cottages, in North Street (Walk 7). The best general impression of the period is provided by the central section of the Shambles (Walk 3); though its timbered houses have been virtually rebuilt in postwar 'restorations', their appearance, if not their structure, is reasonably authentic. The street is also a pointer to prosperity for the better-off craftsmen as well as merchants, for these were, and remained until fairly recently, butchers' houses.

Yet though more solidly built, these houses were still poorly lit, heated, and insulated, and vulnerable to fire. Window-glass and chimneys were still rare, and many rooms were heated, if at all, by braziers. Lists of goods of 15th-century citizens include little furniture beyond beds, benches, and trestle tables, and even the colourful wall hangings of the rich were less for decoration than to conserve heat. Citizens must have spent much time escaping from their homes into the numerous alehouses, or so the many cases of drunken talk and slander would suggest. It is fair to add, however, that there was a slow but real improvement in the quality of the environment. If urinating in public places was still common, there was a growing number of public conveniences, and the 'new privies' on Ouse Bridge had an attendant and a night light as early as 1368. The Corporation was beginning to pave the main streets at public expense (though the paving was of cobbles and not flagstones) and even to introduce a street-cleansing service in a modest way.

Colour and rich furnishings were still lavished almost exclusively on the churches, but so much was destroyed at the Reformation that it is difficult to imagine them in their 15th-century glory. All Saints, North Street (Walk 7), keeps much of its original stained glass, and a long High Church tradition filled it until recently with screens, statues, and little altars in marvellously authentic evocation of its original dark, crowded, and glowing interior. York is of course famous for its medieval stained glass, surviving in far greater quantities than anywhere else in the country, muddled, transposed, and restored though a lot of it is. There is much glass of the 12th and 13th centuries in the Minster, the 12th-century glass of a glowing splendour that no later age was able to achieve, and a sharp contrast to the cool and pearly grisaille glass of the 13th century, of which the Five Sisters window is the finest example remaining. It is, however, the windows dating from the late 13th to the mid 15th century that will be remembered as the most spectacular glories of the art in York.

The late medieval city was well placed as a centre of glass-painting, having both wealthy patrons and access to glass imports through Hull (the better-quality glass was all imported until the 16th century). It had a flourishing glaziers' gild, though the great E window of the Minster, and probably many other York windows, was entrusted to John Thornton of Coventry. Many of the Minster windows still contain the glass originally designed for them, and there are large collections of glass in six parish churches (All Saints,

North Street, Walk 7; St Denys, Walk 5; St Martin-cum-Gregory, Walk 7; St Martin-le-Grand, Walk 4; St Michael-le-Belfrey, Walk 1; and St Michael Spurriergate, Walk 6) and good individual windows in half a dozen others. In these windows one can come closer to the citizens who gave them than anywhere else. The windows portray not only their favourite religious themes but also their furniture and clothing, and even themselves as donors, though these should not be taken as portraits. The figures are invariably represented in the contemporary dress and surroundings of the glaziers' own lifetimes. It is even likely that some Biblical scenes in the windows were inspired by the Corpus Christi plays, and they have been used as a source for reconstructing details of the performances.

Some of the buildings already mentioned date from the third quarter of the 15th century, when York was living on the fat of its earlier prosperity. From about 1475, however, major building came almost to a complete stop. The Abbots of St Mary's greatly extended their imposing house (now the King's Manor, Walk 2) between 1483 and 1502, the Archbishop following suit a little later, but they after all had revenues from rich Northern estates and were not dependent on the city's prosperity. But no more gildhalls and great public buildings were erected, and the one church rebuilt after 1475 (St Michael-le-Belfrey) was a replacement for an earlier church that had become too dilapidated to restore. Very few private houses surviving can be dated between 1475 and 1575. That is the visual evidence for an economic depression that began in the 1460s and worsened steadily for nearly a century, as both population and prosperity shrank. In 1432 Nicholas Blakeburn senior (one of the donors depicted in the All Saints' windows) had left a penny each to 6,400 poor townsmen, implying a total population of 10,000 or 12,000, but by Henry VIII's reign the population was down to 8,000 or fewer, barely half its medieval peak. Tax returns tell a similar story, with York falling from wealthiest provincial town under Richard II to only 14th under Henry VIII. From the 1480s to the 1560s the city fathers were constantly pleading their inability to pay their taxes, citing in evidence in 1555 'the great ruin and poverty of the said city'.

Victorian historians laid the blame for the economic troubles of York and many other towns on the so-called 'Wars of the Roses', the dynastic struggles for the throne between 1453 and 1487.* More recent writers have been rightly sceptical of how much disruption and destruction actually occurred. Only small armies were involved, in a total of six months' campaigning spread over 34 years, and trade and commerce were not generally disrupted. Nevertheless, York was closely involved in the struggles from the first bloody skirmish, which was fought at Stamford Bridge in 1453, and many citizens became retainers of the rival houses. In December 1460 the Duke of York, campaigning to seize the Crown, was defeated and killed at Wakefield, his head being set on Micklegate Bar with a mocking paper crown. Shakespeare's *Henry VI* is more reliable than usual at this point, when Queen Margaret says

> Off with his head, and set it on York gates;
> So York may overlook the town of York.

The Lancastrians' triumph was short-lived, for the Duke's son and heir crowned himself Edward IV (1461–83) and raced north to crush them. He won a bloody victory in a blinding snowstorm on Palm Sunday 1461, at Towton near Tadcaster. York opened its gates without resistance, and he only just missed capturing King Henry 'and Queen Margaret. Taking down the heads of his father and other Yorkist leaders from the gates, he set up Lancastrian heads in their place before celebrating Easter there. The sudden reversal of fortune was a blow to the city, for Edward never forgave York its Lancastrian preference in 1461, and was still less inclined to forgive when York was reluctant to open its gates to him 10 years later in a renewal of the wars.

However, more than royal displeasure was involved in the

---

* The term was not used at the time, for although the white rose was one of the badges of the House of York, the red rose was the badge of Tudor and not Lancaster. In view of the continuing use of 'Wars of the Roses' for Yorkshire and Lancashire sporting fixtures, it is worth stressing that York and Lancaster were titles of nobility and not territorial titles. The Duke of York's main estates were further south, and many citizens and Yorkshiremen supported the House of Lancaster.

city's decline. The cloth industry was moving to the new textile towns of Wakefield, Leeds, and Halifax. The merchants suffered as property rents declined. Epidemics of bubonic plague and something like influenza were particularly severe in the early Tudor period, compounding the decline in population. It becàme harder to find enough wealthy men to serve as Mayors and Sheriffs (they were often out of pocket at the end of their year of office) until in 1526 John Smith simply left York when elected Sheriff, and lived at Shipton Manor to avoid taking office. By 1528 the Corporation threatened to surrender all the city's rights and privileges to the King rather than pay their debts in full, and only financial help by the royal ministers Wolsey and Cromwell staved off civic bankruptcy. To make matters worse, London took more of the export trade, and the growing size of seagoing ships meant that York ceased to be a major port, and had to trade overseas from Hull. One telling indication of York's decay is the contrast between Monk Bar, a handsome 14th- and 15th-century building in good freestone, typical of what the citizens could afford in their age of prosperity, and the Red Tower of *c.* 1490, a markedly economical job in brick.

For a short time there seemed a prospect of reversing the city's decline. Edward IV was no friend to the city, but his younger brother Richard Duke of Gloucester ruled the North sympathetically, if firmly, on his behalf (1471–83), and continued to take a close interest in the region when he became King as Richard III (1483–5). He was what contemporaries called a 'good lord' to the citizens, honouring York with ceremonial visits, grants of privileges and tax remissions, and doing his best to revive its prosperity. When he was seeking political support in 1483 he gave York the unprecedented right to elect four M.P.s instead of the usual two, a privilege shared only by London. Soon after his coronation he spent a fortnight in York with his queen and his young son, whom he invested as Prince of Wales in the Minster. Much to his grief, the boy prince died in 1484 and was buried at nearby Sheriff Hutton, where his supposed tomb is in the church. The Corporation repaid Richard's favours with loyalty, swiftly sending an armed force to help him against Henry Tudor in 1485, though through apparent treachery they were informed of Richard's need too late to reach Bosworth Field in time. On hearing the news of the battle the city fathers recorded openly in their council minutes that 'King Richard, late mercifully reigning upon us', was 'piteously slain and murdered, to the great heaviness of this city'.* Debate still centres, of course, on the character and sincerity of Richard, but this remarkable entry testifies clearly to the Corporation's feelings. Whether, as Canon Raine and others have claimed, the lesser citizens were more hostile to him is not clear; but it is significant that when Henry VII sent an envoy to York two days after Bosworth, he went in fear of being lynched in the streets.

Whether or not Richard, given time, could have solved the city's economic problems, they certainly worsened after 1485. There were, however, two signs of improvement for the city and indeed the whole North, which bore fruit later. One was an attempt by Henry VII to end the old dissensions with Scotland that had provoked numerous wars and a permanent state of lawlessness on the Borders. In 1497 he planned a military expedition against the Scots from York, which he was unable to pursue, but in 1503 he married his daughter Margaret to the Scots king, and she visited York on her way north; the marriage was to produce the Stuart succession to the English throne exactly a century later and so to unite the Scottish and English crowns. The other sign of future peace was the creation of the King's Council in the Northern Parts, a recognition by the Crown that England north of the Humber was too far distant to be effectively ruled from Westminster. It was a special royal council in the York area – originally at the royal castle of Sheriff Hutton – to provide administration and justice for Northerners. It originated in a council of Richard III, but was greatly strenthened by Henry VII and Henry VIII.

When Henry VIII renounced the power of the Pope and

* This famous entry can be seen in place in the original volume, despite Raine's assertion in *York Civic Records*, vol. 1, that it has been lost. The original clearly reads 'mercifully' rather than Raine's 'lawfully'.

made himself head of the English Church (1533) he set in train a series of events that led to the establishment of a Protestant State Church, although that went beyond what he apparently intended. The breach with Rome in itself aroused little opposition, but the attacks on traditional doctrines and religious institutions that followed provoked considerable opposition. Many older histories speak of the Tudor North as much more traditional and even reactionary than the South, dominated in religion by unquestioned Catholicism and socially by the power of great families like the Percies. That is certainly an over-simplification, but there is some truth in it, and in York and in parts of the North the monks, nuns, and friars remained more popular than in other regions. When Henry began dissolving the monasteries in 1536 – including the two priories of St Clement's and Holy Trinity at York – his action was widely resented. In October 1536 an explosive mixture of religious conservatism, provincial grievances, and economic problems produced a widespread Northern revolt. Large forces quickly assembled, restored most of the monasteries already dissolved, and took York without striking a blow. Marching behind a banner of the Five Wounds of Christ, they called their rising 'the Pilgrimage of Grace' for the defence of the Church. They occupied York for two months and clearly enjoyed widespread support. Eventually Henry tricked them into disbanding without a fight, promising concessions, which he never fulfilled. He took his revenge the next year, hanging several monks at York for their part in the revolt, and subjecting the rebel leader, Robert Aske, to the terrible death of hanging alive in chains from Clifford's Tower. In 1541 he made his only visit to the North, accompanied by his new queen Catherine Howard, and was welcomed to York by a penitent Mayor and aldermen kneeling for forgiveness and offering rich presents. The tour was politically satisfactory, confirming his Northern power; only afterwards was it alleged that his queen had committed adulteries at York and elsewhere on the progress, for which she was executed five months later.

The 'Reformation' is really a convenient but misleading

expression for two profound changes – the establishment of a national State Church and the longer process of conversion of the people to Protestantism. Both were resented at York, which was generally traditional in its religious sympathies and depended heavily on the business brought to its tradesmen by clergy, monks, pilgrims, and suitors to the church courts. All the city's monasteries and friaries were suppressed in 1536–9, their sites plundered for building material, their libraries and artistic treasures scattered or destroyed. The ruins of St Mary's Abbey are a reminder of the architectural losses, and near by, in the basement of the Yorkshire Museum, the sculptural losses are also apparent. Among other treasures on display are exquisite fragments of St William's shrine [21] in the Minster, broken up on the King's orders in 1541. Even a small house like the Austin friary had a library of over 650 books, of which only eight are known to survive. Even schools and hospitals were not spared. Henry confiscated St Leonard's Hospital, which still housed nearly 50 sick and elderly, and appears to have effectively closed both grammar schools by seizing their endowments. St Peter's School was apparently closed in 1539 and not re-opened until after 1565, though Archbishop Holgate had founded a new school in 1546. The Minster lost not only its school but most of its plate and endowments; the last Minster treasurer resigned in 1547, stating with pardonable exaggeration that 'all the treasure having been taken, there was no need of a treasurer'. His great house – Gray's Court rather than the so-called Treasurer's House in front of it – passed out of the hands of the church to become a private mansion.

The Protestant Reformation gathered momentum under Edward VI (1547–53), when the parish churches were stripped of most of their Catholic furnishings and plate, and the chantries, where prayers for the dead were endowed, were confiscated by the Crown. Fortunately the stained glass, which in so many towns was destroyed at this time, was largely preserved. The two series of dissolutions – of the monasteries in 1536–9 and the chantries in 1548 – also entailed a revolution in property ownership, since so many city houses and rents had been granted for the upkeep of religious houses and chantry priests. About half the houses in York were seized by the Crown, and sold mainly to London merchants and royal officials. Although many were then sold back piecemeal to local men, there must have been a severe short-term drain of rents to London. There can be no doubt that the citizens were unhappy with the direction of religious policy under Edward, and that the restored Catholic régime of his sister Mary I (1553–8) was more congenial. She was even rumoured in 1554 to be contemplating moving her capital from London to York 'to be among Catholic people'. Certainly many surviving citizens' wills show a reluctance to accept the Edwardian religious settlement and a ready conformity to the Marian reaction.

It would, however, be unfair to depict the Reformation in an entirely negative way, even though it almost certainly aggravated York's economic decay and offended many citizens by attacking cherished rituals and beliefs. Two major positive achievements may be illustrated from a York building and from the career of York's greatest native.* The Pilgrimage of Grace had taught the King the need for effective government north of the Humber to alleviate discontent and avert future revolts. The old council of Richard III and Henry VII had become ineffective, and in 1537 Henry VIII reorganized it as a more powerful King's Council in the Northern Parts, with its headquarters in the York area. When St Mary's Abbey was suppressed in 1539, the site was not sold but retained by the King. The Council moved into the Abbot's house and gradually enlarged it as its headquarters, giving it the name of King's Manor [32], which it has retained ever since. This powerful body ruled five Northern counties from the Manor for a century (1539–1641), making royal government more effective throughout the North and alleviating the sense of provincial neglect and misgovernment that lay behind the Pilgrimage.

Even before the Pilgrimage, a York man in exile had

---

* Coverdale can fairly be so described, because evidence published by J.F. Mozley in 1953 established that he was born in the city, and no one of greater standing in European history is demonstrably a native of York; Alcuin's case is uncertain.

published a book that had an incalculable influence on the course of English Protestantism and on the whole English-speaking world. Miles Coverdale (1488–1568) left his native city to study at Cambridge, and later went abroad to work with Tyndale and others on translating the Bible into English. It was Coverdale who published the first complete English Bible (1535) and whose masterpiece was the official Great Bible of 1539 sponsored by the King's minister Thomas Cromwell. The effect of these books on a public that had previously been forbidden translations of the Bible was immense; and Coverdale's work has endured. The psalms sung in Anglican churches even today are the 1535 Coverdale version, and the Authorized Version of the Bible still widely used, although dated 1611, is largely taken direct from his Great Bible. Coverdale has been rightly called 'a major and too often neglected figure of the English Reformation',* and amends are long overdue for the neglect of his memory at York.

One last effect of the Reformation requires a comment. Most of the suppressions of religious institutions were initiated by the Crown, but the Corporation took advantage of the climate to arrange one of its own by Act of Parliament (1547), involving a reduction in the number of their parish churches. Forty was too many for one decaying city, and they reduced the number by 15, selling off the sites and buildings for their own financial benefit. In general, the more prosperous and imposing churches were spared, and the reduction was drastic enough to allow the city to continue with the same number until Victorian times, when the movement of population out of the walled city centre revived the problem of redundancies. Most of the churches were quickly pulled down for the sake of their stone and lead, but one modest little church, spared for other uses, still stands in St Andrewgate. Not far away, between Aldwark and the city wall, St Helen-on-the-Walls, which was closed at the same time, is of special interest because it was demolished so early that the exact site was forgotten, until excavation in 1973–4

---

* A.G. Dickens, *The English Reformation* (1964), p. 131.

in advance of redevelopment. More interesting even than the re-discovery of the church was the excavation and scientific analysis of over 1,000 graves from the churchyard, which for the first time is providing a picture of the height and physique of the citizens of one ordinary and not very prosperous parish. The average height of adult males was 5 ft 7 in. and of females 5 ft 2 in., and a large proportion were found to have suffered from osteo-arthritis. A high death-rate at all ages meant that only about 9 per cent of the population reached the age of 60.

Peace and War
1560–1689

Elizabeth I (1558–1603) came to the throne at a difficult time for both city and country. York had endured a century of economic decline, aggravated by famine and severe epidemics at the end of Mary's reign. The Lord President of the Northern Council was living away from York at Sheffield Castle, and the city lost much legal business. Fortunately, Elizabeth was in 1561 persuaded to make the King's Manor (Walk 3) the permanent home of both President and Council, and they remained there for the next 80 years. Those 80 years saw a distinct revival in York's prosperity and importance, and much of the credit belongs to the presence of the Northern Council, which by the end of the Queen's long reign was hearing up to 2,000 cases a year, besides acting as an administrative body enforcing the decisions of the Queen's government throughout the North. The roll of Lords President includes two outstanding administrators who were good friends to the city. Henry Earl of Huntingdon was a distant cousin of Elizabeth and was seriously canvassed as her heir in the 1560s, much to the Queen's annoyance; however, once she had overcome her distrust of him he proved an outstandingly loyal and efficient ruler of the North for a generation (1572–95). Sir Thomas Wentworth, later Earl of Strafford (President 1628–41), was equally efficient, though he roused much hostility as one of the chief ministers of Charles I and was finally executed on the orders of Parliament. Most of the Presidents left their mark in extensions and improvements to the Manor; notable are the council chamber remodelled by Huntingdon and now called after him, and a great hall and new ranges added by Lord Sheffield (President 1603–19).

During the rule of the Lords President York gradually

recovered some of its old importance, and by the mid 17th century it was the third largest and wealthiest town in England (after London and Norwich), with a population of about 12,000. Shops and inns flourished, and overseas trade revived, encouraging the merchants to reorganize themselves by royal charter under the grandiloquent title of the Company of Merchant Adventurers (1581). When William Camden, the schoolmaster-historian, visited York about that time, he found it the most beautiful city in the North, 'pleasant, large, and strongly fortified, adorned with private as well as public buildings'. He singled out especially Ouse Bridge, 'a stone bridge, with the largest arch I have ever seen'. He did not exaggerate. The medieval bridge had been carried away by floods, and the new bridge of 1565–6 had a central span of 81 ft. It can now be admired only in drawings and paintings, having been replaced in its turn in 1810–20, but many buildings survive from the construction boom that began towards the end of Elizabeth's reign and continued under James I (1603–25) and Charles I (1625–49). They include fine gabled houses in Stonegate and Petergate, and the so-called Herbert House on the Pavement (Walk 5), grander and more luxurious versions of the medieval timber-framed tradition; brick was not yet fashionable again as a building material.

Growing wealth led to a demand for more comforts, and during the century 1550–1650 chimneys and window-glass became common for the first time in the houses of the well-to-do. Staircases replaced ladders; walls were lined with snug oak panelling instead of being hung with cloths. The Cock and Bottle inn, Skeldergate, incorporates features from its Elizabethan predecessor, which was plainly up-to-date for its time; they include wainscot panelling and timber-framed windows. Other contemporary panelling from demolished houses has been collected in the 'Tudor room' at the Castle Museum. There was also a fashion after 1600 for decorative plaster ceilings, and a fine example, again saved from a demolished house, can be seen in the King's Manor.

However, these houses and furnishings, like the Shambles

houses, are disinfected fragments of a Tudor and Stuart past that was far from 'merrie'. Despite increasing provision of street paving, lighting, and cleansing, it was a dirty, muddy, overcrowded city, where pigs scavenged in the streets, chamber-pots were emptied from windows, and life was very earthy. Not until 1600 did the Corporation erect a wainscot partition 'before the pissing hole' in their inner council chamber off the Guildhall. It was also a brutal and violent time as a hardening of religious divisions broke down the easy-going attitudes of the mid-Tudor Corporation. The turning-point was 1569–70, when the Earls of Northumberland and Westmorland led a Northern Catholic revolt and when the Pope excommunicated Elizabeth and declared her deposed. The Government was gradually driven to harsher policies against Catholic priests and sympathizers. In 1570 many of the city's Catholic church furnishings were swept away, and soon afterwards the Church authorities began to fine Catholics who would not attend Protestant services (recusants). In 1572 the Earl of Northumberland, having been finally captured, was publicly executed on the Pavement for his part in the 1569 revolt, and by 1578 the arrival at York of seminary priests from the Continent was provoking further counter-measures. In the last 21 years of the Queen's reign 27 priests and 14 Catholic layfolk were executed at 'Tyburn' on Knavesmire, all of the priests and some of the laity with the obscenities of hanging, drawing, and quartering, and although the persecution eased after 1603, spasmodic executions of Catholics continued until 1680. The execution that caused most revulsion was that of Margaret Clitherow, a butcher's wife of the Shambles, who was brought to trial in the Guildhall for harbouring priests. She would not plead to the charge, perhaps to avoid the penalties to her family if she were tried for treason and found guilty, and so was sentenced to the terrible punishment of pressing to death (1586). Her martyrdom and saintly character (for which she was canonized in 1970) represent the attractive side of resistance to the Elizabethan settlement of religion; a different side was represented by another York native, the mercenary soldier Guy Fawkes

(1570–1606), a household name because of his share in the Gunpowder Plot (1605). It is unfortunate that York prefers to commemorate figures like Fawkes (or, for that matter, Dick Turpin) rather than Coverdale or Margaret Clitherow.

By the time of the Gunpowder Plot, James I had united the crowns of England and Scotland (1603). The Borders were peaceful at last, and York, which had had no royal visitor since 1541, saw a series of visits by James I and Charles I on journeys between Edinburgh and London (1603, 1617, 1633). James even seems to have toyed again with the idea of making York a capital of 'Great Britain', as the united realms came to be called, but nothing was done. Instead of being a military centre, York was becoming a peaceful social capital for the Northern nobles and gentry who found London too far away but who wanted to develop a modest alternative to the London 'season'. This was a crucial change in its fortunes. The medieval city had thriven on industry as well as trade and the Church; but York's revived prosperity under the Lords President came from its rôle as an administrative and social centre, and it had no substantial industry again until the 19th century. It lay between growing textile towns to the west, notably Leeds, and the port of Hull to the east (neither of which relied as much on York as they had in the Middle Ages), and Newcastle with its booming coal trade was rapidly overtaking York as the largest city in the North.

Gentlemen visited York to shop, to go to law, to vote in county elections at the Castle, or simply for entertainment; bowling, cock-fighting, archery, plays, and races were all staged for their benefit by the shrewd citizens. The first recorded horse race was held between local gentry in 1530, when a silver bell was the winner's prize, and races were held intermittently until established on a regular basis in the 18th century. The richer gentry were beginning to keep up town houses in the city for the winter season. The Fairfaxes built a major mansion on Bishophill, now totally vanished, while the surviving Treasurer's House (Walk 1) is really the private mansion of the Young family. The Archbishops, however, could no longer afford to keep up their palace by the Minster as well as Bishopthorpe. Archbishop Young destroyed the great hall to sell the lead from the roof; and the site was bought by Sir Arthur Ingram (d. 1642), a ruthless financier and self-made man who rose through royal favour. He built a mansion on the site, which, with its gardens, was the grandest house in York. A tourist in 1634 called it 'a second Paradise' filled with 'massy plate, rich hangings, lively pictures, and statues rich, £150 pearl glasses, fair stately £500 organ, and other rich furniture in every room'.

After the success of Crown and Church in enforcing Protestantism at York in the 1570s, the life and worship of the leading citizens had become 'Puritan' or Low Church in spirit. Catholic recusants were a small minority, never more than 100 adults between 1578 and 1676. Most citizens accepted the Elizabethan settlement, and by early Stuart times churches were plain and services simple. Medieval colour was obliterated by whitewash, often covered by Biblical texts; organs were removed; services centred on the sermon and not the communion table. Something of this period can still be sensed where its furnishings survive, like the pulpit in All Saints, Pavement, with its appropriate inscriptions (e.g. 'Preach the word. Be instant in season and out of season. Timo'). In the 1630s the Church authorities began a revival of more Catholic forms of worship – the visitor of 1634 was entranced to see and hear in the Minster 'a fair, large high organ' and 'a sweet snowy crew of choristers'. This, however, shocked the city aldermen, whose religion and politics were beginning to drive them further away from the policies of State and State Church. They preferred to pray with hats on, and to sit round the communion table, practices that earned the censure of the senior clergy by the 1630s.

Charles I's second visit to York (1639) came at an ominous time, when he was raising an army against a Scottish rebellion. It was, however, a cordial visit. He was welcomed at Micklegate Bar with a fulsome speech by Recorder Widdrington, and entertained by Mayor Roger Jaques, whom he knighted, at his house on the Pavement. Between reviews of troops, he distributed the Royal Maundy in the Minster. In 1640 Charles was again in York to deal with a second Scots war. His measures involved the summoning of a Great Council of peers in the York Deanery, but they could only advise him to make terms, and a humiliating peace was signed at Ripon. The Scots wars were nationalist and religious risings against an Anglican religious settlement that Charles was trying to force on his Northern Kingdom, and a major cause of the English defeats was that many Englishmen (including York citizens) sympathized with the Scots on both political and religious grounds. The second war necessitated the calling of a parliament, the famous 'Long Parliament', which sat for over 12 years. It was hostile to Charles's personal rule, and one of its early measures was the dissolution of the Northern Council at York and the execution of Lord President Strafford, who had become the King's chief minister (1641). One of the least substantial charges of treason against Strafford was that he had displayed his personal arms on a royal building; the coat of arms in question can still be seen at the King's Manor. The merits of Charles's rule by royal prerogative are debatable; but the Council had certainly done much in 80 years to provide speedy and efficient justice and order in the North, and to increase prosperity. The Corporation regretted its dissolution, and petitioned for its restoration as soon as it was politically safe to do so, but in vain.

In the years after Strafford's execution, York witnessed, and took a prominent part in, events of great importance – two civil wars between King and Parliament, the execution of Charles I (1649), the first and only English experiment in republican rule, and the restoration of Charles's eldest son as Charles II (1660). Justice cannot possibly be done here to these events, or even to the city's military rôle in the wars, and the story has been told many times already. What perhaps has not been considered sufficiently is what the citizens felt when caught up in the centre of a national crisis. York was the King's temporary capital for five months (March–August 1642), and remained his Northern military centre until July 1644. It was held by a succession of royal governors, under the supreme command of the Marquess of Newcastle. The traditional picture is of a passionately Royalist city, but the citizens really had no choice of loyalty. The Royalist garrison in the Castle and its Parliamentary successor were too powerful to be resisted. The majority of aldermen in the 1630s and 1640s were hostile to Charles's religious policies, and belonged to the tradition that its enemies called Puritan but is better described by the modern analogy of Low Church. Some, nevertheless, supported the King when it came to war, but others were Parliamentarian or neutral. York's M.P.s throughout the 1640s were Aldermen Allanson and Hoyle, who were elected despite pressure from Strafford and who consistently supported Parliament against King. It is also significant that in 1643 and 1644 Newcastle did not trust the Corporation to elect a sufficiently Royalist mayor, and kept Sir Edmund Cowper in office by royal command. As soon as York fell in 1644, Parliament removed Cowper and installed Alderman Hoyle, M.P.; they also purged the Corporation of six active Royalists. Behind all the conflict, most aldermen united to keep control of the city and prevent popular unrest. The really radical groups who seized the opportunity of the civil wars to try to broaden the basis of government had no success at York.

The fall of York in 1644 was a major turning-point in the first Civil War, as Charles I admitted. Parts of Yorkshire were under Parliamentary control, but the North would remain under Royalist domination until York was taken. In the spring of 1644 three Parliamentary and Scots armies gradually tightened their grip round the city, a grip maintained until York surrendered. The episode has been fully treated in L. P. Wenham's *Great and Close Siege of York* (1970), and only the main events need be mentioned here. At first the defenders, under the command of Newcastle, manned a system of trenches and forts well outside the walls, including The Mount, a 'sconce' or fort on the Tadcaster road that has given its name to the road at that point. Soon, however, Newcastle was forced to retreat into the walled city and to burn the suburbs to deny shelter to the besiegers. The only significant battle occurred on 16 June, when the besiegers mined St Mary's Tower and entered through the breach before being driven back. On 1 July Prince Rupert raised the siege, but the next day he was defeated by the Parliamentarians in the decisive battle of Marston Moor seven miles W of York, and a fortnight later the citizens were compelled to yield. Fortunately the articles of surrender stipulated 'that neither churches nor other buildings shall be defaced', a clause that was respected. It saved the Minster and parish churches from the destruction that the soldiers wrought in Lincoln Cathedral; above all, it spared the city's wealth of stained glass. The credit for this apparently belongs to Ferdinando Lord Fairfax (1584–1648), the chief commander of the besiegers and a local landowner, who had a great affection for the city and its antiquities.

The city was quiet between 1645 and 1660, despite plots and rebellions in other parts of England. Members of the purged Corporation played a part in supporting the Commonwealth régime. Alderman Hoyle was a minor government official until he hanged himself on the anniversary of the King's execution, a suicide that provoked a witty and heartless Royalist epitaph:

> All hail fair fruit! may every crabtree bear
> Such blossoms, and so lovely every year . . .
> Yet let me ask one question, why alone?
> One member of a corporation?

Sir Thomas Widdrington (Recorder 1638–62), despite his fulsome welcome of Charles in 1639, became a leading political figure under Cromwell, while employing his leisure to write the first history of York, *Analecta Eboracensia*. Like other Englishmen, however, the Corporation moved with the times when Cromwell died and the republic became increasingly unpopular. Widdrington was one of many who supported General Monck in restoring the monarchy in 1660, and Monck's bloodless capture of York was an important step in the Restoration. He was also aided by Thomas Lord Fairfax (1612–71), Ferdinando's son and heir, whose influence at York was decisive. But it is not surprising that both Charles II (1660–85) and James II (1685–8) regarded the loyalty of York as dubious, and indeed political opposition to the Crown became widespread in York again after 1679. Both kings kept up a garrison in York and a royal governor at the King's Manor, oppressions that were greatly resented. The main guard was quartered in Clifford's Tower, derisively known as 'the minced pie', and in 1684 gutted by fire, perhaps deliberately. Relations between Governor Reresby and the citizens became even more strained under James II, who remodelled the city's charter and interfered with the machinery of local government, as he did in many towns, in an attempt to increase royal power and patronage. The revolution of 1688–9 was generally welcomed at York, which was for the last time at the centre of a national political crisis. On 17 November 1688 Lord Danby and other supporters of William of Orange captured the city without bloodshed and arrested Reresby. The Yorkshire gentry had made sure that they would no longer be threatened by royal power, and the garrison at York was disbanded.

The political revolutions of the crowded 50 years 1639–89 were closely bound up with religious changes, which left a permanent mark on York as on every other English community. Hitherto, despite the Reformation, there had been theoretically only one Church for all Englishmen. The Parliamentarian aldermen of the 1640s and 1650s had not rejected the Anglican Church, but had changed it in a more Protestant direction. After the Restoration, however, it was no longer possible to persuade them and others to accept the old Church order again, and after 1689 the Government abandoned even the idea of a comprehensive State Church. The medieval churches became the preserve of a dominant Established Church, flanked on one side by new 'Nonconformist' Churches and on the other by the Roman Catholics. Those 50 years saw the establishment of most of the separate Christian Churches that have endured to our own day. George Fox preached in the Minster in 1651 and was thrown down the steps for his pains. Soon there were separate congregations of Friends, Baptists, Presbyterians, and Unitarians. The oldest surviving Nonconformist church is the

Unitarian Chapel in St Saviourgate of 1693 (Walk 5) [34], although the Friends' Meeting House in Clifford Street incorporates part of a predecessor of 1674. A few Roman Catholics had always survived in York despite persecution, though no official chapel was built until 1802; but as early as 1686 the Convent of the Institute of St Mary (the Bar Convent) was established in Blossom Street (Walk 16), as a nunnery and a Catholic boarding school. It is the oldest Catholic nunnery in England and one of the earliest girls' schools of any denomination. However, although the main Nonconformist Churches were left in peace, both Catholics and Quakers suffered much persecution; and as late as 1680 a Catholic priest (Thomas Thwing) was hanged, drawn, and quartered on the Knavesmire.

The Age of the Gentry
1689–1835

History's progress does not move in a straight line, despite the optimistic beliefs of the Victorians. York's citizens – or rather the richer ones – had run their own affairs under the Crown's guidance from about 1200 to 1550. They had then suffered more and more interference by the central government under lords president and military governors. The removal of the royal garrison in 1688, however, led only to domination by the local aristocracy and gentry. Municipal self-government had to wait until the parliamentary reforms of the 1830s to reassert itself.

Contemporaries were in no doubt about the real source of prosperity and influence in late Stuart and Georgian York. Daniel Defoe spoke of the city as 'full of gentry and persons of distinction', who 'live at large and have houses proportioned to their quality'. 'Here is no trade indeed, except such as depends on the confluence of the gentry'. Francis Drake, the York historian, agreed: 'Except some few wine merchants, the export of butter, and some small trifles not worth mentioning, there is no other trade carried on in the city . . . the chief support of the city, at present, is the resort to and residence of several country gentlemen with their families in it'. They were right: York had no longer any major trade or manufacturing activity. It was merely a minor river port, of less importance than Hull or Newcastle, or even Leeds, further inland still. It had no major textile industry like its old rival Norwich, which was now outstripping it in wealth and population. Even its administrative importance had diminished after 1641, although it was still of course a shire town and capital of an archdiocese. What gave York a new lease of prosperity and importance was almost wholly its rôle as a social capital, with a winter season for Northern nobles and gentry.

The use of brick at the King's Manor and Bishopthorpe Palace in the late 15th century had done little to change the character of domestic architecture, and timber-framing remained popular and indeed fashionable well into the 17th century. The 'Herbert House' in Pavement (*c.* 1620) had the showy front timbered and jettied, and only the back in brick (Walk 5). (It is questionable how much of York's rather utilitarian timber-framing was intended to show; there is certainly a long-standing and justifiable tradition for covering it over. Pargetting was by no means uncommon, though none has survived the depredations of the 19th century.) The new buildings of the King's Manor used stone, though principally because there was a plentiful supply at hand in St Mary's Abbey. Brick was coming into its own by the Civil War, and Ingram's Hospital in Bootham (Walk 10) is an early example.

In 1645, shaken by the siege and the ease with which the suburbs had been fired, the Corporation ordered that all new houses should be built in brick. A 'Dutch' style developed after the Restoration, with curving gables, pedimented window surrounds, pilasters, and even rustication all in brick. The best surviving example is Archbishop Frewen's work at Bishopthorpe (1660–4), and much restored houses survive in Clifton (Walk 10) and Ogleforth (Walk 1). The grandest example was probably Bishophill House (Walk 7), town house of Sir Thomas Fairfax and later of his notorious son-in-law, the Duke of Buckingham, favourite of Charles II. Buckingham spent much time there after being banished from court and popularized the York winter season of masques, balls, and plays, but the splendours of his house have to be imagined with the aid of distant views in early panoramic engravings, as the house was demolished in the 18th century.

This exotic style was shortlived, and by the 1690s something more classical was taking over. Plain brick walls with stone window surrounds, sometimes linked together by vertical stone strips (Fenton House, *c.* 1700), developed into a style that remained popular till the 1720s, the windows set forward slightly in plain brick bands, sometimes with horizontal bands or cornices as at Cumberland House (*c.* 1700) for Alderman Cornwell (Walk 6) and Red House (*c.* 1714) for Alderman Sir William Robinson (Walk 3). In 1694 the last serious fire in York destroyed many houses in Ousegate, and the new houses built there in the early 18th century have giant pilasters framing and punctuating the upper storeys, a style adopted by the Debtors' Prison (1701–5), probably designed by William Wakefield and one of the most monumental of the city's buildings (Walk 6). The orders were also popular inside, articulating panelled rooms as in the Judge's Lodging (Walk 3) or the saloon of the Queen's Hotel. After the 1720s the orders tended to be confined to staircases and entrance halls, though sometimes with surprisingly Baroque effects even in the 1750s.

Micklegate is, however, the best street in which to observe the architectural and social change represented by the new brick houses for the gentry. An old man told Drake, in the 1730s, that he could 'remember the street "near full of" timbered merchant's houses,' but 'what this street is remarkable for today are the new built houses of Henry Thompson esquire and Mr. Alderman Thompson'. Sadly, these houses (the Queen's Hotel) were demolished four years ago but their reconstruction, incorporating their spectacular rescued interiors, is promised. To the numerous later Georgian houses we shall return shortly.

By the 17th century more facilities for social gatherings and entertainment were being introduced. Tobacco shops were first licensed in 1632, and coffee-houses appeared by the 1660s in imitation of London. The latter were concentrated in Stonegate, and the lane called Coffee Yard was named from them. A permanent waterworks was opened in 1677 in Lendal Tower, on the bank of the Ouse. In 1709 horse-racing began on a regular basis, on Clifton Ings; assemblies for dancing and cards started about 1710; and in 1719 there appeared the *York Mercury,* the city's first newspaper. York became, in fact, the leading cultural as well as social centre of the North. Book printing (previously practised at York in the early Tudor period) was revived with a Royalist press in St William's College (1642) and has been continued ever since. Leading writers and craftsmen resident in York in late Stuart times included Martin Lister (*c.* 1638–1712), the royal physician; Francis Place (1647–1728), the pioneer landscape artist; Henry Gyles (1646–1709), the glass-painter; and John Etty (1634–1708), carpenter. Etty, though scarcely remembered today, was one of the instructors of Grinling Gibbons, and the quality of his surviving reredos in St Michael-le-Belfrey speaks for itself.

Georgian York, in the strict sense of the period of the first four Georges (1714–1830), continued in much the same way, quiet, prosperous, and dominated by the gentry. After the dramatic period of 1639–89 it was rarely the scene of national political and military events, and for that reason some of the older York histories actually conclude their narrative in 1688!* This, of course, is absurd. The most casual tour of York reveals that the city enjoyed a period of real splendour and importance in the 18th century, and the people and buildings are no less interesting because the period was one of peace and stability.

Political history was admittedly quiet if not dull. The medieval system of city government remained intact until 1835, a self-perpetuating oligarchy of Mayor, aldermen, and councillors. The only real change was that the line between citizens and country gentry was becoming blurred – Sir William Robinson, for example, was a country squire as well as a York M.P. and alderman – and that numerous Mayors represented the professions and trades providing services for the gentry – wine merchants, apothecaries, a toyman, and an architect. The peaceful political history of the city was interrupted only occasionally, most colourfully in 1745–6, when the Young Pretender marched south and York was put in a state of defence. After the Pretender's defeat at Culloden, the victorious Duke of Cumberland was entertained by the Corporation at Gray's Court on his return journey to London. Twenty-two rebels were executed at

---

* E.g. J. Raine, *Historic Towns: York* (1893); J.E. Morris, *The Little Guides: York* (1924).

York, and the heads of two were exhibited on Micklegate Bar, the last use of this barbaric practice. These events have been recounted prominently in histories of York; but more significant if less colourful were the great reform meetings held in later Georgian York. Political meetings and parliamentary elections for the whole county continued to be held in York until 1832, and it was there that the Yorkshire Association for Parliamentary Reform campaigned in the 1770s and 1780s, there that William Wilberforce from Hull (1759–1833) campaigned as M.P. for the abolition of slavery and other measures, and there that county meetings in 1823 and 1831 precipitated the events that finally led to parliamentary reform. In viewing the Castle Yard today it is easy to forget those crowded and excited meetings – such as the speech of Wilberforce that so impressed James Boswell: 'I saw what seemed a shrimp mount on the table, but, as I listened, he grew, and grew, till the shrimp became a whale'.

York benefited greatly from the improvements in road transport in the coaching age. Eight roads radiating from it were improved by turnpike trusts operating by levying tolls on travellers. These well-maintained toll roads were frequently thronged with carriers' carts, which played a large part in the prosperity of the district. More important still, York was situated on a main route from London, and the Black Swan in Coney Street was the most famous of several inns catering for mail- and passenger-coaches between York and the capital. During the Georgian age coaches became steadily more numerous and more speedy; the four-day journey from London of 1658–1761 had been cut to only 20 hours by 1836. Nor was water transport neglected. The River Ouse was improved by the building of a lock and dam at Naburn (1757), and the lower Foss was canalized from 1793. These improvements in transport helped a modest growth in York's markets and trade, especially the export of butter to London by boat. Small-scale industries were established: comb-making, toy-making, glass and chemicals, flour-milling, and two humble family firms of confectioners, which eventually became Rowntrees and Terrys. Yet the industrialization that was the making of Leeds and the West

Riding towns passed York by. 'The brutal fact was', says Dr Brooks, 'that, without either water power or cheap coal, York was unable to share in the industrial developments of the period'.*

Instead it was the gentry who provided York with its economic prosperity, who subscribed to the building of the Assembly Rooms (Walk 3) [37], who secured the layout of the New Walk along the banks of the Ouse, who patronized the races (held on Knavesmire from 1730), the theatre (first built on its present site in 1744), and the Festival Concert Rooms (1824–5: now demolished), and it was they who commissioned the fine town-houses in the fashionable streets, Micklegate House and Garforth House (Walk 7), Peasholme House (Walk 5), Castlegate House and Fairfax House (Walk 6). Some aldermen, imitating the gentry, moved in the other direction and started commuting from country seats. It was partly to counteract this that the Corporation built the Mansion House in 1725–7, 14 years before its London counterpart, to be an official residence for the Mayor in his year of office.

The development of public services of various kinds can be traced in the building of the Debtors' Prison (1705), Walk 6; the County Hospital (1740: not the present building); the County Lunatic Asylum (1772–7), Walk 10; the Assize Courts (1773–7) [41] and the Female Prison (1780–3), Walk 6; the Friends' Mental Hospital (1796), Walk 13; the new Ouse Bridge (1810–20), Walk 7; the Cattle Market (1826–38: now demolished); and the Yorkshire Museum (1827–30), Walk 2. Some of these facilities were required to meet a growing population – York's doubled from about 12,000 in 1750 to 26,000 in 1831. Many new private houses were built, and a few new streets were created within the walls, notably New Street, St Leonard's Place, and Parliament Street, while the suburbs expanded considerably. As we shall see, the congestion produced by growing population and traffic led the Corporation from 1799 to make efforts to demolish the medieval walls and gates.

* A. Stacpoole & others, *The Noble City of York* (1972), p. 313.

Only Anglican churches are missing from the usual catalogue of Georgian building types – Dringhouses church of 1725 having been rebuilt – for the 25 surviving medieval churches still sufficed, though their fittings were much improved and survive in surprising quantities. Indeed the Anglicans twice came close to losing their mother-church: in 1829, when the insane Jonathan Martin set fire to the Minster, destroying the furnishings and roof of the choir, and in 1840, when an accidental fire caused equally severe damage to the nave. Miraculously, neither fire destroyed the superb medieval stained glass. New church building was left to the Nonconformists, especially the dynamic Methodists, who made many converts, thanks largely to numerous visits from John Wesley between 1751 and 1790. Their earliest purpose-built chapel of 1759 can still be seen in Aldwark (Walk 5).

Fortunately this great period of building came at a time when architectural taste was at its highest (a situation that no longer held in later building booms, however excellent their individual products might be). High Palladianism, of which Lord Burlington, designer of the Assembly Rooms, was one of the most influential exponents, never really took hold in the city. The Rooms were revolutionary and inconvenient. The local architects were more than competent, and though pattern books were of course consulted, a less rigorously intellectual approach was preferred. William Etty, son of John Etty, probably designed the Mansion House (Walk 3) [26]. After Burlington, national architects did not appear, which was no great loss since York produced John Carr, a mason's son from Horbury, twice Lord Mayor of the city, architect of Fairfax House, Castlegate House, Harewood, Denton, Farnley, and Basildon. Thomas Atkinson was his chief rival in the city, architect of much of Bishopthorpe Palace and the Bar Convent. Carr's firm continued, after his retirement, under the two Peter Atkinsons, the first responsible for No. 51 Bootham [43], while the second designed the elegant new Ouse Bridge.

The beauty of Georgian York is evident in its fine public buildings and its more prosperous streets, especially Micklegate, St Saviourgate, and Bootham. Yet there was a darker side to the city. Poverty was rife, as in every century until the 20th, and many of the poor were crowded together in insanitary conditions. The rich were moving out of the old centre into the suburbs for the first time in York's history, and the older properties within the walls were becoming slums – especially the Bedern, the Water Lanes off Castlegate, and the Walmgate area. Water supply, street cleansing and lighting were still luxuries mainly benefiting the rich. Until the early 19th century, for example, only about half the population enjoyed piped water. Despite the new hospitals, intended especially for the poor, medical services were totally inadequate. The grandeur of Carr's Bootham Park Hospital should not blind us to the fact that treatment of the insane there was notoriously bad from its opening, so much so that Samuel Tuke and other Quakers set up the Retreat as a model mental asylum in opposition. It quickly acquired an international reputation for new and humane methods of treatment, and was the building that attracted most attention from the French economist Blanqui when he visited York in 1823.

Schooling was also poor for a city of York's size, though it is only fair to mention the Blue Coat (boys') and Grey Coat (girls') charity schools, both founded in 1705, which performed valuable work for over 200 years, and the little-remembered stay in Monkgate (1803–40) of Manchester College (Walk 12), the predecessor of Manchester College at Oxford. It was one of the highly-esteemed Dissenting Academies catering for Nonconformists (who were still barred from the universities), and it moved to York simply to place itself under the direction of Charles Wellbeloved, the historian and minister of St Saviourgate chapel. There was also a growth in charitable provision for the elderly and infirm throughout the Restoration and Georgian periods, of which the most conspicuous survivals are several neat almshouses. The oldest still occupied for its original purpose, Sir Arthur Ingram's in Bootham, is of 1630–3 (Walk 10), though it was gutted in the siege of York and had to be reconstructed. Other attractive survivals founded or rebuilt under the Georges include the Merchant Taylors' almshouses in Aldwark (1730), Walk 5; Mary Wandesford's Hospital in Bootham (1739), Walk 10; Dorothy Wilson's Hospital at Foss Bridge (1812), Walk 5; and Anne Middleton's Hospital in Skeldergate (rebuilt in 1828), Walk 7.

Cultural life continued to develop. Apart from the architects already mentioned, Georgian York boasted a remarkable number of craftsmen, artists, and writers. Three generations of the Fisher family were outstanding monumental sculptors in the city, as their numerous works in the Minster and churches reveal. They were excellent at figure work, but their best products, like the Dealtry monument in the Minster, are those showing their exquisitely refined architectural detailing. An outstanding group of doctors included Clifton Wintringham (1689–1748), author of medical works and builder of the Judges' Lodgings, Francis Drake (1696–1771), and John Burton (1710–71), the inventor of obstetric forceps. The two last are better-remembered today for their important historical works, Burton for *Monasticon Eboracense* (1758) and Drake for *Eboracum* (1736), the first great history of York. Burton was satirized as Dr Slop in *Tristram Shandy*, Laurence Sterne's masterpiece, first published in York, and drawing widely on local people for its satire. Sterne (1713–68), nephew of a Minster Precentor, was the outstanding local writer of the period.

Less well remembered, but as important in his own field, was Henry Hindley (1701–71), horologist, whose shop stood on the site of Banks' Music Shop. He was among other things a pioneer maker of telescopes, and another York resident, John Goodricke (1764–86), was the first astronomer to discover variable stars. The culmination of this intellectual and scientific activity was of more than provincial importance. In 1823 W.V. Harcourt (1789–1871), a chemist and local clergyman, helped to found the Yorkshire Philosophical Society (Y.P.S.), which leased St Mary's Abbey from the Crown and built the Yorkshire Museum on part of the site. Even more significantly, the Society was then instrumental in founding the British Association for the Advancement of Science, of which Harcourt became General Secretary, and which held its first meeting in the new museum at York in 1831. At that meeting the geologist Murchison said that 'to this city, as the cradle of the Association, we shall ever look back with gratitude, and whether we meet hereafter on the banks of the Isis, the Cam, or the Forth, to this spot we shall proudly revert'. The promise was kept, and five subsequent meetings have been held in York, the most recent in 1959.

Industry and Tourism:
York since 1835

The Y.P.S. and the British Association were symbols of change as domination by the Yorkshire gentry drew to a close, with the races and assemblies in decline and the Established Church also feeling itself under threat from Roman Catholicism, Nonconformity, and science. (In 1844 the Dean of York felt impelled to publish *The Bible defended against the British Association*.) More immediately, the 1830s witnessed two profound changes that gave back to York, on a more modest level, the political independence and industrial base it had enjoyed in the Middle Ages. One was the series of political reforms for which Yorkshiremen had campaigned so effectively, especially the Municipal Corporations Act (1835), which put an end to the old self-elected council with their deference to clergy and gentry. The new Corporation consisted of councillors elected by the more prosperous householders, and aldermen elected by the councillors, and most of this body was local businessmen. The process had begun that led to democratic local government for the first time. Then in 1839 the coming of the railway stimulated a modest expansion of industry in York.

Even before that a few firms of importance had established themselves, notably the iron foundry of John Walker (*c.* 1801–53) in Walmgate. It achieved national fame after Walker was selected to cast gates and railings for Kew Gardens and the British Museum and was appointed ironfounder to the Queen (1847). It is a success story showing that not all important firms based on iron were situated in the new industrial towns; but Walker was exceptional in relying on barge transport. What hampered York's industrial development, apart from the lack of iron and coal, was its situation off the main roads. Despite its coaches to London, it lay away from the Great North Road (A1), and much commercial traffic passed it by. What saved it was the fact that the new transport by railway not only came into York but made it a major junction and carriage-works; from the beginning it has been a station on the main line from London to Edinburgh. York's first train left the new station in Toft Green on 29 May 1839, proceeding only as far as South Milford, but by 1840 the line extended to Euston via Normanton, and London was within 14 hours' journey. From 1852 a shorter route took the York trains to King's Cross, in only five hours; and in 1871 the present even shorter route via Selby was adopted. Space does not allow a full account of the various railways and their companies; suffice it to say that by 1850 York was the centre of a network radiating in all directions.

The credit for this is generally given to George Hudson 'the railway king' (1800–71), an able, unscrupulous, self-made man. He was active in politics, thrice Mayor, with many financial interests throughout the north-east, especially in the new railway companies. He is said to have persuaded George Stephenson to make York rather than Leeds the focus of railway activity, though his oft-quoted intention to 'mak all t'railways come to York' is a myth.* He and his friends dominated York's political and business life from 1837, lining their own pockets, until his commercial schemes collapsed in 1849 with the exposure of financial frauds. His railway empire in that year amounted to over a quarter of the total British network, and extended to London, Bristol, and Kelso. After his fall, the Corporation erased his memory with Stalinist thoroughness. His portrait was removed from the Mansion House; the new Hudson Street leading to the station was renamed Railway Street; and the statue erected near the station was that of Hudson's rival George Leeman. York owes Hudson a good deal; an act of reparation was made on the centenary of his death when Railway Street was rechristened George Hudson Street.

The railway became the characteristic form of travel to

* A. J. Peacock, 'George Hudson and the Historians', *York History* no. 1 (n.d.), pp. 30, 31.

Victorian York. The King of Saxony travelled there by rail as early as 1844, and Charles Dickens, a frequent visitor, always came by train. The railways became almost at once the largest employer of labour in the city; the station and engine and carriage works between them employed over 1,200 men in 1855 and 5,500 in 1900. A new suburb developed in Holgate, largely for railway workers. The visible signs of railway success were manifested in a fine series of public buildings: the new station [50] and adjoining hotel by Thomas Prosser (1877–8), and the N.E.R. headquarters offices of 1900–6. Nor was it only the railways as a direct employer that mattered so much to York; they also stimulated an expansion in other local industries, especially confectionery. Joseph Terry & Co. expanded rapidly from the 1850s, and Rowntree & Co. from the 1880s. These were, however, only belated responses to the new transport opportunities, and more must be said of the black side of early Victorian York.

The 1830s and 1840s saw not only the domination of Hudson but a growing awareness that the city was insanitary and overcrowded, and that conditions were even worsening. A cholera epidemic in 1832 killed 185 people, nearly 1 per cent of the population, and it was particularly severe in the insanitary districts of Walmgate and the Water Lanes. A special burial ground had to be opened in Thief Lane, part of which is still preserved opposite the railway station. Even so, despite medical agitation, little was done to improve public health, and the Irish famine of 1845–7 made things worse by driving starving and vagrant Irish to settle in York in large numbers and in overcrowded conditions (at the census of 1851 there were 1,928 Irish in York, forming over 5 per cent of the population). In 1847 typhus raged among the Irish, and in 1849 cholera struck York again; these two were the city's worst epidemics of the century. Public health improvement was very slow, and the death-rate actually rose after 1870 while that of England as a whole was falling. There was no slum clearance at all in the 19th century with the single exception of the Water Lanes in the 1870s, when those notorious slums were razed and a new thoroughfare,

Clifford Street (Walk 6), created in their place. Not until the 1890s did water-closets outnumber privies in York.

The Irish were seen by many Anglicans as a religious threat. Roman Catholics had enjoyed full civil rights since 1829, and now formed a greater proportion of the city's population than they had since the 16th century. St George's church (Walk 5) was built for the Walmgate Irish in 1850 and designed by J.A. Hansom, while the central Catholic chapel in Duncombe Place was replaced by the present church of St Wilfrid (1864) to designs by George Goldie (Walk 3). (Hansom and Goldie, two of the major Catholic architects between Pugin and Bentley, were both born in the city.) The churches are Gothic, and the prominent tower of St Wilfrid's, interfering with the newly-created view of the Minster, seems a deliberate challenge to the Established Church. The Nonconformists, on the other hand, still built in the classical style as a conscious reaction to such Catholic associations. A high point was reached in 1839–40, when both Congregationalists and Methodists built imposing chapels in St Saviourgate (Walk 5) with Ionic porticos. The Salem Chapel has been demolished, but the Methodists' fine Centenary Chapel survives. It was avowedly built as a 'cathedral of Methodism', in commemoration of the centenary of the movement. New opportunities came for the still-expanding churches when Priory Street was laid out in 1854 across the grounds of Holy Trinity Priory. By an irony of history the monks' precinct became and remains a concentration of Free Churches. Alongside the surviving Trinity church (Anglican), the Methodists built Wesley Chapel in 1856, the Baptists a chapel in 1868, and the Presbyterians St Columba's in 1879 (Walk 7). The Baptist chapel, unlike the others, was in Gothic style, symbolizing the Free Churches' belated following of Catholics and Anglicans in architectural fashion. Altogether about 30 Nonconformist chapels were built in the 19th century, and their congregations out-numbered those of the Established Church. The Anglicans themselves still had sufficient ancient churches for the city centre; indeed, with the movement of population into the suburbs they were beginning to be faced with the problem of redundancies. However, new Anglican churches were built in Victoria's reign to serve the new suburbs and the growing dormitory villages like Dringhouses (Walk 16) and Heworth (Walk 12), and some rebuilding took place. The most ambitious, though an extraordinarily old-fashioned design, is the massive rebuilding of St Lawrence's church (Walk 13) outside Walmgate Bar (1883–92).

Population growth is the key factor in the development of modern York. The population of 29,000 in 1841 increased by 26 per cent over the next 10 years, in large part through the impact of the railways, and continued to grow steadily until it reached 105,000 in 1951. The built-up area has expanded out of all proportion even to this increase in population, and the city is now 28 times larger than its walled medieval predecessor, expansion brought about partly by a growth of suburbs and dormitory villages as the population has deserted the old centre, but much more by a decline in crowding as more families have been able to live in separate homes with their own gardens. Traffic pressure has led to much road-widening, a process that began long before the motor car. Sydney Smith (1771–1845), the clerical writer and wit, once complained that York's streets were 'the narrowest in Europe; there is not actually room for two carriages to pass'. Such sentiments prevailed from the 1840s, and many of the older, narrower streets have been widened, often to the great loss of York's architectural heritage. Terraces of artisan housing were crammed into nearly every available acre within the walls, especially on Bishophill and in the Walmgate and Hungate areas, many degenerating into slums. The Bishophill area, however, largely laid out in the grounds of the old Fairfax/Buckingham mansion as its street-names indicate, is still an attractive survival, and is now likely to be conserved rather than replaced. More artisan housing spread well outside the walls, in Layerthorpe, the Groves, Clementhorpe, and South Bank, while the more prosperous citizens built larger houses in Clifton, Heworth, and the Mount.

Nineteenth-century York witnessed both architectural gains and losses on a large scale. No city can remain a museum, and some replacement of the building fabric was inevitable even in the absence of large-scale industrialization. This was accelerated, however, by an influential body of citizens in favour of 'improvements' for traffic and health reasons, many of them necessary; and they raised up in opposition, for almost the first time in York, a vocal body of conservationist opinion. The first battle was over the defences, which the Corporation tried to demolish entirely during the first half of the 19th century. In fairness to what must now seem an appalling policy, it should be remembered that most other corporations had already pulled down their walls and gates in the 18th century as unfashionable traffic obstructions. Fortunately the Archbishop challenged the Corporation in the courts in 1807–12, and from the 1820s influential citizens campaigned to save the walls, assisted by Sir Walter Scott and by the York-born artist William Etty (1787–1849). The Corporation did succeed in demolishing several posterns, some short stretches of wall, and the barbicans to all the gates except Walmgate Bar, but by 1860 the principle of preserving the rest was accepted, and in 1878–89 they were fully restored. There were more grievous losses elsewhere: the picturesque medieval/Tudor Ouse Bridge, demolished in 1810, which had at least a seemly successor; the gateway to Holy Trinity Priory (1854); and the most imposing of the parish churches, St Crux (1884–7), which had formed an effective ending to the Shambles. Most of the old timbered houses were also swept away. The scale of the demolition is indicated by the fact that until the 1840s there were still six elaborate houses with 15th-century 'spur' porches, not one of which now survives, though the porch of one has been preserved by being moved to another house in Trinity Lane.

Victorian York continued the Georgian tradition in a fine series of public buildings, which can be more fairly assessed now than they were a generation ago. It also continued a Georgian tradition of employing local architects. A few national figures appear: Street and Bodley at the Minster, Butterfield at St Mary Castlegate, Pearson at Clifton Parsonage, and a few unexpected figures like Huon Matear and

Edmund Kirby obtained plum jobs, but mostly it was left to the local architects. At the very beginning of Victoria's reign came the new street of St Leonard's Place, with the De Grey Rooms (1841–2) and the handsome crescent of houses opposite (1844–5), Walk 3, still in the Georgian classical tradition, in contrast to the later Gothic Theatre Royal and the Italianate Art Gallery, which completed the ensemble. Clifford Street (Walk 6) provides another Victorian panorama, dominated by Matear's Law Courts and Police Station of 1890–2. Banks, offices, and educational institutions proliferated, at first in classical or Italianate style, and after 1850 in a variety of period revivals and pastiches. St Helen's Square provides good examples of the early period by local architects, Pritchett and Watson's Savings Bank (1829–30) [26] on one corner and G.T. Andrews's Yorkshire Insurance (1840) [47] on another. New school and college buildings abounded: good examples include St Peter's School, Clifton (begun 1838), Walk 10; St John's College, Lord Mayor's Walk (begun 1841), Walk 11; and the Mount School (begun 1856), Walk 16. The last was and is a Friends' girls' school, an indication of the Quaker concern for education; their corresponding boys' school was founded in Bootham in 1823, but is less obvious because it is housed in and behind a fine series of Georgian private houses adapted rather than rebuilt. After 1870 came universal primary education and the gradual provision of undenominational 'Board' schools, of which Walter Brierley's Scarcroft Road School (1896) is outstanding (Walk 16). At the end of the century Edmund Kirby designed the Dispensary in Duncombe Place (Walk 3) and Barclays Bank in Parliament Street (Walk 6) in shiny bright-red brick and terracotta. A generation ago they were despised as tasteless, and it represented a major change of values when in 1970 Barclays decided to reconstruct behind Kirby's façade rather than demolish it.

The 19th century also saw the development of specialized shops rather than businesses simply run from a ground-floor front room in the home. The old pattern can be seen in early photographs of the Shambles (and in one surviving shop there), for the butchers long continued to trade over wooden shutters let down to form a counter. The next stage was the provision of graceful early-19th-century bow windows, which can be seen on Hillyard's wine shop in Ousegate and on a shop and former shops in College Street. The multiple store made its appearance soon after mid century, leading to the present rather dreary appearance of several central streets as well as to an improvement in shopping. Leak & Thorps led the way in 1868 by demolishing a fine coaching inn in Coney Street for their premises. Outstanding among smaller shops are Nos. 5–7 Feasegate, for they were built of cast-iron and plate glass by William Walker (son of John Walker) as early as 1884 (Walk 4).

The fine architectural legacy of Victorian York should not make one forget that there was much desperate poverty, though slum clearance since the 1920s has destroyed most of the visual evidence. The conscience of York – and the nation – was awakened to the size of this problem by a local Quaker businessman and philanthropist, B.S. Rowntree (1871–1954). As a young man, before taking over the management of his family firm, he carried out a detailed sociological investigation of every wage-earning family in the city in 1899.* The results appalled many people who assumed that poverty in cathedral cities was less severe than in the large manufacturing towns. Using sophisticated methods for that time to calculate the cost of a nutritious diet and other necessities, he found that '20,302 persons, equal to 43·4% of the wage-earning class, and to 27·84% of the total population of the city, were living in poverty'. This, he was shocked to find, was about the same as the extent of poverty in the East End of London as recently measured by Charles Booth. Fortunately, Rowntree and his friends were able to use their influence to attack poverty both nationally and locally; and he lived to have the satisfaction in old age of compiling two more surveys of York that revealed great improvements: by 1950 poverty had nearly disappeared. His father, Joseph Rowntree (1836–1925), was one of the pioneers of improvement in the York district, for in 1901 he

* Published in 1901 as *Poverty: a Study of Town Life.* His later surveys were *Poverty and Progress: a Second Social Survey of York* (1941) and *Poverty and the Welfare State* (1951).

began to build a garden suburb of 500 homes at New
Earswick (Walk 11), not exclusively for his employees, and
letting at 5s. a week to people earning about 25's. Rowntree
then handed over the village to a trust separate from the
firm, one of three charitable trusts he founded, still very
active at local, national, and international levels.

New Earswick was designed by Sir Raymond Unwin, who
was also the architect of the first true garden city at
Letchworth. It is one of a number of outstanding designs of
the turn of the century in York at a time when English
architecture was still experimental and influential; others
include the Art Nouveau interiors of Elm Bank Hotel (1898)
by Penty and Penty and George Walton of Glasgow (Walk
16) [53]. The Pentys designed other excellent buildings in
the city after a startling conversion from Waterhouse Gothic
to Arts and Crafts in the 1890s. But the outstanding architect
of the period was Walter Brierley, whose firm was descended
from John Carr's. His schools are original, powerful, and
wholly convincing, in the manner of, but excelling, Robson's
London board schools; and his own house in St George's
Place (1905) is one of the best of its date in England (Walk 16)
[54].

In the same year of 1905 the locomotive repair works were
moved from York, and the railways gradually lost ground to
confectionery as the largest employer of labour. Both
Rowntrees and Terrys expanded considerably, to the point
where large new suburban factories were needed in the
1920s; but these giant buildings, still dominating the skyline
to north and south respectively, witness as much to debased
architectural taste as to commercial growth. Rowntrees in
particular expanded enormously, until by 1939 they were
employing almost 30 per cent of York's insured working
population. Confectionery and the railways remain the
largest employers today.

Since the First World War, much of York's history is the
history of any 20th-century community and need not be
recounted in detail: the growth of public transport (trams
and then motor-buses) and of private transport, increasing
public services, libraries, schools, hospitals, gas and electri-

city; the demolition of the worst 19th-century slums; and the ever-extending suburbs to cater for extra population as well as rehousing. One new suburb was started after 1919 at Tang Hall, and the healthy and elevated district of Acomb also began a growth that has made it today much the largest of the suburbs. In the decade 1901–11 the infant mortality rate, above the level of many industrial towns in the 19th century, at last dropped below the national average, though there was a temporary return to poor conditions in the 1920s; only since 1930 has York consistently been healthy relative to the country at large. The continued movement of population from the centre led to further church redundancies. St Helen's was nearly pulled down in 1910, and in 1937 Christ Church was demolished, 'the little grey building which made delightful the junction of Shambles and Colliergate, now reduced to the ideal municipalised stretch of clean pavement with seats for pensioners'.* Hitler's war caused less damage than steady erosions of this kind. The one serious attack was a 'Baedeker raid' on 29 April 1942, which destroyed the Guildhall and adjacent church of St Martin, and severely damaged the railway station. Even so, in this relatively unscathed city, 87 people were killed during enemy attacks and 9,500 houses were damaged.

The post-war years have seen a developing conflict between two possible future rôles for York: as a primarily business, shopping, and administrative centre for a wide region, welcoming population and traffic growth, or as a modest-sized historic city increasingly dependent on cultural and tourist interests. The conflict is not yet resolved, but the pressures for conservation have so far enabled York to avoid, by the skin of its teeth, the fate of towns like Worcester. This is due largely to the energy and vision of one man, Alderman J.B. Morrell (1873–1963), yet another philanthropic businessman in the Quaker tradition. A much respected city councillor for 40 years, he it was who in 1938 persuaded the Corporation to buy and adapt the disused castle prison to house Dr J.L. Kirk's magnificent collection of

---

* A.G. Dickens. *The East Riding of Yorkshire with Hull and York* (1954), p. 19.

'bygones', thus creating the first and still the best English folk-museum. In 1940 he published *The City of Our Dreams,* a vision of what a replanned post-war York could be like, which, though many of its ideas now seem old-fashioned, was well ahead of its time (it was mostly written in 1935). He became in 1946 the first chairman of York Civic Trust, a body that has done more than any other to conserve the historic fabric of the city centre. He played a large part in organizing York's first Festival of the Arts as part of the 1951 Festival of Britain, a festival so successful that it has become a distinguished if not quite regular triennial event. He was active in founding the Borthwick Institute of Historical Research (1953) and the York Institute of Architectural Studies (1956), and beyond all this he was an active campaigner from 1949 for the establishment of a University of York, which has since subsumed the institutes. It was he who persuaded the Rowntree Social Service Trust to buy Heslington Hall as the nucleus of the proposed University, and to help ensure the choice of York as one of the new Universities in 1960 he donated £100,000 from the Morrell Trust.

Despite the activities of Mr Morrell and others, the existence of York as a historic town remained under serious threat until the early 1970s. Traffic continued to increase and to overload the narrow, historic streets, often leading to short-sighted and ugly road-widenings. York has been demolishing its past for 1,900 years, but never perhaps with the vigour and futility of the post-war years, when, unlike every previous period, it seems to have had nothing of interest, latterly nothing at all, with which to replace what had been taken away. Gaps await filling for years. Skelder-gate has been raped and North Street has almost vanished. Dilapidated, medieval Little Shambles made way for the new Market Place. St Andrewgate continues to disappear, though at least here the redevelopments are promising. The development boom of the 1960s produced some frightful mistakes: the concrete horror of Stonebow House; the gloomy canyon of Rougier Street; supermarkets in the wrong places and in the wrong materials: while at the same time decent Georgian and Victorian buildings decayed for lack of money or through planning blight. Even major buildings were not exempt: John Carr's own house in Skeldergate was demolished after war damage; Pritchett's Salem Chapel and Penty's Davy Hall have gone; and the Queen's Hotel in Micklegate was demolished after being found unsafe, though there at least the long-promised reinstatement may be in sight.

The turning of the tide came with a Historic Buildings Grant Scheme started by the Corporation in 1966, their designation of the entire historic core as a Conservation Area in 1968, and the publication in 1969 of a report on York by the architect and planner Lord Esher on behalf of the Government. There is no room for complacency, as most of the plans put forward by Esher and by the Corporation themselves remain unimplemented over 10 years later, despite plenty of opportunity to put them into practice. There is still only one true pedestrian street (Stonegate, since 1971), a very slow progress compared to Norwich; traffic still continues to thunder along Deangate past the foundations of the Minster; of the series of schemes by Esher for revitalizing decayed central areas, only one (Aldwark) is being implemented, and that with painful slowness.

Yet it would be unfair to end on a negative note. There have been many recent developments that augur well for York's future. One was the establishment in 1962 of the University at Heslington (Walk 13) [56], which has not only restored to the city something of the academic importance it has lacked since the 8th-century School of York, but has also provided, in the design of grounds and buildings, the best 20th-century architectural ensemble in York. The 1967 additions to the Theatre Royal are equally fine in a quite different way, and both together give hope for a better-designed environment. A major restoration of the Minster in 1966–72 has left it safer, one trusts, and certainly cleaner and lighter than it can ever have been since it was completed in 1472. The opportunity was taken, in strengthening the weakened foundations of the central tower, to create an impressive Undercroft Museum in the heart of the concrete foundations, where visitors can view the foundations of the Roman and Norman buildings that preceded the present cathedral. In 1971–5 there was a major battle over a Corporation proposal for an inner ring road, which would have reduced cross-town traffic but at the cost of spoiling the attractive Georgian suburbs of Bootham and the Mount. The scheme was shelved indefinitely by the Secretary of State for the Environment in 1975, while the less controversial outer by-pass was implemented (1974–6) to divert the busy A64 out of the built-up area.

One positive result of the ring-road battle was the establishment of York Archaeological Trust (1972) to initiate rescue archaeology in advance of the proposed road and of other developments. By then the historic buildings above ground were fairly safe, but many important archaeological traces below ground had been destroyed without record in post-war redevelopment. The Trust has done much to provide archaeological evidence for York's past to set alongside the better-known documentary record. Its work has been invaluable for the Viking period, for which York is the most important site in the British Isles other than Dublin, but for which documentary records are almost totally lacking. The timbered Viking houses discovered in Coppergate in 1976 are only the most spectacular of many important finds. Meanwhile, the Corporation has been taking a much more positive attitude to tourism, appreciating that tourists have become a vital ingredient of York's economic well-being.* It appointed a Director of Tourism in 1969, and in 1975 (European Architectural Heritage Year) it opened a converted redundant church as St Mary's Heritage Centre to tell the 'York Story'. The Civic Trust, which had already converted another redundant church into St Sampson's Old People's Centre, made its own contribution in 1975 by an excellent restoration of Peasholme House, a major house of *c.* 1750, probably designed by Carr. Yet another landmark in 1975 was the merger of the York and Clapham

---

* Especially as in 1974 local government reorganization took away the county borough status York had enjoyed since 1396, and made it a district of North Yorkshire. The failure to secure York rather than Northallerton as the new county capital was much regretted by Yorkers, but may well help York to discover its true rôle.

railway museums and their reopening by the Duke of Edinburgh as the National Railway Museum in a spectacular new home at York. It is not surprising that this city of 100,000 should now be coping with some 3 million visitors a year, double the number that came in 1970. Dr Nuttgens has argued cogently that a better future lies ahead for York as 'a tourist delight' rather than 'a thriving regional centre',* but if the balance tilts much further towards tourism then the preservation of the attractions that draw so many visitors will have to become the overriding priority.

* Patrick Nuttgens, *York: the Continuing City* (1976), p. 116.

The Walks   Preliminary Note

The best way to see York is to walk aimlessly about; not as the inhabitants, intent on their shopping, nor the day trippers, baffled in search of their coach-park – for York is a confusing place – but slowly and observantly, with plenty of time for the great things and for the multitude of minor delights. No one knows the whole of York. One has only to step a yard from an accustomed path, or out of a new front door, or glimpse a reflection in a shop window for a scene visited a hundred times to reassemble itself in a new and unexpected way.

Exaggerated claims made for the city have made its real quality difficult to assess: extravagant restoration has been as calamitous as vandalism: yet it remains a wonderful place, perhaps at its best in the early morning and evening. At night, yellow floodlights have replaced the moon, making power cuts a secret pleasure.

York is not a large city, but its interest is widely and by no means thinly spread. Half the walks deal with the suburbs, which are full of surprises; half with the city centre, which is full of tourists. The walks are designed to show what is best in the city, which frequently means passing what is worst.

Some of the walks are lengthy, and people with time should certainly do them in stages. For Walks 5 and 7 parts of the city walls provide a complementary return route; for Walk 1, an exquisite supplement. Suburban walks end at a point convenient for public transport.

For readers with limited time, Stonegate, the Minster, the Close, the walls from Monk Bar to Bootham Bar, and the Museum Gardens should encourage an early and more leisurely return visit.

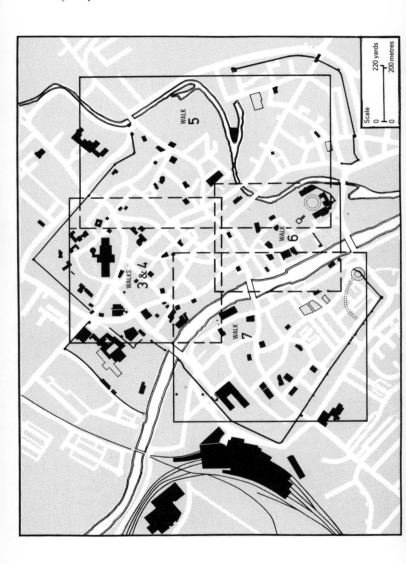

WALK 5

WALK 6

WALKS 3 & 4

WALK 7

Scale
0   220 yards
0   200 metres

York Minster

(*The Cathedral Church of St Peter*)

This account owes much to two publications. Dean Addleshaw's 'Four Hundred Years' (1962, republished in *Architectural History*, vol. 10, 1967), a scholarly list of the contributions of all artists, architects, and craftsmen who worked on the Minster between 1590 and 1960, provides the basis of almost all the attributions of fittings and monuments. *A History of York Minster* edited by Aylmer and Cant (1977) is full of invaluable matter, but special mention must be made of the chapters by Dr E.A. Gee and Dr J. Harvey on the medieval building history, and by D. O'Connor and J. Haselock on the stained glass. All the information about master masons derives from Dr Harvey's chapter, though the author occasionally takes issue with him on matters of interpretation.

☆

St Gregory the Great's mission to re-establish Christianity in Britain (597) did not reach the North until 625, when Ethelburga, sister of the Christian King of Kent, arrived as second wife of Edwin of Northumbria, accompanied by Paulinus – one of St Augustine's original followers – and assurances on their freedom to practise their faith. Edwin, initially cautious, was baptized on Easter Day 627 in a newly-built wooden church. Paulinus fled following Edwin's death in battle (632), leaving the completion of the new stone church to King Oswald, and the purposed establishment of an Archdiocese of York in abeyance for a century. Oswald buried Edwin's remains in the porticus of St Gregory. Further disturbances followed Oswald's death (642) and the allegedly irregular consecration of Chad in 664. St Wilfrid arrived in 669 to find Edwin's church in disrepair, restored it, and glazed its windows. Ecgbert became first Archbishop in 735, and restored the church after a fire of 741. There may have been another fire in 764 – fires are recurrent in the Minster's history. Alcuin relates that he assisted Archbishop Aethelbert and Eanbald (Aethelbert's successor as Archbishop) in building a great new church, *c.* 780; but whether this replaced the earlier church, or stood adjacent, or was somewhere else entirely, remains as problematical as the site of Edwin's church itself.

Excavations during the restoration of 1967–72 provided evidence of the Roman headquarters building, of a 10th-century cemetery, of the Norman church, but nothing that could confidently be claimed as part of a pre-Conquest church. Wherever it stood, it was burned on 19 September 1069, eight days after Archbishop Ealdred, who had crowned William the Conqueror, had been buried in it. Archbishop Thomas of Bayeux repaired it, but started his grand new church after further damage in 1079. Bede's assertions about the two earliest churches seem to dispose of the theory that Edwin merely adapted part of the headquarters building. Many of the buildings in the Close, and the Saxon cemetery, are within a degree or two of the Roman alignment, whereas Archbishop Thomas's new church was swung through an angle of approximately 42° – to the permanent confusion of the city's street pattern and aesthetics – and aligned E and W with uncommon accuracy. Did this allow some patched remnants of the old church to remain in use while the new was being built? Perhaps they still await excavation beneath the Dean's Park.

Archbishop Thomas's church was probably completed by his death in 1100. It was as far from being unique as it was from being a classic Norman church. It had a long apsed chancel with narrow passage aisles; a crossing the full width of this; squarish transepts with eastern apses; and an aisleless nave. Between transept apses and choir aisles were stair turrets, which survived until the end of the 14th century and are critical to an understanding of the Minster's development. The scale was enormous, 362 ft long with a nave 45 ft across.

There was another fire in 1137. What followed this is not entirely clear, but when William Fitzherbert (St William of York) died in 1154 he was buried not in the eastern arm as archbishops normally were but in the nave. Works to N, S, and E of the transepts* seem to have been in progress both before and after the rebuilding of the choir – the part worst affected by the 1137 fire – by Archbishop Roger de Pont L'Eveque, *c.* 1155–75, but what these were, and how far they were completed, remains mysterious.

Archbishop Roger's choir was of the greatest refinement and magnificence, though not so 'Transitional' in character as his later work at Ripon. It was raised high on a crypt – as at Canterbury – the W parts of whose aisles flanked the remains of Thomas's choir, and whose eastern part formed a complete, aisled, cruciform church. At the end of the 12th century a new W front was added, of towers set closely together flanking a porch. During the early 13th century additions to the W end of Ripon Minster and the E end of Kirkham Priory left them both close in plan to the late-12th-century church at York.

Archbishop Walter de Gray started work on a new S transept *c.* 1220, part of a scheme involving also the rebuilding of the central tower and the N transept, for which the Treasurer, John le Romeyn, was responsible. Both builders died in 1255, by which time the work was probably completed. Though enormous in scale, the transepts were carefully related both to Archishop Roger's choir and Archbishop Thomas's turrets, but made no provision for a new aisled nave.

The next project was the octagonal chapter house, initially – *c.* 1275–80 – a separate building, but quickly linked to the N transept by the mysterious, marvellous vestibule, completed *c.* 1290, when the builders at last turned their attention to the nave.

---

* The evidence is confusing and has yet to be published.

York exported its best saints: Paulinus, Chad, Wilfrid, John of Beverley; St William, canonized 1226–7, was a somewhat doubtful case. However, the pilgrims came, and in 1284 his remains were translated from the nave to the usual position behind the high altar.

Work started on the new nave in 1291. If there was ever such a thing as a new beginning for the Minster it was here, and not as so often stated in the transepts. The scale presupposes a choir of equal magnitude, where the transepts seem set out to embarrass such ambitions. The nave design formed the basis, with modifications, for that of the rest of the cathedral; sadly some changes were made before its own long-delayed completion in *c.* 1360. In 1361 work started on the Lady Chapel, E of Roger's choir, which for the time being was left untouched, but the new work was unfinished at Archbishop Thoresby's death (1373) and was not completed until the early 15th century. Archbishop Roger's choir was abandoned in 1394, by which time the sacristies and so-called Zouche Chapel would have been built and work may have begun on the choir. The glazing of the E window in 1405–8 indicates some degree of structural completeness, but work on the vaulting was still in progress in the 1420s.

At the beginning of the 15th century the matter of the central-tower piers was exercising the master mason, who removed Archbishop Thomas's turrets, ingeniously shuffled elements of the 13th-century transepts to provide access to the nave and choir aisles, and recast the tower piers and arches. There was no intention of demolishing the tower, nevertheless some part of it collapsed in 1407, and Henry IV sent his master mason, William Colchester, to supervise the reconstruction. Colchester's grand design of a lantern with a belfry above and possibly a spire on top of that was never completed. Western towers were substituted to hold the bells. The building of the three towers is not satisfactorily documented; it seems probable that the existing central tower was long left incomplete while work was in progress on the western towers, and that all three date from *c.* 1433–73. The fabric could, therefore, have been regarded as complete at the consecration in 1472.

The 1547 Act abolished chantry foundations, and the confiscation of treasures and vestments begun under Henry VIII continued under Edward VI, though there was some replenishment of stock under the Marian régime. The greatest collection of medieval stained glass in Britain survived the 1644 siege by a miracle and the direct intervention of Lord Fairfax. 'Improvements' took place. Archbishop Lamplugh's sanctuary arrangements were replaced by Dean Finch's, when he cleared away the huge wooden screen that separated the high altar from the revestry, where St William's shrine had stood, and envisaged a Baroque reredos by Hawksmoor. Repaving of 1728–38 to designs of Lord Burlington and William Kent produced a seemly Greek-key pattern on an enormous scale, substitute for countless medieval graveslabs. In 1770 John Carr surveyed the roofs, and in 1798 replaced the medieval painted wooden panels of the chapter house vault with new ones in plaster.

On 1/2 February 1829 Jonathan Martin, religious fanatic, set fire to the choir stalls after Sunday Evensong. The fire spread slowly. It was not until salvage operations had started that the organ blew up setting light to the wooden vault. Sir Robert Smirke carried out a faithful restoration and the Minster was reopened on 6 May 1832. On 20 May 1840 the nave vault was burned and the SW tower gutted, after a clockmaker had taken a naked light into the tower. Sidney Smirke did a similarly excellent reinstatement between 1840 and 1844. The stained glass survived both fires, though seriously damaged. G.E. Street restored the S transept (1871–80), rebuilding the clerestory and interfering with the elevations. G.F. Bodley (Minster architect 1882–1907) added the flying buttresses to the nave (left unfinished when the medieval builders gave up the idea of a stone high vault) and the huge pinnacles on the N side. The glass, removed during both World Wars, was releaded after the First, and reorganized after the Second under the supervision of Dean Milner-White. Successive structural restorations culminated in a massive scheme (1967–72) by Bernard Feilden designed to underpin the central tower and the E and W fronts, and to clean the interior (and unfortunately the exterior). Work is currently in progress (1979) on the S transept vault.

York Minster is England's largest (surviving) medieval church. Its aims are everywhere spectacular, often beyond realization: its vaults are of wood; its central tower is unfinished. Curiously, it does not dominate the city. It is set back. The resonance that even the smallest hill would give is denied it. Fortunate occupiers of upper storeys see it differently. Interference in the scale of its surroundings inhibits their setting it off to advantage. Nocturnal flood-lights dye it yellow: a full moon after midnight is magical. Neither does it dominate the Plain, except to the N, for the moraines hide it, but from the surrounding hills it points the horizon magnificently, alone since the destruction of the gasometer.

The paraphernalia of tourism has struck with the need to raise money. Info-bars, 'minutes of history', signposts, labels, chewing gum, and a one-way system engendering queues on wet days. There is no admission charge to the consecrated parts; only the tower, chapter house, and undercroft (is consecration only pavement deep?). It used not to be like this. It is best in the evenings, but the clutter remains.

A chronological visit is not easy but is the only way properly to understand the building.

The Crypt and Undercroft Museum

Layers of history, and structural division, have made the undercroft a baffling place. It comes in four sections, whose interest is not matched by accessibility: the Undercroft Museum, the crypt below the sanctuary, Archbishop Roger's crypt, and the mains electricity room (not normally access-ible). Roman work, at an unmistakable angle, is surrounded by Archbishop Thomas's footings, much encased in recent concrete: Archbishop Roger's crypt, partially demolished, partially rebuilt *c.* 1400, surrounds the stub of Thomas's choir, encased in turn in Smirke's ingenious vaulted pas-sages, its rhythms further interrupted by several centuries of medieval footings.

Undercroft Museum

This is one consequence of the recent restoration. It lies beneath the central tower, in and around Archbishop Thomas's transepts, the E end of his nave, and the W end of his choir where the treasury is securely situated. A sense of orientation is important. The first space is outside Thomas's S transept, whose buttresses have traces of plaster with faint red lines to represent joints. The interior, at this level, has rough herringbone masonry. The Roman headquarters building is set at 42°. The reconstructed 4th-century wall painting in reds, ochres, and grey-greens with figures, masks, birds, columns, and the outline of a window is inside Thomas's nave. In the angle between the Norman nave and N transept is an early-13th-century well. The broken end of the mid-13th-century plinth cut off by the 14th-century nave stands in front of the older transept wall.

Some of the better pieces from the 10th-century cemetery are displayed: a grave-slab comparable with that in All Saints' Pavement (see p. 206) and a mid-10th-century shaft with superb Scandinavian animal ornament on three sides and an enigmatic 'blessing' on the fourth. Also early Norman capitals with volutes and heavy leaf forms; a stone slab with 13th-century lettering stating that it fell on Roger of Ripon leaving him unharmed through St William's intercession; worn 12th- and 14th-century figures from the W front.

Thomas's crossing, largely encased in Feilden concrete, lavish with bolts, is only visible flanking the entrance to the treasury, where nothing of Thomas's choir footings can now be seen. Mostly it is post-1829 work with the floor cut away to show Roman remains beneath.

The treasury houses an exceptionally fine collection of Yorkshire church plate and the 'William Lee Collection of York Silver' as well as some of the Minster treasures: the early-11th-century horn of Ulphus, the episcopal rings of Archbishops Sewall de Bovill, Greenfield, and Bowet, a magnificent Tazza of 1660, candlesticks of 1664 and 1676, the plate given by Archbishop Harcourt in 1830; Archbishop Walter de Gray's ring, chalice, and paten, the head of his early-13th-century pastoral staff in Walrus Ivory, and his superb painted coffin lid of *c.* 1255, found beneath a mortar bed when his monument was rebuilt. Geoffrey de Ludham's pastoral staff of *c.* 1260 is exquisitely carved wood.

Thomas's footings, reusing much Roman material, can best be appreciated under the S transept, where the entrance to the eastern apse can still be seen.

The Eastern Crypt

Parts of Archbishop Roger's crypt were reassembled *c.* 1400 to provide a new platform for the high altar and St William's Shrine. The rest was buried and forgotten until the 1829 fire. Some of the bases of the monolithic shafts are old capitals reversed – most of the bases were left *in situ* – flat foliage and scallop shells decorate. A row of little stick-like men contrast oddly with the extreme refinement of some of the detailing. Norman vaulting ribs are reused and there are Norman arches to the aisles with chevrons flanking roll moulds. The lavatorium near the N entrance has an enchanting plughole. A trapdoor near the N wall covers a Roman column base and part of Thomas's apse footings.

The 'Hell Cauldron' seems part of the late-12th-century work, oddly barbaric: Hell, a monstrous mouth, flames, within and without, being stoked vigorously. The contrast with the exquisitely refined, Byzantine-influenced, mid-12th-century Virgin and Child relief could not be more marked. Fourteenth-century Virgin and St Anne. Medieval floor tiles. Font cover by Comper, 1946. Early-15th-century iron entrance grilles.

Archbishop Roger's Crypt

What remains of Roger's crypt (*c.*1154–74) lies to the W, in Smirke's cross-vaulted passages, recently sparsely converted into a shrine for St William. Originally, it formed a miniature church, almost symmetrical on both axes; five aisles of five bays, the central, double one leading to transepts. Massive cylindrical piers [11] in the outer arcades held up the superstructure, decorated with diagonal chequerboards and spiralling zigzags, reminiscent of Durham except that the execution and refinement, like everything else of Roger's work, is exquisite; classical bases, thin detached shafts and splendid multi-scalloped capitals. Smaller cylindrical piers supported the crypt vault; it was these that were reused in the eastern crypt, though their bases with delicate leafy spurs were left *in situ.* Lozenge-shaped piers, with attached corner shafts, led to the transepts, where there was another change of design to four shafts set in a diagonal square. Single shafts marked the bay division of the aisles, triple ones the responds of the main arcades. The outer walls (accessible only to the agile) had buttresses, again shafted, on finely moulded plinths. The outer aisles extended westwards for two bays flanking Thomas's footings (herringbone masonry), through sumptuous doors into porches roughly quadrant-shaped to accommodate the stair turrets leading to the Norman crossing tower. These porches formed the approach to the crypt. Some sad little remnants of the S door and porch remain in position.* A ladder gives access to the footings of Thomas's S transept apse. Perpendicular arcades stand on rockeries of chevron, against which discarded late-12th-century statues lean. Much more remained of the N porch and door but this was dismantled during the restoration and has not been reconstructed. The N crypt aisle is little better than a junk heap, though the junk is of the greatest interest. In the mains electricity room at the W end of the N aisle are the remains of Thomas's other transept apse, and the arch at the foot of his N stair turret, compromised by pipes and tubes.

Roger's choir must have been a work of great splendour, but at present only its details can be assessed, not its form. It had some waterleaf capitals, adventurous use of zigzag, rolls set with bobbin-like ornaments, a stone vault. His church at Ripon is austere in comparison.

* The refectory door at Kirkham Priory is perhaps the closest approximation to them in style.

The Transepts

The rebuilding of the transepts, *c.*1220–55, should be seen rather as a completion of Roger's work than as a new beginning; indeed, there was no attempt to replace anything of Thomas's church that could be usefully adapted; the tower piers remained as the core of the new ones (as they still remain as the core of the present ones), establishing the tower's size, and the two turrets were kept, flanking the entrance to Roger's choir, and generating the transepts' original plan. This had a narrow, blank bay fronting the turrets on the E, and providing excellent abutments for the tower, then each transept had three bays with E and W aisles, all on a very large scale.

South Transept

Archbishop Walter de Gray started work on the S transept in *c.* 1220. Dr Gee suggests that the outer walls of the W aisle were built first, and that one of many changes of plan moved the W arcade further W than originally intended, accounting for the narrowness of that aisle.

The S front is a monument to changed minds and ill-advised interference. The inner arch of the shallow porch has remains of sumptuous, undercut stiff-leaf (and a restored 15th-century door). The outer arch was largely renewed (1871–80) by Street, whose agonizingly acute trio of gables replaced something equally awkward of the 18th century. Small lancets at the sides. Large lancets above are fitted into a space intended for something else. The enormous rose (or wheel) window in the gable is uncomfortably near the top and out of line with everything below. Turrets, again by Street, are the prosaic results of much thought. (The calm majesty of the Beverley transept fronts provides an instructive comparison here as that between the two W fronts will prove later.) The aisle elevations are scarcely more satisfactory, the windows hemmed-in by string courses and buttresses poking gablets above the parapet. The clerestory is small, much rebuilt by Street, arcaded, with little canted buttresses between the bays.

Inside, majestic space compensates for much. The view
looking N [13] is far grander than that looking S. The design
follows Whitby in developing the final proportions of Selby
nave into Gothic form. The triforium, the grandest expression of this North-country type, dominates; divided and
subdivided beneath its enclosing arches, it is too elaborate
for what happens below, and too large for what happens
above. The central bay is wider than the others so the round
enclosing arches of the former become bluntly pointed in the
latter. Detailing everywhere is rich; Purbeck marble, excellent stiff-leaf, dog-tooth, and billet. The aisles have 13th-
century stone vaults, to which the window arches are
unhappily related. The intended high-roof form remains
mysterious, since, presumably, both the rose window and the
stepped lancets of the N transept were meant to be seen
internally. There are vaulting shafts on luscious corbels, and
curious little ribs starting across the spandrels of the
triforium, but if these were meant for a vault they cannot
relate to the present clerestory. The existing pointed
wooden barrel vaults, masquerading unconvincingly as
ribbed vaults, are much-restored work of the 15th-century.

South transept fittings:

East side. Archbishop Thompson, d. 1890, in Bodley's
ultra-refined Gothic: effigy by Sir James Hamo Thorney-
croft.

East aisle. Archbishop Sewall de Bovill, d. 1258; Purbeck
slab on trefoiled arcade. Archbishop Walter de Gray, d.
1255: the finest monument in the Minster [14], and the finest
of its date in England. Purbeck marble effigy under a gablet,
with shafts on sprays of stiff-leaf. Purbeck canopy on
(originally) 10 columns with trefoil arches; freestone superstructure, gabled and arched; pretty finials by Bernasconi,
1803–5; the painted marble coffin lid in the treasury was
found during restoration. Archbishop Godfrey de Ludham,
d. 1264, Purbeck slab. Dean Duncombe, d. 1880, by Street:
prickly canopy on columns not so structurally daring as the
Gray monument; effigy by Sir Edward Boëhm; popular if
sentimental choir boys. The Minster's one substantial piece
of medieval screenwork stood in this aisle: like several other

things it has not reappeared since removal during the recent restoration.

Glass of *c.*1434 in the five E windows: SS. William, Michael, Gabriel, John the Baptist, and the Virgin. Much white glass, an economical scheme to let in light. The figures (some ludicrously out-of-scale heads given at the restoration) are, for once, related to the altars that stood below. Trite modern heraldry. Two lancets by Kempe, *c.* 1890, in S wall.

South wall of transept. Peckitt windows in the lowest tier; St Peter (1768), Abraham, Solomon, and Moses (1796), shortly to be reunited with their original plinths, after years of dissonant appendages. The next tier has SS. William, Peter, Paul, and Wilfrid, early-16th-century, the worst medieval glass in the Minster. Rose window, a Peckitt sunflower, central in a sunburst; roses on twisting stems of the early 16th century.

West side. Chapel of St George, West Yorkshire Regiment, 1926–9, fittings by Sir Walter Tapper, magnificent wrought-iron screens in association with W. Bainbridge Reynolds, among the few 20th-century fittings in the Minster worthy of their surroundings.

Glass in S lancets by Tower (Kempe and Co.), 1907: early-13th-century grisaille at the top. West windows. Fragmentary Te Deum panels, mid-15th-century, said to be from St Martin Coney Street.

North Transept

Work must have progressed quickly. John le Romeyn, the treasurer, was responsible for both the N transept and the new central tower. It seems probable that he first recased Thomas's tower arches since the S transept must have been well advanced before the N transept was started. This is a much more assured design; everywhere an improvement on the earlier work. Inside, the bays have settled for a single width; the triforium is smaller (the incipient vaulting ribs have disappeared), the clerestory is larger; the detail is everywhere richer; animals appear among the stiff-leaf; the rich rere-arches of the windows are better related to the vaulting compartments. Outside, smaller buttresses are stopped at the window springings, and the clerestory is no longer divided into bays. The cusped doorhead from Chapter House Yard* has affinities with the w door at Byland. Above all, the N front in its broad, noble simplicity transcends the agitated muddle of the s front in one of the grandest creations of the Early English style [13 and 15]; five great lancets of equal height, splendidly restrained beneath a clear but not overstated cornice, and stepped lancets in the gable. The turrets have been spared the unhappy terminations of the other transept. Close set arcading beneath the lancets, outside, has alternating shaft sections giving a tiny turn from perfect symmetry.

Transept, chapter house, vestibule, and tower form far the most memorable external grouping of the Minster.

North transept fittings:

East side. Clock face by Bodley, painted by W.A. Powell (*c.* 1883); mechanism by Henry Hindley, 1750; 16th-century men-at-arms belong to an earlier clock. Rear Admiral Cradock, d. 1914, by F.W. Pomeroy.

East aisle. Astronomical clock, 1955, vacillating stylistically; architect, Sir Albert Richardson; sculptor, Maurice Lambert; painter, H.J. Stammers. Mid-18th-century gates to St Nicholas's Chapel. Altar is tomb of Archbishop Rotherham, d. 1500. Archbishop Greenfield, d. 1315, beautiful cusped arch under a gable with large finials and flanking pinnacles; arcaded tomb chest with a brass, rather under life size, the earliest surviving episcopal brass.

Windows are characteristically rich products by Kempe, of 1899–1903, incorporating fragments of a *c.* 1434 scheme similar to that in the s transept.

North Wall. The original, *c.* 1250 grisaille glazing of the Five Sisters Window survives, mysterious, pearly grey, lightly articulated with geometrical colour. Leaf patterns that covered the white glass are traceable intermittently. It seems possible that the order of the lights has been changed, and that the second from the E was intended as the centre light. The account of its design in *Nicholas Nickleby* is not

---

* Between the choir and the chapter house.

historically accurate. Late-12th-century panel of Habakkuk feeding Daniel in the Lion's den does not fit with any other Minster glass and probably belonged to Roger's choir.

West side. Statue of Christ by Fisher, *c.* 1761.

West aisle. St John's Chapel (King's Own Yorkshire Light Infantry). Fittings by Tapper, 1925, magnificent grilles to the transept, in collaboration with Bainbridge Reynolds. Entrance screen, late-17th-century, originally round the Lamplugh monument. Thomas Haxey, d. 1425, a grim cadaver in a cage under a marble slab. One of several Bodley tablets above. Opposite, Burma memorial (1852–3) by Edward Richardson; tablet with bronze 'St Michael' by Eleanor Fortescue Brickdell (1921); bronze tablet with beautiful raised lettering, in mother-of-pearl border, by Voysey and Bainbridge Reynolds (1922).

Glass in W windows from St John's church. Excellent scenes from the life of John the Baptist, *c.* 1430. Four-light window, crammed into two: late-15th-century glass commemorating Sir Richard York; 14th-century donors incorporated. North windows by Reginald Bell, 1933, incorporating medieval glass in colourful medallions.

The Norman nave must have been sufficiently splendidly rehabilitated at the end of the 12th century for its rebuilding to be unthinkable at this stage. Certainly the idea of an aisled nave was not taken into account with the planning of the transepts. The considerable juggling of elements that was later needed to rationalize the situation is better discussed in connection with the 15th-century rebuilding of the central tower. It was to the chapter house that the builders next turned their attention.

The Chapter House

The chapter house is the largest in England, octagonal and hugely buttressed [15]. Evidence for its dating is problematical and conflicting. According to Dr Gee, masons' marks suggest a starting date of *c.* 1260, shortly after the completion of the transepts; but details of tracery and stall canopies indicate intimacy with Parisian architectural fashion of *c.* 1280, while, on the other hand, stiff-leaf carving lingers even into the vestibule. It need not have taken long to build, and a later rather than an earlier date seems more likely. The buttresses suggest a change in plan, from a stone vault with a central column to a timber dome without one: the raking flying buttresses belong to the first stage. The buttress S of the vestibule has the tall, cruciform pinnacle but not the horizontal flyer, suggesting that these came at different stages of the work, and that the vestibule had been started before work on the chapter house roof had reached the point where the need for the upper flyers became apparent. Like the pinnacles, these are traceried, and bristling with gablets and finials, a treatment reaching its apogee in the staircase turret. Calm is restored above by the octagonal cornice and vast octo-pyramidal roof. The window jambs are set back at right angles – an important motif in the Decorated work at York – with the tracery near the inner wall face. The tracery is some of the grandest of the late-13th-century: paired outer lights, acute central light pressing the three great multi-foiled circles upwards so that there are none of those distressing holes in the composition that mar the E window of Lincoln. All the forms are still firmly enclosed within circles; loosening up starts in the vestibule and progresses in the nave.

What the interior loses in mystery, with the omission of the central column, it gains in impressiveness of volume, with which Southwell (the only other English chapter house on this plan) cannot compare. However, Southwell has a stone vault, where the magnitude of the project led the York designer to the ultimate frustration of a wooden vault (or rather dome), though the ingenuity required in the design of the huge space-frame roof, its massive centre-post suspended over the central boss, may have been some compensation. Scale models explain the structure. Originally the vault was boarded and painted (Halfpenny's *Gothic Ornaments*, plate 102), but the panels were replaced in plaster (under Carr's direction) in 1798. In the 1844–5 restoration by Sydney Smirke the vault was repainted by Thomas

Willement. The partial reinstatement of Willement's designs
in sharp colours will not be to everyone's taste. The loss of the
original roof is made more poignant by the recent reappear-
ance of two of its panels – beautifully restored, and displayed
in the undercroft – which show it to have been a work of the
highest artistic quality. Minton tile floor. Over the door, 13
niches once housed statues of Christ and the Apostles.

The stalls [16] are among the glories of York. Each canon's
seat is a shallow octagonal niche, the back angles on Purbeck
shafts, the front pair free, dropping pendants; capitals and
pendants alike with exquisite foliage, part still stiff-leaf, the
rest naturalistic. Above this, gablets, wide ones alternating
with others narrow as split pinnacles, all with glorious leafy
finials below a swaying vine cornice. Between the gablets,
heads and little figure subjects are beautiful or amusing at
the carver's whim (dental problems may have been a
speciality of one mason). That some of this delightful work is
the result of Smirke's excellent restoration should not impair
one's enjoyment.

Minor treasures are on display, and a splendid 15th-
century chest with St George and the Dragon.

Six of the seven windows belong to the original glazing
scheme of *c.* 1285. The tall lights have four bands of subject panels (mostly in geometrical surrounds), the details
strongly treated with lively heads, alternating with grisaille,
which has naturalistic leaf forms. Clockwise from the door,
scenes from the life of 1 St Katherine, 2 St William, 3 and 4
both concerned with the life of Christ. No. 4 has had an
unfortunate history: in 1845 it was renewed by Barnett who
carefully copied the originals, respecting the general iconographical scheme. In 1959 Dean Milner-White substituted
for this a hotch-potch of grisaille from another window,
15th-century panels of the life of Christ, and 16th-century St
Thomas Becket panels – more of which series is in St
Michael-le-Belfrey. The result is not a success. No. 5 has
panels of St Peter, 6 St Paul, while 7 disrupts the general
scheme both by dealing with five saints (Thomas Becket and
Margaret, Nicholas, John the Baptist and Edmund) and for

the first time introducing canopies over some of the scenes, anticipating the windows in the vestibule.

Perhaps the chapter house was already finished in 1284 when Edward I came for the Translation of the relics of St William.

The Vestibule

The Vestibule is one of the strangest and most moving creations of the English Geometrical style: L-shaped, linking the NE corner of the transept with the W entrance to the chapter house. The designer set himself tasks that were beyond reasonable accomplishment. The walls were designed as screens; arcaded (inside) below, glazed above, under flat-soffitted arches whose outer edges are defined by thin mouldings, and thinner shafts down the flanks of the supporting buttresses. That an unfathomable change of plan necessitated some of these arches taking the oddest shapes seems not to have troubled the designer at all in his search for the ultimate Gothic aim of a building supported entirely on its buttresses. These grow upwards into tall, square pinnacles linked back to the wall-face by traceried screens.

In Chapter House Yard these intellectual conundrums are given up in favour of simply letting the building happen as it would, like slicing off of window lights by buttresses. (Gargoyle of St Nicholas, with three boys in a boat, being stoned by a devil on a higher pinnacle.)

The tracery is remarkable – sometimes scarcely believable – and its analysis is beyond the scope of this book. The E–W arm has five-light windows with noble circles subdivided into pointed and rounded trefoils, really rose window designs like the nave clerestory. The N–S arm has much less organized tracery, narrower windows, springing higher up; one next to the transept is only two lights with piled up trefoils like a French apse window. Next to it is the most extraordinary window, seeking to reconcile the two springing levels by setting between them traceried gablets bisected, not quite accurately, by the continuing mullions. (This window's resemblance to one at Troyes will appear more important when we deal with the nave.) The same geometrical dottiness informs the transept entrance: paired arches under a gable below a transom beneath paired arches under a large arch bisected vertically – excellent 15th-century wooden grilles.

If the exterior suffers from these awkwardnesses, the soaring interior triumphs over them. The French Court style influences are here most apparent. Tracery, wall arcading, and multi-membered vaulting shafts become one glorious, unified, rippling surface, under the stone vault. The bay next to the chapter house, entirely encased within its buttresses, invents yet another form of elongated tracery to fill the side walls, but uses the chapter house tracery pattern above the doorway, an exquisite composition with a restored statue of the Virgin under a canopy on its central pillar, and little pedestals in the quatrefoil above suggesting a former crucifixion sculpture. The original doors have superb, chaste, swirling ironwork of the late 13th century. The sculptural work is of the highest quality, both in the capitals and in the round bosses in the wall arcade [17], still occasionally stiff-leaf, mostly naturalistic; but including a few animals and little subject carvings, like the crucifixion of St Peter on the S jamb of the chapter house door. Only the entrance to the transept is a little thin, thin tracery under an arch reorganized from the hood moulds of 13th-century lancets with the vaulting accommodating itself as best it can around the transept buttresses.

The chapter house vestibule is English Gothic at its finest. Moreover, it keeps its original glazing scheme, and even some traces of its painted decoration (there was more until the recent cleaning) and so gives as complete an impression of a great medieval interior as can be found anywhere in the country. The glass develops the theme of Chapter House window 7 with alternating bands of grisaille, and single figures under canopies, *c.* 1285–90.

Two 13th-century Vestment chests with splendid iron

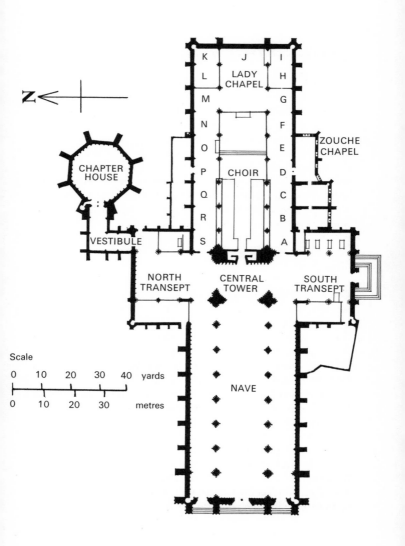

N

K
J
I

LADY
CHAPEL

L
H

M
G

N
F

ZOUCHE
CHAPEL

O
E

CHAPTER
HOUSE

P
CHOIR
D

Q
C

R
B

VESTIBULE

S
A

NORTH
TRANSEPT

CENTRAL
TOWER

SOUTH
TRANSEPT

Scale

0   10   20   30   40   yards

0   10   20   30   metres

NAVE

scrollwork; the Great Banner (1916) was designed by Sir Walter Tapper.

The Masons' Design Office

Over the vestibule vault is the lofty L-shaped space that was used by the later medieval master masons as a design office. The level floor was covered with gypsum in which window tracery, piers, mouldings, etc. could be set out full size, scratched in the surface with a pointed instrument. The earliest of this confusion of superimposed drawings seems to be William Hoton's design for the Lady Chapel aisle windows of *c.* 1361. The room has its original scissors truss roof, crisp 13th-century detailing where it butts against the transept, and a garderobe contrived for the workmen above one of the buttresses in the E wall.

The Nave

Once the vestibule was completed, the same masons started work on the new nave; but where the Early English transepts and central tower had taken 35 years to complete, the nave was to take almost 70 years, with the long delays, and consequent changes in plan, that were to pervade the later building history of the Minster. Archbishop John le Romeyn laid the foundation stone on 6 April 1291.

The Master Mason was Master Simon, whose grand design [19] was one of the most ambitious of the English Geometrical style. Its enormous proportions were dictated by the footings of Archbishop Thomas's N and S walls being used for the new arcade piers (parts of Thomas's structure are still *in situ* behind the triforium, towards the E end); so the nave became the widest (106 ft) and almost the highest (93 ft) in England, still low by Continental standards despite French influences evident elsewhere in the design. The N and S aisle walls could have been well advanced before it became necessary to demolish any of Thomas's building.

Master Simon's Geometrical design was with small exceptions adhered to, despite changing taste, until his death in
1322, by which time the aisles would have been complete
with the great pinnacles on the s side (their companions on
the N side and the flying buttresses they are meant to support
were not added until Bodley's restoration, 600 years later),
together with the clerestory and the lowest part of the w
front.

The nave tracery has been accused of monotony, one
design each for the aisles (triplets of quatrefoils) and
clerestory (great circles with quatrefoils in lozenges derived
from rose-window designs), which ignores the main premise
of the design, that unity, and not mere geometrical ingenuity, is what matters. The aisle windows are under decorative
gablets outside, which should be compared, like much else in
the nave, with the gatehouse at Kirkham Priory; the
clerestory windows, following the vestibule design, have
tracery set back on the inner wall face, under flat-soffitted
arches outside.

Inside, the design is a little over-delicate in the beautiful
wall arcading, understated in the vaulting shafts, majestic in
the arcades with benefactors' heraldry in the spandrels, and
revolutionary (for England) in the combination of triforium
and clerestory. The inner-plane tracery makes it possible for
the mullions to run through both stages, the division defined
by a row of gablets. The central triforium openings had
statues: one marvels at the sensibility that has recently placed
a cubical light fitting in front of each of the remaining ones.
The resemblance of the whole design to the nave at Troyes
has often been remarked, but where at Troyes the
clerestory–triforium combination occupies the whole space
below the quadripartite vault (Master Simon's original
intention for York), at York the composition remains
essentially a hole-in-the-wall in the less daring English
manner.

The very beautiful doorway in the N aisle N wall has the
Virgin under a canopy, censing angels and heraldic carving
all of the highest quality. The doorway led to St Sepulchre's
Chapel.

Whether apprehension or economy led to the abandonment of a stone vault remains doubtful. Archbishop Thoresby was still seeking timbers to complete the original wooden lierne vault in 1355. Faithfully reinstated after the fire of 1841 it remains something of an embarrassment, a confession of failure, an uneasy compromise. Recent redecoration has left it with the impact of a Georgian Gothick drawing-room ceiling.

St William was buried near the E end of the nave and after his translation to the choir in 1284 the original burial place remained one of special sanctity. In the 1330s Archbishop Melton gave money towards the glorious 'tomb' of which there are fragments in the Yorkshire Museum (Walk 2).

The West Front

There are archaeological arguments suggesting a change of plan at the W end, and architectural reasons for refuting them. The western piers are larger than the others – supporting the towers – and their responds on the N and S walls are larger than the ordinary vaulting shafts, cutting off a half bay of the wall arcading – suggesting a change: countering this last, the same thing happens on the W wall, allowing the W aisle windows to appear centrally between the buttresses outside and centrally in the E tower arches inside, indicating considerable sophistication in the setting out.*

The splendid uncertainties of the new W front are due to its 150 year building programme and the unwillingness of each succeeding designer to follow the intentions of his predecessor. The W front of Beverley, the result of one building scheme, is full of capricious variations contributing much to its charm; its impression is one of unity and height contrasting with the breadth of York, with which the towers argue ineffectually.

* The idea that the intention was to retain the late-12th-century w front seems unsustained by an early-14th-century drawing of York in the British Museum showing the old front partly erased with the first stages of the new front drawn in below. The old front was probably the last part of the Norman nave to be demolished, but its retention would have made the new nave impossibly short with a narrow w bay and irresolvable anomalies in the w terminations of the two aisles.

Order is maintained to the level of the aisle parapet. Concordant tiers of niches encase the buttresses, broken by larger frontal niches for narrative sculpture of which uninformative fragments remain. This display is given up as soon as the flanking buttresses are passed. Round the W door, Dr Harvey detects a change of designer to Hugh de Boudon, marked by an incursion of ball flowers and ogees and a cramping of niches (though mouldings and ornaments otherwise follow through, suggesting this may be a needless complication); scenes from Genesis are among the carvings. Much of this was excellent restoration of 1802–16 by William Shout and Michael Taylor; since cleaning, the detail has proved sadly less than perdurable; the doorways are crumbling and ravaged.

Little more than the width of the W window was settled at this stage, and when, after a long break, work was resumed *c.* 1335, under Archbishop Melton, the new designer, probably Ivo de Raughton, used the Curvilinear style. The large buttresses finish in variously traceried gables; a band of niches under nodding ogees no longer subscribe to the firmly gridded discipline below. In the centre is the most elaborate Curvilinear window in England: eight lights are paired and paired again under heavy ogees forming the lower half of the heart-shaped centrepiece supporting an ogee vesica above, and linked back to the enclosing arch by sharply turned loops. The centre mullion, diminishing, almost bisects the composition. Blunt-ended mouchettes droop and swirl within this heavy framework, with none of the variety of form that just sustains the Carlisle and Selby windows. It is famous, splendid, and not quite a success; too large or not large enough; the long lights leave a sense of vacuity in the middle of the front, and the great 'heart' rests uneasily on its central mullion as though it might drop out at any minute. Nor is the space in which the window exists adequately defined: the upper wall has rippling niches that conveniently fill up any space; across this thin buttresses flank the steep gable that clashes with the monster-infested cornice, and, after breaking into tracery, with the low-pitched nave roof, which has its own swirling tracery design, stepped battlements, and openwork pinnacle. The inside face of the wall follows exactly the same stratification of Geometrical, nodding ogees, and convenient ripples.

The middle stages of the towers must have followed immediately, though under another mason and more plainly treated. Two worn Evangelical symbols on the SW tower are late-12th-century (probably part of the surround of a majestas, the other two flank the apex of the W window inside;* three statues on the buttresses of the NW tower are also late-12th-century.) Proper towers were intended, probably not of great height, and with two windows to each face: some fragments of these are fossilized among the battlements over the main cornice of the W front, below the NW tower.

By c. 1430 the weakness of the central tower abutments and foundations had become apparent, and the scheme for the great belfry was abandoned. Western towers were substituted c. 1432–72, to a design probably by William Waddeswyck. They are not a success; the feeblest part of the building, overladen with niches; buttresses retracting at the top beneath the tray-like cornice on which huge pinnacles teeter. Ruskin referred to them as 'paltry'. The SW tower has 13 bells; the NW one, Big Peter, weighing $10\frac{1}{2}$ tons, heard at midday and on state occasions.

Nave fittings:

Fine Eagle lectern given in 1686. Pulpit by Comper, 1948. Choir stalls (1948), Dean's and Canons' stalls (1952), and Archbishop's throne (1959) all by Sir Albert Richardson; intended for traditional ceremonial, unconformable to fancy liturgical layout. The dragon in the N triforium is a copy of that which supported the medieval font cover. Chapel of the Lord's Prayer, 1963, by Francis Johnson – unfortunate fairground Gothic.

Brass to James Cotrel, d. 1595, at E end of S aisle. Much renewed, 15th-century four-centred arch intruded into the wall arcade in the N aisle has been claimed as a monument to Archbishop Roger.

---

* I am grateful to Christopher Wilson for pointing this out to me, and for much else.

The early-14th-century stained glass has suffered more in the s aisle than in the N. The scheme, to which there were early exceptions, had two bands of subject panels under canopies, between bands of grisaille. The tracery panels have been extensively replaced by garish Peckitt designs. Recent intrusions are more subtly distressing. The windows are described from the SE corner, clockwise.

1 Probably given by Archbishop Greenfield: supposedly St Nicholas panels, much obscured: bishops, kings, and cups in the borders. Dark, rich colours against which a recently intruded *c.* 1180 panel jangles horribly. Peckitt tracery. *2* Dishevelled with cropped canopies. Nativity panels – a two-headed Virgin in one – donor below; bishops, saints, and falcons in borders. Feeble panel by Harcourt Doyle (1959) centre bottom. *3* Given by Robert de Riplingham. Scenes from life of St John the Evangelist. Original tracery glass with SS. Catherine and Margaret and an angel. Gorgeous colours, much restored. *4* Given by Canon Stephen de Mauley. Martyrdoms of SS. Stephen, Andrew, and John Baptist above members of the Mauley family, liberally heraldic. Largely renewed by Burlison and Grylls, 1903. *5* Jesse tree, restored by Peckitt (1789) especially discordantly, and again in 1950. Much added to, with late-14th- and 15th-century heads. Reticulating branches form vesicas with an elongated one for the Virgin. *6* Made up at the recent restoration. The best panels are SS. Edmund and Edward the Confessor in the outer, upper lights, flanking St William crossing Ouse Bridge. Annunciation, St Gregory, and St John of Beverley below. *7* Mostly displaced glass, found in the chapter house windows. Martyrdoms on chequered backgrounds above, and in side lights. Three panels of *c.* 1350 in lower centre light, belonging to a series of which more remains in the choir. Joachim in the Wilderness, Joachim and Anna, the Annunciation, the first and last exquisite panels showing Parisian influence, the Annunciation based apparently on a Duccio design.

The two w aisle windows were ordered in 1338–9 to complement the great w window. *8* A majestic crucifixion between the Virgin and St John; sumptuous canopies with

lesser saints. Shrill Peckitt panels at the foot of the centre
light and in its companion opposite. *9* The W window is the
greatest of English stained-glass windows. It was paid for by
Archbishop Melton, who also gave the stone tracery. The
achievement of Master Robert, the glasspainter, is techni-
cally and artistically brilliant. The scheme is simple. Above
the trellissed base, tiers of archbishops and apostles under
gablets; then the Annunciation, Nativity, Ascension, and
Resurrection each spread over two lights like the Coronation
of the Virgin, centre top. The tracery panels, defying
iconography, are given grisaille glass. (There are 55 substantial tracery panels at York, to 8 lights, compared to 45 to the 9
lights at Carlisle.) The window has rightness of scale and
subject-matter, with richness of detail, refined yet telling.
The figure of St John (three lights from S, upper tier) is one
of the grandest in the Minster [22]. Dean Milner-White's
cosmetic treatment to Peckitt's heads is an improvement.
10 The Virgin and Child between SS. Catherine and
Margaret; smaller saints in the gorgeous canopies, smaller
figures still in the borders of the Virgin's panel.

11 A made-up window with the merit of not pretending
to be part of the scheme. Pentecost and Ascension panels
(English, 16th-century) flank St Christopher (16th-century),
whose anatomical peculiarities are due to his upper half
being French and his lower half English. Small 15th-century
saints. Sixteenth-century French 'Nativity' under a charming, formal arrangement of trophies, griffins, and angels.
12 Gablets instead of canopies mark interference in the
lower parts. Nativity scenes above and Coronation of the
Virgin in the tracery. Jesse panel of *c.* 1180 at the foot of the
centre light. *13* Martyrdoms of SS. Peter and Paul flank a
made-up Coronation of the Virgin above penancer's panels.
Figures of masons in the borders. The other four windows in
this aisle are among the loveliest in the Minster, two sadly
obscured by old protective glazing outside. *14* Virgin
between donors below the martyrdoms of SS. Laurence,
Denys, and (?) Vincent. Martyrdoms of SS. Edmund and
Stephen are in the medallions. Christ in Glory with SS. Peter
and Paul in the tracery. *15* Pilgrims approaching St Peter

holding his church. Above is a Passion scene spread over three lights; Christ and angels in the tracery. Along the bottom borders, a monkey's funeral, a fox stealing a hen, and a hunting scene. *16* The Bellfounders' window given by Richard Tunnoc, who presents the window to St William between panels of bellmaking scenes; St William panels above. Monkeys play instruments in the centre light borders: the preponderance of yellow bells, elsewhere, is a consequence of restoration. SS. Peter and Paul in the tracery. *17* Given by Peter de Dene, the finest of all the early-14th-century windows in the aisles. The life of St Catherine with the donor centre bottom. Much important heraldry including a splendid series of kings, queens, knights, and nobles, all wearing heraldic surcoats.

The nave clerestory windows were again designed on a banded scheme of white glass, heraldry, white glass, figure subjects, white glass, and rich, dark colour in the tracery. Much use was made of earlier material, in both subject panels and coloured patterns. The decision to remove the glowing tracery glass to store, replacing it with insipid new work, seems an indefensible piece of meddling. The upper, subject bands are being reorganized; five windows in the S side complete at the moment, the two eastmost with Barnet panels (1845) from the chapter house; the three western ones with late-12th-century panels.

The Choir

The scale of the new nave demanded an eastern arm of corresponding magnitude, and in 1360 Archbishop Thoresby addressed himself to providing one. He began with the four bays of the Lady Chapel set out to the E of Roger's transepts so that the greatest progress could be made before any demolition became necessary; though the eastern part of Roger's choir and the transepts must have been demolished earlier, it was not until 1394 that it became necessary to transfer services to the new vestry.

The aisle walls were built first, to a design, not too inspired, by William Hoton junior; mechanical tracery, large buttresses with heavy pinnacles, its one original feature is the setting back of the wall face above the window springings outside so that the crockets above the windows stand free of the wall. Robert de Patrington was appointed master mason in 1369, and he was responsible for the much more adventurous design of the arcades, and of the triforium and clerestory, which develop the theme established in the nave, with inner-plane tracery still having some curvilinear features; but combining this with an external stone screen to the clerestory of three divisions to the bay in a rhythm syncopated to that of the tracery.

Archbishop Thoresby died in 1373, after which there seems to have been little progress until the early 1390s.

The E front impresses by size [24], if not by subtlety or co-ordination. Obvious variations of pinnacle and parapet are matched by lesser ones like the unsettled forms of the lowest tier of buttress niches. But the great window with its ogee hood shooting far above the gable is much more successfully integrated in the design than the W window. Below it is a popular range of heads; above it, a statue perhaps more likely to be St Peter than Archbishop Thoresby. The tracery is the work of the third master mason to work on the eastern arm, Hugh de Hedon, who was also responsible for the five western bays of the choir. Hedon kept to the main lines of the Hoton–Patrington design, reducing the buttresses and pinnacles and modifying everything else to suit his more purely Perpendicular tastes. His most original invention was the quasi-transepts, which form the central bay of the whole eastern arm, transepts projecting upwards but not outwards, like enormous dormers, with much prolonged and transomed versions of his new clerestory windows down the front faces. In his clerestory Hedon reverts to the usual practice of setting the tracery on the outer wall face, thereby compromising the internal unity of triforium and clerestory. Another of Hedon's inventions is the double-plane tracery in the lower parts of the E window and the transeptal windows, stiffening the structure, providing gallery walks, displaying unfathomable logic in making it possible to have larger windows for the display of stained glass and difficult to enjoy them fully.

The choir is full of large and small felicities; the overwhelming, unintended space as one passes beneath the choir screen; the more involved spatial effects in the aisles, confined below, opening above and diagonally into the choir and vertically into the transepts. The wall arcades are more broadly treated than in the nave, though still delicately; their original impact difficult to gauge beneath the plethora of later monuments. The little canopies crowning the vaulting shafts, instead of capitals, are a pretty feature. Stone vaulting for the choir does not seem to have been contemplated. The wooden vault, a copy made after the 1829 fire, is much more successful than the nave vault, though no less unfortunate in the effects of its recent decoration.

The original arrangements of the choir make Hedon's design more comprehensible. The high altar stood in the transept bay, between the St William and St Cuthbert windows, and behind it a huge wooden screen separated sanctuary from feretory, where St William's Shrine stood, separated from the Lady Chapel by a second, stone screen. Sanctuary and feretory stood on the platform above the early-15th-century crypt built from the remains of Roger's crypt.

Choir fittings:

Stalls, screens, and the stone screen behind the high altar all date from the restoration after the 1829 fire; and are probably more correct reproductions of what was there before than would have been possible later in the 19th century. The work was supervised by Sir Robert Smirke: the stalls by Coates; tabernacle work by Robert Hume; stone screen by the Minster masons under John Scott. A fragment of the original stone screen is in the garden of Moreby Hall. Charming Art Nouveau choir-stall lights. Organ by Elliot and Hill, 1832. Spanish silver altar cross made in Aquilar, *c.* 1570, in a gorgeous mixture of Gothic and Renaissance styles.

Early-15th-century clerestory windows, popes flanked by kings and bishops; heraldry below, small saints in the tracery, much damaged in the fire, probably from Thornton's workshop.

The fittings and glass of the choir aisles and chapels are described bay-by-bay starting at the W end of the S aisle. The plan (p. 109) shows a key to the bays.

A The stone screens at the entrance to the choir aisles are one of William Colchester's devices for propping up the central tower: statues designed by Bodley, 1905. Gates given by Dean Finch, *c.* 1710, ornament concentrated on the standards and along the top. Cast-iron railing round the organ pipes, designed by Heindrick Franz de Cort, 1804, to surround Archbishop Gray's monument. Vaulting ribs at cross-purposes.

B Undistinguished military memorials: the Duke of Clarence was popular when stationed locally, 1887–91; George Vyner's death promoted glorious memorial churches at Skelton and Studley Royal (see excursions, p. 298). The 'York Fiddler', half-length, 18th-century figure.

Martyrdom window; parts of four windows, subjects conveniently identified by modern labels. Early-15th-century upper panels belong to the scheme that survives complete in the next bay and the N choir aisle. The panels of St Gregory and St John the Baptist are a little later. The Te Deum panels belong to the window in St George's Chapel. Embarrassing Stammers panel in the middle.

C 1st North Riding Regiment of Foot brass (1859), by J. Hardman Powell. William Mason, d. 1797, and Henry Dixon, d. 1854, prickly brass confection by Skidmore (1862). Mason might have been surprised but not, one hopes, unamused.

Glass of *c.* 1420, influenced by John Thornton (see E window): holy families, Zebedee and Salome, Joachim and Anna, Mary Cleophas and Alphaeus, above panels of the childhood of the Virgin, marriage of Joachim and Anna in left light, a lovely panel.

D Lieutenant Colonel Oldfield, d. 1850, an ambitious product by Skelton. 'Europa Transport' memorial, 1854, by J.B. Philip, alabaster, marble, and brass, one of the best

Victorian tablets. Mrs Hodson, d. 1636, already 'classical' with pediment and cherubs.

The Oxford Jesse, late-14th-century glass by Thomas of Oxford, from New College, given to William Peckitt in part-payment for a new window. Greenish with rich, crowned figures, an important example of the new 'soft style' glass painting. The tracery panels are part of a 'Doom'.

E William Wickham, d. 1840, chaste Greek. Sir William Gee, frontal, his wives and children in profile, amid heterogeneous classical elements, dated 1611. The trapezoidal area above had, till recently, traces of painted strapwork decoration. Archbishop Matthew Hutton, d. 1605, effigy with *rigor mortis* above kneeling family; elaborate surround, liberal with strapwork. Charming label stops to the crypt entrances, *c.* 1400. Tapestry of the Last Supper, 16th-century Spanish, the original donor and his lady kneeling in the foreground.

St Cuthbert window: probably the latest of the choir windows, given by Thomas Langley, Bishop of Durham, showing Archbishop Kempe with his cardinal's hat, which he received in 1443. St Cuthbert is surrounded by Lancastrians and ecclesiastics, jewels annealed to some of the richer robes. Monkish subjects above give a preponderance of blue. A pallid copy of the St William window. In the clerestory, figures of St William and Archbishop Scrope.

F Henry and Edward Finch, by Rysbrack (1729); twin busts exhibiting a proper disdain for the passer-by; designed to go round a pillar, it has lost much of its plinth. (Several of the choir monuments have enjoyed a peripatetic existence, losing parts on the way.) Nicholas Wanton, d. 1617, surprised in his delicate niche. John Brooke, d. 1616, and Edmund Bunney, d. 1617, show a passing fancy for painted wood; Bunney exchanges his heart for a gospel in a landscape littered with texts. Archbishop Lamplugh, d. 1691, by Grinling Gibbons; standing figure in a curtained niche, viewing the Lady Chapel with understandable scepticism; semicircular pediment with cherubs, one weeping, one disgruntled. Opposite, Archbishop Dolben, d. 1686, reclining beneath flying cherubs. Milner and Visick panels by Stammers, delicate, but not wearing well.

The glass is a N French crucifixion of the early 16th century, from Rickmansworth; good, but very foreign. Heraldry below of Princess Elizabeth, daughter of James I; Archbishop Lamplugh, by Henry Gyles, *c.* 1690, and Archbishop Williams as Bishop of Lincoln (1626).

G Minor monuments by Taylor and Fisher. Brass to Elizabeth Eynnes, d. 1585, gentlewoman in waiting to Queen Elizabeth I. William Burgh, d. 1808, by Westmacott, chilly statue carrying a cross.

Late-14th-century glass. SS. James, Edward the Confessor, and John the Evangelist, under pepper-pot turrets like some in the Lady Chapel clerestory (*c.* 1373); scenes from the childhood of Christ, much patched and darkened.

H All Saints' Chapel (with *I*). Screen by Tapper and Bainbridge Reynolds (1930) after one in Siena. William Wentworth, Earl of Strafford, d. 1695, 'as full of good deeds as of days'. The grandest and finest of the post-Reformation monuments [45], convincingly attributed to John Nost. Life-size figures and an urn in a Corinthian surround; a virtuoso performance, especially the Garter robes. Wentworth heraldic brasses on the family vault outside the chapel.

Glass: good 15th-century figures of Isaiah and King Edwin; Trinity panels inadequately occupy the central light.

I South wall. Anne Bennet, frontal figure in a niche, flanked by harpies (1615) by Nicholas Stone; good.

Sixteenth-century French glass with Adam and Eve being driven out of the Garden of Eden accompanied by the seven deadly sins. Seventeenth-century 'Salutation' panels below, from Rouen.

East wall. Archbishop Piers, d. 1594, strapwork exploding round a tablet. William Palmer, d. 1605, tiny and refined.

Late-14th-century glass. Central panel St James of Compostella, one of a series of *c.* 1350 panels (see clerestory and *M*); uninformative panels around glow gorgeously in morning sunlight.

J The Lady Chapel has settled uncertainly for a central

altar, among borrowed and inharmonious fittings. Bodley's reredos (1905) carved by Laurence Turner isolated above blue curtains.

Monuments anticlockwise. Archbishop Tobias Matthew, d. 1628, restored effigy on a tomb-chest by Sydney Smirke. Archbishop Bowet, finished *c.* 1415, spectacular, elliptical arch occupying the whole bay; panelled beneath, edged with turned-up vaults between pendant canopies, original statues in the canopies above; much damaged in the fire: the archbishop's chantry chapel was in the E bay of the aisle. Archbishop Sharp, d. 1714, by Francis Bird; reclining before a flatly Baroque reredos prolix of inscriptions. David Kindersley's 1957 slab to Archbishop Garbett is a model of good lettering. Neither Mrs Matthews, d. 1628, in a curtained recess, nor Archbishop Frewen, d. 1664, ladies sliding off the pediment, has much to recommend it. Archbishop Scrope, d. 1405, has plainly quatrefoiled tomb, and Archbishop Markham, d. 1807, one by Salvin with brasses by Willement.

The E window (1405–8) is the greatest monument in stained glass of the International Gothic style of the 15th century. John Thornton of Coventry who painted it received four shillings a week, five pounds a year, and ten pounds on completion. God the Father at the apex (Thornton's monogram in smaller lights) reigns over a multitude of tracery saints and angels; the creation and fall of men above the gallery, with the Revelation of St John the Divine below, and a superb series of ecclesiastics, kings, and York saints along the base. Individual panels – one with 22 figures – are masterpieces of design, calling for binoculars; if the effect is less than totally successful that is the fault of its iconographical complexity rather than any deficiency of the designer's. White and silver stain figures against ruby and blue backgrounds, scattered green, gorgeous orange apples in the Garden of Eden.

The Lady Chapel clerestory windows are in two groups. Two on the N and one on the S are late-14th-century with saints under pepper-pot turrets, like those in bay *G.* Two others on the S are of *c.* 1350, figures under gablets with subject panels above from the Annunciation to Joachim to the life of the Virgin (others of the series in the E aisle windows and bay *M*). Binoculars are needed, again, for the splendid little figures in the side shafting. O'Connor and Haselock suggest these were originally in St Sepulchre's Chapel, N of the nave, of which Archbishop Melton licensed an enlargement in 1333.

K St Stephen's Chapel (with *L*). East wall; altarpiece by Street and Tinworth (1879) made for the high altar, in painted and gilded terracotta.

Early-15th-century glass, not by Thornton, large crucifixion group with the Virgin and St John; four St Stephen panels and another of the *c.* 1350 figures; original tracery, glass, angels back-to-back ingeniously filling the subsidiary lights.

North wall. Numerous attractive, minor 18th-century tablets and cartouches; Lionel Ingram (*c.* 1630) dark and gabled.

North French glass, late-16th-century panels of St James the Great.

L Ironwork from the Watson Wentworth monument, *c.* 1724.

John Dealtry, d. 1773, by Fisher, allegorical figure on a plinth, architectural details of exquisite refinement [46].

Glorious figures of SS. Stephen, Christopher, and Laurence, *c.* 1340, probably by the artists who designed the W window. Lamentable infil below.

M Minor Fisher tablets. Dorothy Langley, d. 1824, grittily Gothic. Admiral Medley, died Savona, 1747, bust and trophies on a sarcophagus with a battlepiece delicate yet spirited; swags of sea shells; grey, white, and ochre; by Sir Henry Cheere. Lady Mary Fenwick, d. 1708, curious, three cartouches, three inscriptions disparately lettered, bust against a cut-away vaulting shaft. Formerly it had an involved pediment.

Six more *c.* 1350 panels, more readily studied, prophets and Passion scenes of very high quality.

N Sir William Ingram, d. 1623, frontal figures between caryatids with obelisk hats. Henry Swinburne, d. 1624, kneeling between disaffected persons balanced on globes under 'Gothic' canopies. Opposite, Thomas Watson Wentworth, d. 1723 (lacking its pyramid back), by William Kent and G.B. Guelfi, figures in classical costume, leaning against an urn.

St Vincent belongs to the series in Bay *L*. Early-15th-century SS. Edward the Confessor and Peter are not on same level of achievement but superior to what happens beneath. *O* Henry Belassis by Nicholas Stone (*c.* 1615), old-fashioned and an early work but the best Minster monument of its period [34]; a cherub blowing bubbles in the spandrel. Archbishop Savage, d. 1507; stiff effigy beneath an arch, the panelled soffit with the faintest traces of painting. Delicate chantry above by Sir Albert Richardson, 1950.

The St William window is one of the Minster's masterpieces. Scenes from the saint's life and miracles – some 'borrowed' – *c.* 1423, probably by John Thornton. Like the E window difficult to read but a marvellous record of medieval life and costume. The suggestion that it was originally two windows opposite one another is architecturally unconvincing.

P, Q, R, S The four W aisle bays have numerous brasses in thick marble frames of the 1880s and 90s, for which Bodley must be responsible, two late 'Gothic' monuments with indents for brasses, and a number of monuments settled here from elsewhere. Archbishop Sterne, d. 1683, in a recess below a rather undersized pediment, cherubs and a pretty swag; a good monument whose sculptor has not yet been identified. Archbishops Musgrave, d. 1860, and Vernon Harcourt, d. 1847, have effigies by Matthew Noble (the Musgrave tomb chest by Raphael Brandon). Dr Beckwith, d.1845, by J.B. Leyland, has been deprived of his tomb chest, too fulsome on his benefactions for later tastes. Laura Burton Dawnay, d. 1812, 'for her character and other particulars see the Gentleman's Magazine for May MDCCCXII'. At the W end of the aisle under three tiers of triple canopies, above a tomb chest with tracery remarkably unflowing, exquisite, worn effigy of Prince William of Hatfield, second son of Edward III and Queen Philippa. Sir

George Saville, d. 1784, by Fisher, lacking the finesse of his best work.

The 'Gudbrandsdal' tapestry of the Epiphany (*c.* 1625–50) and the English Annunciation Banner, *c.* 1670, have recently been set in glass cases designed to reflect the windows opposite.

The glass of these three bays is closely related to that of the choir clerestory, all of the 1420s and probably from Thornton's workshop. The aisle scheme has large figures of saints under splendid canopies above scenes from each saint's life. Several of the large figures are taken from the same cartoon, a standard medieval practice. *P* Given by Robert Wolveden, Treasurer; SS. Chad, Paulinus, and Nicholas. *Q* Given by Thomas Parker, Canon; SS. John of Beverley, Thomas Becket, and William. *R* Given by Archbishop Bowet; St Paul, the Virgin, and St Peter. This window suffered sadly in the fire, but the glorious wings and lily crucifix in the Annunciation panel confirm its original splendour.

The Vestries and Zouche Chapel

South of the choir, a range comprising consistory court, vestry, and the so-called Zouche Chapel present problems for the historian. Their design is consistent, with narrow, heavily mullioned, heavily barred windows. Archbishop Zouche's chapel is supposed to have been started in 1350, two years before his death, but the W aisle buttresses of the Lady Chapel were built against Roger's choir transepts and the E wall of the chapel is built against Thoresby's buttresses, that is after 1361. Neither could the tierceron vaulting of the chapel have been completed until after the demolition of Roger's transepts, and the vaulting of the other two rooms reuses Norman work (as in the crypt). However, there are some signs of alteration when the entrance from the chapel into the new choir aisle was formed (different leaf carving on the capitals). All of this strongly suggests that this is a late-14th-century building and that the chapel is the new vestry to which services were transferred in 1394 – a supposition that may be confirmed by the range of late-14th-century cupboards with charming ironwork and the pretty well canted out in the SW corner – and that Archbishop Zouche's chapel was somewhere else.

Two misericords in the chapel are all that remain of the medieval choir stalls. The E window has fragments of medieval glass from the 'Mauley window' in the nave, and three mid-15th-century figures, including Archbishop Kempe. Most of the other windows have medieval quarries. The SE window by Ervin Bossanyi (1944) was put here in 1975, strong but alien; ill-advisedly adapted for a space that it was not intended for, but the only recent glass in the Minster worth noting.

The Central Tower

The new choir was not completed until the 1420s. At the beginning of the 15th century work had reached the point where something had to be done about the crossing. The eastern arch, designed for Roger's choir, would have been inadequate as an entrance to the new choir, the others were still related to the roof of the Norman nave, and the original roofs of the Early English transepts, and there was still the problem of Thomas's turrets and their Early English fronts cluttering the ends of the aisles. The complex and daring scheme involved recasing and presumably heightening the tower arches; swapping the adjacent wide and narrow bays in the E and W walls of the transepts, reusing the original material; removing the turrets altogether, and providing the transepts with new, wooden 'vaults'. The Early English tower was to be retained. The self-confidence of medieval masons was astonishing. Not surprisingly, in 1407, part of the tower fell.

Henry IV sent his master mason William Colchester to oversee the work, and Colchester planned a new tower on the grandest scale, with a belfry above the lantern stage (a much larger version of the tower at Durham), but by his death in 1420 work seems only to have progressed to roof level. The lantern stage was built in the 15th century, but the inadequacy of the foundations, which has given so much recent trouble, must have already become apparent: the belfry scheme was abandoned and the western towers built instead, so that, even in its truncated form, the central tower was not completed until *c.* 1473. The majestic simplicity of its design, pairs of windows flanked and separated by tiers of niches, should have been (but was not) an inspiration to the designer of the western towers.

The screens at the W end of the choir aisles are part of Colchester's ingenious system of support. (During the work on the tower the remaining pier in the W arcade of the N transept had to be replaced, involving more structural daring.) The beautiful wall arcading below the lantern and the bosses of the original vault are worth closer study (binoculars) than the windows glazed by Matthew Petty in 1471, with the cathedral arms dismally repeated 48 times.

The Choir Screen

The choir screen has always been assigned to the end of the 15th century as the work of William Hyndeley, master mason *c.* 1473–1505, because of his alleged rebus of a hind lying down.* The Kings of England from William I to Henry VI are asymmetrically disposed, seven to one side, eight to the other. After 1461 Edward IV should have been included; after 1485 Henry VII, though it might have been politic to ignore his immediate predecessor. It seems most probable that the screen was built in the mid 15th century before Henry VI's deposition. (Dr Harvey attributes the design to the reign of Henry V – an even number of kings – feeling apparently that while the Middle Ages could not have conceived so lop-sided a thing, they could have happily executed it if circumstances demanded.)

All but one of the statues are original, strongly individual-

---

* Hyndeley may have repaired the screen after a fire of 1464.

ized figures under elaborate and variously vaulted canopies. The statue of Henry VI (1810) is by Michael Taylor, the original having been removed because of the King's sanctity and replaced by one of James I who was without such embarrassing attributes. The stucco angels and much repair work revealed by recent cleaning are by Bernasconi (1803–5). The pretty lierne vault in the porch has a Coronation of the Virgin on the central boss. The inner porch has a fan vault hidden darkly under the organ. The excellent iron gates were given by Mrs Wandesford, *c.* 1702.

The Minster is open from 7.00 a.m. to 5.00 p.m. in winter and until dusk in summer. the Undercroft Museum and treasury, chapter house and central tower, for all of which a charge is made, are closed an hour earlier. On Sunday mornings visitors are encouraged if they attend the services, but not otherwise. Guided tours and access to the eastern crypt and Archbishop Roger's crypt should be arranged in advance through the Tourist & Information Officer, St William's College, York.

Walk One

(The area covered by this Walk is shown on the map for Walk 8, pp. 234–5.)

The Close

Once York had a proper Close, walled, gated, and filled with Prebendal Houses packed round little spaces from which the Minster loomed hugely so that you must have had to crane your neck to take in the view. Whether it was comparable to Salisbury, Wells, Winchester, or Norwich is matter for speculation. Early illustrators, anticipating history, cleared the ground, or, excellent at retailing facts, found topographical nuances beyond them.

The wall was built in 1285, enclosing roughly the northern quarter of the Roman city, Chapter House Street (*via decumana*), Ogleforth, Precentor's Court, and many of the individual buildings following or parallel to the Roman alignments; the Minster by this time established – if it had not been so from the first – at 42° to them, a dissonance with endless townscape repercussions. The gates were at Lop Lane (Duncombe Place), Minster Gates, College Street – the only survivor – and in Ogleforth near the corner of Chapter House Street. The College of the Vicars Choral in Bedern (see Walk 5) stood outside, but connected by a bridge.

'Improvements' had probably been contemplated before Dean Cockburn arrived in 1822 with ideas for something grander than the existing medieval muddle. The Ingram House N of the Minster and the Old Deanery to the SE were demolished, but plans to clear the whole area E of the Minster in front of St William's College were fortunately left incomplete. New buildings were designed by J.P. Pritchett and R.H. Sharp, in competent, uninspired Tudor. In the 1860s Dean Duncombe demolished parts of College Street and lent his name to the disastrous developments in Duncombe Place, whose buildings are too big for a foreground and too far off to be an effective background.

In 1902 the Minster Chapter allowed the construction of a new street through Dean Cockburn's layout, to shorten the journey from Monk Bar to the new station. It was called Deangate, though Dean Purey Cust, to his credit, opposed the scheme. Recent meddlings have been on a smaller scale but no less pernicious.

Precentor's Court and Dean's Park

The best entrance to Precentor's Court now is from Petergate, through a passage by the Board Inn, on foot and unexpectantly. It is a little square, three-quarters delightful, and an alley wholly so, framing between a garden wall and a terrace of little *c.* 1700 houses with wood mullioned and transomed windows, a view of parts of the W front towering out of sight round the corner [3]. Fenton House (No. 9) is also *c.* 1700 (a moment when the canons of York were evidently making themselves comfortable), altered outside but the door and window above probably original, a little gazebo on the roof, and the original heavy balustered staircase like others at Nos. 5 and 10. No. 10 has a late-Georgian front, a medieval stone wing encased in Victorian brick, several charming Regency fireplaces, and a fragment of St William's Shrine under the staircase. The back of the Purey Cust Nursing Home intrudes, and medical aesthetics beyond leave something to be desired.

Sharp left at the entrance to Precentor's Court, facing across the windy promenade in front of the Minster are the Walker iron gates (1839) to the Dean's Park and the stone archway into the grounds of the Purey Cust Nursing Home, Brierley, 1914, simple, slightly French; and beyond another wall the New Residence, R.H. Sharp, 1824–7, stone, Tudor with an oriel. The Park is the most successful of Dean

Cockburn's creations, though scant compensation for what has gone. The Archbishops had a palace here from the 12th to the mid 16th century, though latterly they preferred Bishopthorpe. In the reign of James I what remained passed to Sir Arthur Ingram, one of the Secretaries of the King's Council of the North, who built a house and garden described as 'A place . . . so pleasant to all the sences as art and nature can make it'. Charles I stayed there in 1642. In 1817 the Dean and Chapter terminated the lease˙and the building was demolished. On the NW of the Park (in front of where Pritchett intended a terrace of houses) is part of the Great Hall, probably Archbishop Roger's work of the late 12th century, worn but of great refinement – taken down by Archbishop Young (1561–8).

The Chapel, built *c.*1230 by Archbishop Gray, was rescued from ruin (1806–11) by William Shout, mastermason of the Minster, for use as the Minster Library. The entrance gable is Shout's design, an amazingly convincing piece of Gothic Survival antedating Rickman's first *Attempt to Discriminate the Styles of Architecture* by several years, and certainly superior to any Commissioners' Church Gothic of the 1820s and 30s. The end facing the Deanery has most medieval evidence; the style is characterized inside and out by groups of lancets under round-headed arches. This has been the largest English Cathedral Library since Archbishop Matthew's widow gave his collection of 3,000 volumes (then the largest private library in the country) in 1628. The Gospels of *c.* 1005–10 form the greatest treasure. There are Dean and Chapter Archives from the 14th century; manuscripts from the 12th; Books of Hours; printed books from the 15th century, including the Nuremberg Chronicle; and the Hailstone Collection, outstanding on North-country history.

Winter trees set off the noblest Minster view [15].

J.P. Pritchett's Deanery (1827–31), Tudor, very up to date with a hot-water system, stood next to the Library until it was pulled down when Rutherford and Syme's new Deanery was built, 1938–9, at a perverse angle to its surroundings, with worn-out Georgian conventions flatly imposed.

Minster Court

Minster Court, Minster Yard, Chapter House Street, and College Street have the best of what remains of the Close. Minster Court is three-sided, variously dated, unified by white paint, and a most desirable place in which to live. The high roof over No. 2 belongs to a 15th-century hall, arched-braced with carved bosses. In front Elizabethan extensions, recast but with a delightful early-17th-century ceiling of ovals and lozenges. The left wing is early-Georgian; good staircase, the handrail spiralling boldly at the foot; Rococo ceiling and fireplace in the Saloon upstairs. The right wing has another early-Georgian staircase, but was much extended and recast in the early 19th century.

Minster Yard, a capricious street, starts here, proceeds in a horseshoe hugging the Minster closely to St Michael-le-Belfrey church. Deangate and College Green have confused its line, pointless renaming of its middle stretch as the Queen's Path its identity.

Treasurer's House and Gray's Court

The Office of Treasurer, established late in the 11th century, was abolished (temporarily) in 1547, since, all the 'Treasure' having passed to the Crown, it had become redundant. The medieval Treasurer's House, now called Gray's Court, edges endways into Minster Yard (Georgian, tampered with, up a long garden, with a 1730s doorway), between Minster Court and what is now called Treasurer's House, in fact the Young family mansion added at right angles to the old house in the early 17th century, and brought up to date by the Squire family in the first half of the 18th. The whole group was called 'The Great House' until a process of subdivisions started *c.* 1725. Frank Green bought Treasurer's House in the late 19th century and together with Edwin Gray, of Gray's Court, and their architect Temple Moore restored the group, 1897–1906; a restoration informed by taste if no great regard for historical accuracy.

Treasurer's House belongs to the National Trust. Its garden is quintessential York: terraced; formal before the not-too-formal front, where Young, Squire, and Green elements combine beautifully but indeterminably; terracotta statues; half a glorious Ash and garden walls full of medieval stones worn to amorphousness – the Minster is magnificent beyond; in a corner, gravestones of a dog and parrot, both venerable. The centrepiece of the house (early-17th-century) has the delicious solecism of large classical columns perched on pairs of smaller ones. The Dutch gables are of *c.* 1700.

Inside, much material was imported or moved about at the restoration. The Entrance Hall decoration is based on some in Clifton House Tower, Kings Lynn. The West Sitting Room has an almost Baroque fireplace moved from the Hall. The Dining Room has dark mid-18th-century panelling and fireplace with overmantel, its swirling pediment and basket of fruit crammed in beneath the massive early-18th-century ceiling refurbished with sumptuous Rococo twirls [39]. The Hall (familiar from ancient railway posters) is Temple Moore's creation, open to the roof as it had never been before. Temple Moore also created the Drawing Room out of two smaller rooms, repositioning fireplace and door surrounds. It is perhaps the most beautiful room in York. The staircase is early-18th-century and very handsome, planned round a rectangular well, inside an L-shaped landing. Beds dominate the upper rooms. Princess Victoria's Room has a lovely, linear, Kentian fireplace of *c.* 1755 from Micklegate House. The run-through panelling of *c.* 1600 in the Tapestry Room was found beneath wallpaper. At the other end of the house, Temple Moore's decoration of the King's Room in pink with green and blue squiggles is not attractive. The house is beautifully maintained and furnished.

John Goodricke (1764–86), the deaf and dumb astronomer, discovered 'variable stars' in observations from the house. Though he died so young no other citizen of York has exercised so much influence on the history of thought, except Alcuin.

Gray's Court opens off Chapter House Street: again York at its best; Cobbles and pleached planes; gateposts with belligerent lions framing pretty gardens by the walls. The back of Treasurer's House deploys five more-or-less symmetrical architectural elements, brick and stone, in a composition of total asymmetry, disarmingly tied together by bits of cornice: mullioned windows, bald Venetian windows with dislocated pediments, sashes and ovals jostle.

Gray's Court is more resolutely brick. Much of it – the pretty oriel on columns and the big bay on the right – archaeologically unreliable, delightful restoration by Temple Moore. The columns supporting low, four-centred arches along the front are more intelligible inside, certainly late-12th-century, interpreted variously as a portico, the central columns of a great hall, or (most probably) post-Reformation reuse of material from a demolished church. The back wall of the Entrance Hall (and of the gallery above) is late-12th-century work undoubtedly *in situ*, but what one sees is the outside face of the wall with window and string course, and corbel table behind the gallery panelling. The staircase (1900) belongs to the restoration, when the gallery was also reconstructed; it had been subdivided but much of the panelling of *c.* 1600 survived. Some of the stained-glass medallions (late-17th- /early-18th-century) may be the work of Henry Gyles; three of the ladies have distinctly cynical inscriptions. The fireplaces, with oval overmantels, and doorcases are 1740s work for Canon Jaques Sterne – uncle of Lawrence Sterne – who also added the beautiful Dining Room (the Sterne Room), Rococo ceiling, and fireplace with exquisite portrait medallion of Augusta, Princess of Wales. The Bow Room – *c.* 1846 with classical fireplace – is part of extensive irregular additions to the back of the house by J.B. and W. Atkinson.

Chapter House Street, Ogleforth, and College Street

Chapter House Street is cobbled, with cottages growing out of old walls, and a strategic tree setting off the bulk of the

Minster to perfection [2]. At the other end the Old Rectory has a Dutch gable above the rendering, and an odd neighbour, the Tower House, seen from the walls, a conceit, a cylinder with a Victorian chalet on top. Townscape disintegrates in Ogleforth, restored houses on one side face gaps on the other. One of the gates to the Close, the church of St John del Pyke ('at the Minster Gate'), and Archbishop Holgate's Grammar School, founded here in 1546, have all gone. Cromwell House (*c.* 1700) has windows in projecting bands, under little cornices. A post-Restoration brick house, lavishly pedimented, expensively rebuilt, used as a store.

By turning right and into Goodramgate and then right again College Street (formerly Vicar Lane) can be entered through the one surviving gate to the Close, 15th-century timber-framed, next to the National Trust Shop, where George Hudson had his draper's shop. St Mary ad Valvas church and the Chapel of the Countess of Huntingdon's Connexion (*c.* 1749) both stood here, and Elizabeth Lumley who married Laurence Sterne in 1741 lived here.

St William's College

St William's College, the College of Chantry Priests of the Minster, was built 1465–7, by extending the Prior of Hexham's slightly earlier house round a courtyard. At the Dissolution it was granted to the Stanhopes, then to the Jenkins family. Charles I's printer had rooms in it. By the end of the 18th century it was tenements. Since Temple Moore's restoration of 1906 it has been used for Diocesan purposes. The Prior's House is that at the Minster end of the courtyard (Hall, Chapel, and Study below, with a large Hall above). The rest of the courtyard and elevation [30] follows the original design of a stone ground floor and timber-framed upper floors on deep-coved jetties – with figures of the Virgin and St Christopher flanking the door and others probably representing the 'Months' under the coves in the courtyard. The pretty oriels on the front, and most of those in the courtyard, date from the restoration, when the excellent range of Georgian shopfronts was wisely left alone. Some idea of what the building was like before restoration can be gauged – for the moment – by the NE end of the courtyard, behind which good panelled rooms and a staircase of *c.*1700 survive. The door from the courtyard, the hall ceiling, the big brick staircase at the back, and panelling in the Bishop's Chamber were added by Tobias Jenkins in the late 17th century. (The original door – 15th-century – with wicket is kept in the Entrance Hall.)

The medieval layout of the back wing had screens passage, buttery, and kitchens on one side, a new chapel on the other, and a two-storeyed hall in the centre, whose arched-braced roof survives at one end of the MacLagan Room. (At the back the Hall was stone to its full height and had large stone-traceried windows with four-centred heads.) The rest of the MacLagan Room was originally small chambers with partitions under the tie beams. The House of Laymen has diagonally set ties at the end, which may be the framing for former passages. The Painted Chamber has the last vestiges of painted decoration, of more antiquarian than aesthetic interest.

Minster Yard

The swathe of paving and setts and the feebly obtrusive fence round the Minster are recent and regrettable. Minster Yard keeps up appearances with ragged determination. No. 4 is an early-18th-century house with a late-18th-century front between wings dating from the 14th to the 19th century; timber framing, Dutch gable, *c.*1600 panelling. The Old Residence, SE of the Minster, is a good house of *c.*1727, the windows of the middle floor delicately amended a century later. A vivid impression of the looming immensity of the Minster in the Close before Dean Cockburn can be gained by standing in its doorway.

Deangate's noise and traffic are shocking intrusions, the more so since the road should never have been permitted, let alone encouraged, by the Chapter in the first place. Attempts are being made at the time of writing to have it closed. The medieval Deanery, in whose Great Hall Charles I held his Great Council of Peers in 1640, stood here. Dean Cockburn's layout survives as two Tudorish buildings with turrets. The more imposing of them, the Song School, was first built as St Peter's School, 1832, and designed by J.P. Pritchett. Neither it nor its neighbour has sufficient presence to command the space (though it does have a very good view). The backs of Petergate houses, pleasant enough, were not meant to be *seen*; Dr Shand, sensing the deficiency, contributed twin Scottish-Baronial spires in slate and doubtful taste. Dean Fountaine's crest of an elephant is seen on a rainwaterhead near Minster Gates, above the Roman Column from the Headquarters Building, found during the Minster Restoration and erected here instead of in the Museum – not beautiful; Palladio would have learned nothing from it; it is possible it is upside down.

St Michael-le-Belfrey

Minster Yard ends at St Michael-le-Belfrey, largest and most consistent of York churches; generally said, with some disregard to facts, to be the only one built all at the same time. First mentioned in 1294, probably older still, it was rebuilt by John Forman, Minster mason, 1525–36. Its Tudor style is no longer really Perpendicular; four-centred arches with curving tracery. The side to Petergate is the more elaborately treated, the characteristic York buttresses developing diagonally-placed pinnacles. The W front with an open turret on an arch (cf. St Helen's church) was rebuilt by George Fowler Jones, 1867, to an amended design.

Inside four-centred arcades are richly treated in contrast to the plainness of the rest, as though they had been bought by the yard and dropped in. Splendid, dark, Corinthian reredos, 1712, by William Etty, decidedly Baroque; sumptuously carved altar rails with semi-circular centre. Etty also probably carved the Royal Arms (now set on the Gallery, 1785, Victorianized). There are several medieval benches, and the huge slab in the nave floor has been identified as the medieval mensa from the High Altar of the Minster. Mayoral Boards of 1711, 1804, 1808. The church is full of massive pews.

The walls are covered with monuments, many by local sculptors, Fisher, Flintoft, Taylor, Tilney. Among the more interesting, in the N aisle: Thomas James, d. 1732, Mannerist; brasses to Francis Farrer, d. 1680, and Thomas Dawny, d. 1683, both signed Joshua Mann: at the E end of the S aisle an excellent group centred on Robert and Priscilla Squire (d. 1707 and 1711 respectively), life-size figures on a reredos background, with original iron railings, attributed to John Nost and Andrew Carpenter; and a magnificent Baroque cartouche to Maria Drake, d. 1728, designed to fit round a column; and many others worthy of attention.

The early-14th-century stained glass in the E window is from the previous church. Panels of the Annunciation, Resurrection, and St Peter notable. The remaining old glass is of the 1530s and 1550s, an important collection, showing strong Flemish influences; in the S aisle four windows with large standing figures above groups of Donors (their pallid, Eastern companion by J.W. Knowles). In the N aisle three windows were *created* in 1960 out of the dense jumble of glass that formerly filled the E window of the aisle. Large saints again in the middle window; small figures, much made up, in the westmost window, and four panels concerned with the life of Gilbert Becket (father of St Thomas) in the eastmost window (more of this series are in the E window of the chapter house).

The following appears in the Parish Registers: 'Christeninges, 1570. Guye Fawke sone to Edward Fawke the XVI day of aprile'.

☆

The Dean's Park is generally open during daylight hours. The Minster Library is open Monday to Friday, 09.00–17.00; tel. 25308. Treasurer's House open April to October; tel. 24247. St William's College, open daily, closed

Sundays during the winter; tel. 24426: contains a Brass Rubbing Centre and useful restaurant. Written permission is needed to visit the interior of Gray's Court from the College of Ripon and York, St John, York. St Michael-le-Belfrey is open in the summer months but closed during the winter; Vicarage, 86 East Parade, York; tel. 24190.

Walk Two

(*The area covered by this Walk is shown on the map for Walk 8, pp. 234–5.*)

The Museum Gardens

The discovery of the Kirkdale Cave fossils in 1821 led to the foundation of the Yorkshire Philosophical Society to promote the building of a suitable museum. In 1827 the Society was granted part of the precinct of St Mary's Abbey and, with characteristic 19th-century self-confidence, they excavated the site, built their museum on part of it, and laid out charming gardens over the rest to a scheme devised by Sir John Murray Naesmith. St Leonard's Hospital, Multangular and Anglian towers, St Olave's church, and the King's Manor on the gardens' periphery are included in this chapter.

At the entrance to the gardens, the lodge (1874) and drinking fountain are engaging pieces of Victorian nonsense; the former certainly by George Fowler Jones, the latter probably so. The city wall originally stretched from Lendal Tower (Walk 3) to St Leonard's Hospital.

St Leonard's Hospital and the Multangular Tower

King Athelstan is said to have founded a hospital dedicated to St Peter in 936. Royal patronage under William II and Stephen, who rededicated it to St Leonard, led to its becoming one of the grandest of such charitable institutions, with accommodation for 229 patients, of which only a corner, part of the Infirmary of *c.* 1240, remains. The vaulted passage (Roman coffins), still with round arches, was always open and led to St Leonard's Landing; behind it, part of a vaulted undercroft; above, a chapel with triple lancets and oculus in the gable wall. (Late-12th-century vaulting under the Theatre Royal gives some idea of the extent of the original premises.)

The hospital wall facing the Gardens stands over the Roman fortifications; a six-sided interval tower has been excavated below it. Abutting, on the NW, is much the most imposing relic of the Roman fortress: a stretch of wall standing almost to its full height – with characteristic small ashlar facing, tile lacing course, and rubble core – and the Multangular Tower, the W angle of the fortress, 10-sided, set outside the quadrant curve of the main wall, and with a squarish building divided longitudinally projecting inside at 45° into the fortress [5]. All this is of early-4th-century Constantian build. The upper part of the tower (thinner walls of large ashlar, with restored cross-bow slits) is late-13th-century, as is the city wall, which here turns NE, and stands 2–5 ft outside the Roman wall (with the stubs of an interval tower), the boundary wall of St Leonard's Hospital inside that, and the *c.* 1266 wall of St Mary's Abbey outside and below the city wall bank. This section of the Abbey wall was never fortified after the licence to crenellate of 1318, as one can see from a remaining fragment past the set-back in the path beside the King's Manor. A convenient door in the city wall gives access to these complexities; also to the 'Anglian Tower', a post-Roman, pre-Conquest refurbishing of the Roman fortification, rubble, vaulted, much patched in brick. It was most exciting when one crawled into it along a tunnel. Beyond, cobbles elucidate the stratification of the ramparts. The Roman wall briefly reappears in the garden at the end of St Leonard's Place, whose construction involved the demolition of a length of the city wall (see Walks 3 and 8).

St Mary's Abbey

St Mary's Abbey was one of the richest and most splendid of English Benedictine houses. It was already in embryonic, if poverty-stricken, existence when it found favour with William II in 1088. Alan, Earl of Richmond, had given the church of St Olaf to monks who had fled successively from Whitby and Lastingham. William gave them a grant of land and laid the foundation stone of their new church in 1089. The Abbey prospered hugely. By 1132 Benedictine discipline had become so lax that a group of monks left, ultimately to found the great Cistercian monastery at Fountains, amidst an acrimonious dispute between Archbishop Thurstan, who supported them, and Abbot Geoffrey, who did not.

Repairs of some magnificence, which followed a fire of 1137, were still in progress at the end of the 12th century.

In 1270 Abbot Simon de Warwick began a new church. Major expenditure elsewhere in the very early 14th century suggests that it was completed by then, and the E and S ranges of the claustral buildings followed immediately, suggesting a comfortable rather than an ascetic life. The central tower was damaged in the great storm of 1377. From 1483 the Abbot's house was greatly extended. In 1539 the Abbey was surrendered (without martyrdom) to become Royal residence and home for the Council of the North.

The eastern arrangements of the Norman church are outlined in the grass; long apsidal chancel, apsed aisles, squared outside, two more apses diminishing outwards to the E of each transept. A fragment of gritstone pilaster survives from the N transept wall, embedded in a much larger 13th-century buttress. Recent investigation of the choir footings uncovered a great display of Norman worked stone neatly coursed; as Abbot Simon's foundations are said to be 26 ft deep in places, they may well account for a great deal of the Norman church.

Abbot Simon's church had an aisled nave of eight bays, transepts of three bays with eastern aisles, beyond which the choir extended a further eight bays. What remain are the outer walls of the N nave aisle [18] with its transept arch, part of the W front, and some lower courses of piers and walls on the S side. It must have been one of the most beautiful and unified products of the English Geometrical style, justifying – for once – the Camden Society's predilection for 'Middle

Pointed'. It indulged in none of the French 'experiments' of the Minster chapter house and nave. It was built quickly. Signs of a break in construction half way along the nave are unaccompanied by any material change in the design. Only the W front, perhaps, does not conform.

The forms are large; there are none of the discrepancies in scale that disturb the Minster nave. Wall arcading, eschewing cusps, has two or three simple traceried elements to each bay; only the haunched N door, framing William Etty's monument, disrupts the scheme. Windows alternating two and three lights with one and three cusped tracery elements are flanked by sharply pointed arches following the wall rib of the vault inside, and dying into the massive buttresses outside (seen from St Olave's churchyard); but the W window of the aisle was designed to fill the whole compartment below the vault. Detached shafts, an element of the design, have not survived; those flanking the windows came centrally over the wall arcade bay below. Such niceties abound. The capitals of arcade and vaulting shafts, window jambs and mullions are kept on a level; those of the triforium develop into capitals for the tower piers and the string below the triforium marks the springing of the tall windows in the W transept wall. One crossing pier remains full height: it is a faultless amalgamation of the forms of two large and two small piers; comparison with the Minster tower piers is illuminating. One triforium bay survives over the arch to the nave aisle, still on the large scale of the Minster transept, four lights in pairs with large and small cusped circles. Detached fragments indicate a stone high vault; evidence for the clerestory is inadequate.

Standard wall arcading continues across the W nave wall inside but gablets escaped from the W front are intruded on either side of the door. The W front is crowded with cusped arches under gablets in tiers of varying height. The canted inner angles to the buttresses suggest turrets. As at the Minster this display is given up as soon as the flanking buttresses are passed.

The cloister was neither large nor particularly regular; one corner survives, outside the Museum, with slightly tapered nave aisle buttresses, larger rectangular ones to the transept, larger because of the greater wall height. A fragment of wall arcading (trefoils under an arch and gablet) is preserved, like other visible remnants of the monastic buildings, in the Museum basement.

The E and S ranges were measured in splendour with the church; the former with slype, vestibule, and chapter house, and an undercroft beneath the dormitory; the latter with warming house and common hall below the refectory. With the exception of parts of the chapter house vestibule of *c.* 1200, which must have been considered sufficiently splendid to keep, all this is work of the early 14th century. South of Abbot Simon's transept the slype gave very restricted access to the Abbey cemetery E of the church. The W portal to the vestibule had piers of great refinement, attached shafts separated by the subtlest of hollows with detached shafts at the cardinal points. The E portal, also *c.* 1200, was opulent in comparison, cruciform piers chevroned into carved pyramids and surrounded by detached shafts, and sumptuously chevroned arches. The R.C.H.M. account (developing the theory of Prior and Gardner) suggests that the great series of statues [12] excavated at the site, or rescued from elsewhere in the neighbourhood, formed caryatid vaulting shafts; prophets in the vestibule, apostles in the chapter house. English sculptors never produced anything grander than these heavy, heavy-headed figures with long sweeping drapes over one arm and sudden lively folds around the feet; they are among the noblest and least-known examples of English art of the end of the 12th century. In the early 14th century the statues were removed and the vestibule was reconstructed as a vaulted room, three by three bays, with elegant compound piers, like those flanking the comfortable warming house fireplace elsewhere in the basement.

The Abbey Gatehouse and St Olave's Church

The Abbey Gatehouse to Marygate keeps late-12th-century work in its outer arch, irregularly arcaded flanking walls, and in the remains of vaulting, but has lost its inner arch and an intermediate arch that probably held the gates. Buildings of *c.* 1466–98 surround it: St Mary's Lodge, to the SW, restored in the 19th century; the substructure of the gate chapel NE, below St Olave's church tower; and the N wall of the church itself.

When St Olave's was founded by Siward of Northumbria, *c.* 1055, the dedication was to St Olaf. It was given to the monks from Lastingham in 1086, and, though quickly replaced as the monastic church, it remained within the precinct serving its parishioners outside the walls. There is 12th-century work in the S aisle footings but the nave reached its present size in the late 15th century. The church was used as a gun platform during the 1644 siege, repaired, then largely rebuilt in 1721-2 in what is engagingly described as 'post-Gothic Perpendicular'. The niche over the N door may be from the Abbey Gatehouse. The nave columns remain classically Tuscan despite half-hearted Victorian attempts to medievalize them. George Fowler Jones's chancel of 1887–9 was much improved, and the S chapel formed by Francis Doyle, 1908. Thirteenth-century head of a woman in a quatrefoil over the S door. Fragment of 14th-century stone screen, very rich, on chancel step. Fifteenth-century glass in the E window has not been subjected to 'informed' restoration. Nineteenth-century glass is uniformly dull but there is a small (1957) window by Stammers in the S chapel. War Memorial chapel (1953) and font cover (1963) by George Pace. Rest for a wooden leg in 3rd pew from front on N of nave. Monument to William Thornton, Joyner and Architect, d. 1721, lushly floral above cherubs. Minor tablets by Fishers and Michael Taylor. Tombs of the Wolstenholme family, carvers, and of William Etty, artist, d. 1849, in the churchyard.

Low in the precinct, near the river, is what is said to be the Abbey guesthouse, the hospitium – early-14th-century stone below half-timbering, very much rebuilt 1930–1 when the roof pitch was raised. Late-medieval arch and wall adjoining do not represent the Abbey river wall, which was further W.

In a coppice, ruinous, crumblingly awaiting restoration is

the Observatory. Built 1832–3 to house instruments given by
Dr Pearson, whose conical summer-house roof – said to have
been designed by Smeaton – it incorporates.

The Yorkshire Museum

William Wilkins was official architect for the Philosophical
Society's new Museum of 1827–9, but the work was supervised by R.H. Sharp and J.P. Pritchett. The elevation with a
Greek Doric portico is a typical Wilkins product, aridly
handsome. Pritchett, left to himself, could have produced
something more lively. The dignified Corinthian main hall
has skylights in its coffered ceiling. The interiors have not
been treated respectfully.

The Tempest Anderson Hall is altogether more remarkable; added in 1912 to designs by Edwin Ridsdale Tate, who
carried on Wilkins's style (more or less) but turned it into an
essay in reinforced concrete with the shutter marks showing,
in the manner of the 1960s. Raked seating with botanical
rooms beneath, and the need to accommodate the Chapter
House remains in the basement, create wonderful anomalies
in the elevation that would have given staid Wilkins
apoplexy.

The Museum may well be found disappointing. Thinning
of exhibits in recent years, preparatory to distant reorganization, seems premature. Even major items disappear into
store for no very good reason. The curatorial staff could not
however be more helpful. They desperately need more
space and better facilities.

The Kirkdale Cave fossils, discovered 1821, form the core
of the fossil collection, but the most imposing fossil exhibits
are the Ichthyosaurs from Whitby. Part of the fine geological
collection is usually on display. Natural history concentrates
on the locality. The bird room has period charm.

Among pre-Roman material the Arras chariot burial is
outstanding and there is extensive material from Stone,
Bronze, and Iron Ages, some of it compromised for lack of
provenance.

The Roman collection, of international importance, is split between the Museum and the Hospitium, monuments and inscriptions mostly in the former. The best lettering records the building of the SE gate (*c.* 108), though even this takes Trajanic subtleties in variation of size to extreme lengths. Monumental Constantine pursing his lips is less moving than a beautiful woman's head. Gravestones are both military and domestic (Aelia Aeliana [6], touchingly embraced by her husband). An impressive statue, probably intended as Mars, guards the public exit. (Some of the odder manifestations of Roman culture are confined to the basement.) The Hospitium dustily exhibits very large objects – a pavement from Oulston – and some of the thousand complete Roman pots in various wares; also glass, pins, keys, compasses; a harpy, part of a candelabrum and a table leg in stone; building elements in terracotta; the Fremington Hagg collection of metal objects; cooking pots from Knaresborough. A Roman lady's hair is marginally less obscene than funerary casts in gypsum; mummies are wholesome by comparison.

Material from the Minster and Coppergate excavations is not yet prominently displayed. There is a good collection of Dark Ages metalwork. The Ormside Bowl, late-8th-century, is one of the finest surviving pieces of Anglian metalwork, fusing native Anglo-Saxon and Mediterranean styles. The Gilling Sword, 9th-century, is an outstanding recent acquisition. The Newgate Shaft is innovatory, lively York work of the 10th century with flat animal ornament in the Scandinavian tradition; also Anglian and Anglo-Scandinavian clasps and brooches [8], Jellinge-style fragments, and 11th-century grave slabs.

Medieval and Tudor pottery is well represented; Yorkshire pottery of the 18th and 19th centuries outstandingly so.

The Museum's greatest treasure is its medieval sculpture. Other Abbey material includes sculptural elements of both Norman churches, late-12th-century capitals from the cloister, a superb series of voussoirs of *c.*1200 and of bosses of the late 13th century, an imposing fragment of a 'Coronation of the Virgin', and the splendid bronze Infirmary Mortar [20],

1   Streetscape: Stonegate

2   Streetscape: Chapter House Street

3   Streetscape: Precentor's Court

4   Streetscape: Shambles. A photograph taken early in the century when it was still predominantly the Butchers' street (*photo: Yorkshire Architectural and York Archaeological Society collection*)

5   Roman York: The Multangular Tower, the western corner of
the Roman fortress

6 Roman York: Monument to Aelia Æliana (Yorkshire Museum)

7 Pre-Conquest York: The tower of St Mary Bishophill Junior

8 Pre-Conquest York: Anglo-Scandinavian scabbard chape
(Yorkshire Museum)

INITIVM EVANGE
LII DÑI NRI IhV
XPI SCDM MATHCM

LIBER

GENERATIONIS IhV
XPI FILI DAVID·
FILII ABRA
HACD·

ABRAHAM AVTE GENIT ISAAC
ISAAC AUTEM · GENUIT IACOB IACOB AUTE·
GENUIT IUDAM ET FRS EIUS IUDAS AU
TEM · GENUIT PHARES ET ZARA DE THA
MAR · PHARES AUTEM · GENUIT

9 Pre-Conquest York: The Gospels, Minster Library (*photo: Minster Library*)

10 Norman York: St Margaret Walmgate. Doorway from St Nicholas

11 York Minster: Archbishop Roger's crypt, late-12th-century

12 St Mary's Abbey: Statue of Moses, probably from the chapter-house vestibule, *c.* 1200 (Yorkshire Museum)

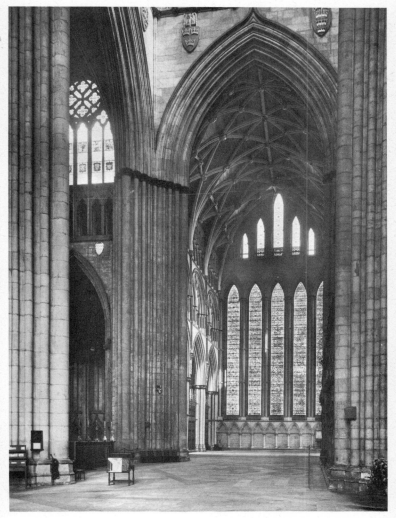

13   York Minster: The N transept. Finished by *c.* 1255

14   York Minster: Monument to Archbishop Walter de Gray, after 1255 (*photo: N.M.R.*)

15   York Minster: North transept, finished by 1255. Chapter house
probably completed *c.* 1284 and vestibule by *c.* 1291. Central tower
by William Colchester

16   York Minster: Chapter-house canopies. Late-13th-century

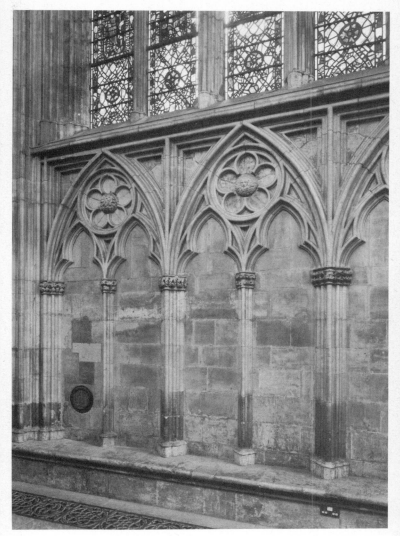

17 York Minster: Wall arcading in chapter-house vestibule, finished *c.* 1291

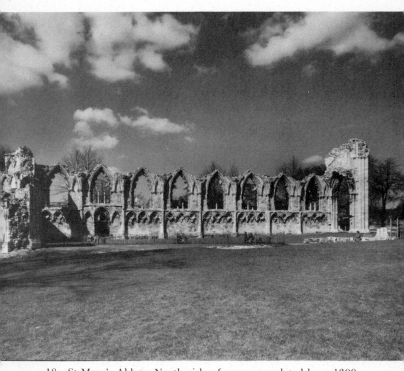

18   St Mary's Abbey: North aisle of nave, completed by *c.* 1300

19 York Minster: Nave, 1291–1355. Vaulting replaced after the fire of 1840

20 St Mary's Abbey: Infirmary mortar, 1308 (Yorkshire Museum)

21 York Minster: detail from the tomb of St William, *c.* 1330s,
probably Ivo de Raughton, now in the Yorkshire Museum

22 Fourteenth-century stained glass: York Minster. West window. Figure of St John. 1338 (*photo: the Dean and Chapter of York*)

23   Fifteenth-century stained glass: St Martin le Grand. St Martin
window. 1437

24   York Minster: East front. 1360–1408

25 Churches: St Michael Spurriergate. Late-12th-century arcades, heightened. Eighteenth-century fittings

26 Churches: Holy Trinity Goodramgate. Thirteenth- to 15th-century; fittings of the 17th and 18th centuries

27 Churches: St Martin le Grand. Early-15th-century, restored after war damage by George G. Pace, 1961–8

28   Fortifications: Micklegate Bar. Twelfth-century arch; 14th-century upper stages

29 Fortifications: York Castle. Clifford's Tower, by Henry de Reyns, 1245–62, and forebuilding of 1642–3, on the motte of William the Conqueror's castle

30 Medieval Public Buildings: St William's College, 1465–7.
Regency shop fronts and restoration by Temple Moore, 1906

31 Medieval Public Buildings: Merchant Adventurers' Hall. Foss-gate; late-14th-century

32 The King's Manor: Originally the house of the Abbot of St Mary's, late-15th-century, much altered in the 16th and 17th centuries

33 Sixteenth-century interiors: panelling in Stonegate

34 Seventeenth-century monuments: York Minster. Monument
to Henry Bellassis, by Nicholas Stone

35 Nonconformity: Unitarian Chapel of 1692–3, with Walker ironwork of 1852

36 Georgian Public Buildings: The Mansion House, 1725–32, probably by William Etty. On the right The Savings Bank, 1829–30, by Watson and Pritchett

37 Palladianism: The Assembly Rooms, by Lord Burlington, 1730, after Palladio (*photo: Yorkshire Evening Post*)

38 The Georgian Interior: Queen's Hotel, Micklegate, completed
1727, awaiting reconstruction

39 The Georgian Interior: Treasurer's House Dining Room, mid-18th-century

40   The Georgian Interior: Garforth House staircase, Micklegate,
possibly by John Carr, finished 1757 (*photo: N.M.R.*)

41   The Georgian Interior: York Castle. The dome of the Crown
Court, 1773–7, by John Carr (*photo: N.M.R.*)

42   The Georgian House: Castlegate House, 1761–3, by John Carr

43   The Georgian House: No. 51 Bootham, by Peter Atkinson
Senior, c.1800

44   Regency: Tower Place Terrace

45 Classical Monuments: York Minster. William Wentworth, Earl of Strafford, d. 1695. Probably by John Nost

TO THE MEMORY OF JOHN DEALTRY MD
WHOSE SKILL IN HIS PROFESSION WAS ONLY EQUALLED
BY THE HUMANITY OF HIS PRACTICE,
ELIZABETH, HIS AFFLICTED WIDOW, DEDICATES THIS MONUMENT.
HE DIED MARCH XXV, MDCCLXXIII,
AGED LXV.

HERE O'ER THE TOMB WHERE DEALTRY'S ASHES SLEEP,
SEE HEALTH IN EMBLEMATIC ANGUISH, WEEP!
SHE DROOPS HER FADED WREATH "NO MORE", SHE CRIES,
"LET LANGUID MORTALS, WITH BESEECHING EYES,
"IMPLORE MY FEEBLE AID; IT FAIL'D TO SAVE
"MY OWN AND NATURE'S GUARDIAN FROM THE GRAVE".

47 G.T. Andrews: Yorkshire Insurance Building, St Helen's Square, 1840

46 Classical Monuments: York Minster. John Dealtry, d. 1773, by Fisher

48   J.P. Pritchett: Cemetery Chapel, Fulford, 1837

49   County Hospital, 1849–51 by J.B. and W. Atkinson

50   York Station: Designed by T. Prosser, B. Burleigh, and W. Peachey 1871–7

51 Victorian Townscape: Clifton Green

52　Industry: Leetham's Mill, 1895–6, by W.G. and A. Penty

53   Art Nouveau: Elm Bank overmantel, 1898, by George Walton working with Penty and Penty

54   W.H. Brierley: Scarcroft Road School, 1896

55 W.H. Brierley: Bishopbarns, St George's Place, built for himself 1905

56   York University: College Buildings of 1965 by Robert Matthew,
Johnson-Marshall and Partners.

covered in beasts in quatrefoils and inscribed 'Fr Will[elmu]s de Towthorp me fecit AD MCCCVIII'. There is fine 12th-century material from St William's Chapel (Walk 7) and parts of two 12th-century doors in pristine condition. Two later medieval masterpieces from the Minster are both associated with St William and were found together in Precentor's Court (Walk 1) where more remains buried. The first, sadly fragmentary, is the Tomb from the nave [21], which formed a glorious platform for one of the reliquaries: work of the 1330s of the very highest quality, rivalling the Percy Shrine at Beverley, nodding ogees dense with foliage and figure subjects, below pillars sumptuous with saints under canopies. Archbishop Melton contributed towards its cost. It may be the work of Ivo de Raughton. More survives of the Frosterly marble shrine base of *c.* 1470–2, designed by Robert Spillesby, from behind the high altar; a work of equal if rather more mechanical luxuriance; the marvellously inventive vault forms and the mass of minute carved detail are delightful.

The King's Manor

Back to back with the Yorkshire Museum is the most complex and confusing though not the most beautiful of York's secular buildings. It grew intermittently over at least four centuries (probably much longer) and for half that time within its existing boundaries so that architectural development always seems three or four layers deep. The R.C.H.M. account runs to 11,000 words leaving much unanswered.

The Abbot of St Mary's was, in temporal terms, the equal of all but the grandest barons; in the North only the Prior of Durham was grander. There is no reason to think that he was already other than very adequately housed when, in 1483, Abbot Boothe retained Richard Cherryholme, bricklayer, for a work for which his successor Abbot Sever was still paying when he moved to Durham in 1502. Abbot Sever's building survives much altered. When later in the century Archbishop Rotherham enlarged the Palace at Bishopthorpe (probably using the same craftsmen) he left the 13th-century hall and chapel and built his new house at right angles to it. Nothing in what remains of Abbot Sever's house can convincingly be identified as hall or chapel so it is probable that he also kept the old house, adding the new U-shaped house to form a courtyard, less divorced from the rest of the monastic buildings than it seems at present. The new building, of brick, with black vitrified patterns and an early modern use of terracotta windows, forms the SE part of the existing King's Manor.

After the Dissolution the house became headquarters of the Council of the North and the Abbey was converted into a short-lived Royal residence, where Henry VIII and Queen Katherine Howard stayed in 1541. By the 1560s, however, the Palace had become dilapidated and a start had been made on the long series of additions to the Manor House. There are four wings to the N of Abbot Sever's house, closely set. The eastmost is of 1560–70, started by the Earl of Rutland; the westmost is a recasting, *c.* 1575, by Henry, Earl of Huntingdon, of the NW end of Sever's building to provide a council chamber on the first floor above the kitchens. (Huntingdon also added a porch in the NE corner of the courtyard, and a building running SW from Abbot Sever's House.) Back to back with these, facing each other across a narrow space, two other wings are part of enormous additions started by Lord Sheffield *c.* 1610, at the suggestion of James I, to provide an adequate new Royal Palace. Most of the new work was to the W of the old house. A new hall over an arcaded kitchen at the SW corner linked by two-storeyed galleries and an ante-room to Huntingdon's council chamber at the NW corner. West again and linked by a cross gallery was another range, on the grandest scale, probably intended as a gallery back to back with staterooms. Nothing inside matches the sophistication of Sheffield's new entrances on the E front, and it seems probable that the enormous project remained unfinished. (Parts of the building were used to repair St Mary's Tower after the siege.) Thomas Wentworth, Earl of Strafford, continued the work between 1628 and *c.* 1640 in a much more provincial style.

His four-year-old daughter wrote complaining that the workmen were inattentive unless she was superintending them. Charles I stayed in the Manor in 1633 and 1639 but his Great Council of Peers, 24 September–18 October 1640, was held in the Great Hall of the Deanery. The Long Parliament assembled in November, immediately impeaching Strafford, and the Council of the North was abolished. When Charles came to York in 1641 the Court was at Sir Arthur Ingram's house.

The house was attacked during the 1644 siege after the blowing up of St Mary's Tower (see page 253). The house was kept under repair during the Commonwealth, and in 1667 became in part residence of the Governor of the City of York, in part Popish School under Father Lawson.

Multiple ownership came with the 18th century. Sir Tancred Robinson did much internal work to the NE wing; the hall became an assembly room. Francis Place (artist), Mr Lumley who ran a school, and Thomas Wolstenholme, carver and gilder, lived here. Occupation of the SW part of the building by the Manor National School (1813–1922) involved new building by J.B. and W. Atkinson; and of the rest of the building by the Blind School (1833–1956), a memorial to William Wilberforce, much ingenious restoration under Brierley. In 1963–4 the building was again restored by Feilden and Mawson for the University, and is now the Institute of Advanced Architectural Studies.

Entrance is usually from the E, from Exhibition Square. Abbot Sever's house, in brick, is to the left; Rutland's wing in reused stone, much amended by Sir Tancred Robinson, is to the right. One tiny terracotta window remains to the extreme left; most of the others have been replaced by mullioned and transomed windows of plastered brick *c.* 1560. Both of Sheffield's elegant 1610 doorpieces are now on this front (the right-hand one used to face the courtyard), James I's initials on the plinths of their termini figures: Strafford's huge overdoor with Charles I's arms is not an improvement.

Another of Abbot Sever's terracotta windows faces the lane to the Museum Gardens, but much of this side has again been picturesquely improved by Brierley – before the hall is reached – and by the Atkinsons – beyond it. Brierley's Headmaster's house (1899–1902) stands to the W, at right angles to the front: a brilliant, loving pastiche; stone patched with brick; alternating gables and bays, up and out; nowhere quite obvious; symmetry subtly evaded.

The N side of the house is the most picturesque range of buildings in York. From left to right: Rutland's wing ending in a bay; Sheffield's with a delightful range of dormers and regular mullioned windows (an oriel of the late 15th century is visible in a tiny yard behind the Feilden Link); Sheffield again,* stone below, but patched and pilastered in brick above in repairs after the Restoration; Huntingdon's Council Chamber brick with an oriel, which like the rest of Huntingdon's work reuses 13th-century plinths from the Abbey; then Sheffield again behind cycle sheds and educational links; finally the Atkinsons' grittiest addition, projecting at right angles to the Museum Gardens boundary.

The first courtyard has traces of original windows and diapered brickwork, and of the galleried arrangements for the upper floor. Late-13th-century plinths again reused in Huntingdon's brick porch. Sheffield's stone cross wing is symmetrical but not quite on the same axis as the entrance, involving a sideways shift in the plan of the courtyard. The little arcaded frieze was repeated on the outer W wing. The Hall is in the corner, above an arched kitchen, approached through Strafford's doorway (Charles I's arms again) up a flight of Brierley stairs. Strafford's door in the cross wing bears his own coat of arms.

The further courtyard is less regular. What is old is mostly Sheffield's work – the back wall of the cross range showing traces of demolished buildings – much altered by the Atkinsons who extended the cross wing northwards, built the 'cloister' and the rather raw building in the NW corner. Sheffield's great cellar (persistently misattributed to Henry VIII) has an almost four-centred barrel vault, and a fine early-14th-century doorway reused in one of the dividing walls. Remnants of its original superstructure are recorded

---

* Both Sheffield's ranges have moulded plinths found again on the outer w wing.

in engravings, but it was another Atkinson building that was demolished for the 1964 Feilden and Mawson building, when the vault was found to be medieval stone laid with flat surfaces below and carved and moulded surfaces on top. No record was made before it was bitumenized beneath the respectfully modern studies above. Ironically, they now house the Centre for Medieval Studies.

Good medieval ceilings remain in the NW wing, as well as doors and fireplaces, and an open timber roof, not in its original condition, in the SE wing. The cross wing has several gross doorways of the Strafford era on the way to the Huntingdon Room, which has its original plaster frieze with Huntingdon heraldic elements, and a remarkable 1570s fireplace with long voussoirs carved with masks, cartouches, and arabesques: another room with similar frieze, but its medieval ceiling exposed, has been opened into it. The little domed feature in the Hall ceiling relates to its use as an Assembly Room in the 18th century. An early-17th-century ceiling rescued from North Street (Walk 7) has been installed in the NE wing.

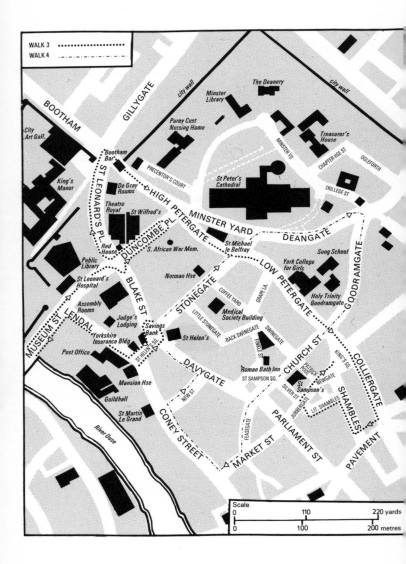

WALK 3 ·············
WALK 4 –·–·–·–·–·–·

BOOTHAM

City Art Gall.

King's Manor

St Leonard's Hospital

Assembly Rooms

MUSEUM ST.

LENDAL

Judge's Lodging

Yorkshire Insurance Bldg

Post Office

Mansion Hse

Guildhall

St Martin Le Grand

River Ouse

Public Library

BLAKE ST.

DUNCOMBE PL.

Bootham Bar

De Gray Rooms

Theatre Royal

St Wilfred's

Red House

S. African War Mem.

ST LEONARD'S PL.

GILLYGATE

city wall

PRECENTOR'S COURT

HIGH PETERGATE

Minster Library

Purey Cust Nursing Home

St Peter's Cathedral

MINSTER YARD

The Deanery

city wall

Treasurer's House

MINSTER YD.

CHAPTER HSE ST

OGLEFORTH

COLLEGE ST

DEANGATE

Norman Hse

St Michael le Belfray

LOW PETERGATE

Song School

York College for Girls

Holy Trinity Goodramgate

GOODRAMGATE

STONEGATE

COFFEE YARD

LITTLE STONEGATE

Medical Society Building

Savings Bank

St Helen's

ST HELEN'S SQ.

GRAPE LA.

BACK SWINEGATE

SWINEGATE

FINKLE ST.

CHURCH ST

KING'S SQ.

COLLIERGATE

DAVYGATE

Roman Bath Inn

St Sampson Sq.

St Sampson's

PATRICK POOL

NEWGATE

SILVER ST.

JUBBERGATE

LIT. SHAMBLES

SHAMBLES

NEW ST.

CONEY STREET

FEASEGATE

MARKET ST.

PARLIAMENT ST

PAVEMENT

Scale
0 · · · 110 · · · 220 yards
0 · · · 100 · · · 200 metres

Walk Three

St Helen's Square

St Helen's Square is at the heart of York: administratively, since the Council Offices are discreetly hidden behind the Mansion House; historically, for beneath it lie the remains of the Roman Porta Praetoria; commercially, for Coney Street and Stonegate, both Roman in origin, have adapted to commerce in their different ways; and architecturally, as will become apparent.

The Mansion House [36] was long and untenably ascribed to Lord Burlington (other national figures have been canvassed as its architect), despite its manifest provinciality. It was built and decorated 1725–32. Its most likely architect was William Etty, whose name appears in the accounts, not specifically as designer. Civic pride need not have prompted the Corporation to look further afield for an architect since no other city had hitherto provided such a residence for its chief citizen. The London Mansion House was not started until 1739. York's Mansion House has a dignified unsubtle elevation: a giant portico sitting on a shelf over an arcaded basement, the architect evidently at a loss how to join the two. Very fine late-Georgian railings and lamp-posts. The stair-case has triumphal arches at the bottom, and rather crowdedly at the top as introduction to the stateroom occupying the whole of the upper front of the house. Corinthian pilasters flank civic portraits, augmented by columns flanking the prettily painted door, and by pediments, a distinctly provincial touch, over the two end fireplaces, framing the civic and more ebullient Royal arms. The eight civic portraits are Sir John Lister Kaye by Joseph Highmore, 1738; George Lane Fox by Thomas Hudson,

1758; King William III, by Anthony Highmore, his only known oil, copied from Kneller; Charles Watson Wentworth from Reynolds' studio, *c.* 1781; Sir William Mordaunt Milner by Hoppner, 1799; George IV as Prince of Wales, again by Hoppner, a copy of Reynolds' portrait; Baron Dundas by John Jackson, 1822. Elsewhere are portraits of Drake, the York historian, John Carr, and George Hudson dominating the staircase. The panelled rooms downstairs are the usual setting for the splendid insignia and plate for those fortunate enough to see them.

The earliest surviving City Seal is of the 13th century. Of the two state swords, the one of 1416 belonged to the Emperor Sigismund (the scabbard has silver gilt mounts of 1586), the other was presented by Sir Martin Bowes in 1549. The Cap of Maintenance of 1580 is somewhat dilapidated. The Great Mace, silver gilt, was made by Claudius Tirrell in 1647. The gold Lord Mayor's Chain is of 1612 and that of the Lady Mayoress, the earliest to survive, is of 1670. Waits's chains probably 1565.

Of the plate, the following are among the most noteworthy items: Gold Cup by M. Best 1673, given by Marmaduke Rawdon; silver gilt Standing Cups, London, 1680, by William Holmes, 1789; and among the silver items, the Posset Cup, Seth Lofthouse, 1703; Chamber Pot, M. Best, 1673; Pair of Tankards, M. Best and J. Plummer, 1675; Monteith, Seth Lofthouse, 1700; Soup Tureen by Peter Podie, London, 1797, and a Tea Urn by Walter Tweedie, London, 1781, both given by John Carr; and the Centre-piece with *Justice* by W. Pitts and J. Preedy, London, 1797.

Guildhall Yard is down the passage through the right-hand end of the Mansion House. The Guildhall was built 1447–59 to designs of Robert Couper (though there had been a Common Hall in the city for two centuries), the Corporation and St Christopher's Gild sharing the expense of the new hall. The building was gutted in the York blitz of 1942 and rebuilt to the original design, 1958–61, under the direction of Romilly B. Craze. It is a broad, stone, perpendicular envelope round a timber-arcaded interior, with an arch-braced roof. Stained glass by H. Harvey, 1960. Regrettable light fittings, pallid heraldry. The old Council Chamber escaped the fire and still has its 15th-century roof and panelling inscribed over the inserted Rococo fireplace:

Cameratum et ornatum
Fuit conclave hoc sumptibus
Johannis Hewley Militis
1679
Ricardo Shaw Mayor

Beneath the Guildhall, Common Hall Lane, inauspiciously approached through a door behind the civic rockery, opens on to the riverside, the last vestige of the Roman river crossing. The Council Offices are even less auspiciously approached down a passage by the Guildhall (or with more dignity through the Guildhall itself). They concentrate architecturally on the river side, a highly successful design of 1891 by E.G. Mawbey and Alfred Creer, successive city surveyors: variations on the Guildhall elevation, with a little extra panache when it came to dealing with the corner turret.

It is only recently that St Helen's Square has achieved its present dignity. When the Mansion House was built it was simply a complicated road junction (known says Drake as 'Cuckold's Corner'). The first 'improvements' came with the clearing away of St Helen's churchyard (1745) to ease the passage of carriages going to the new Assembly Rooms. Harker's Hotel remained a blunt promontory between Davygate and Coney Street until the 1920s. Its removal was a mixed blessing. New shops and offices replaced it, designed by T.P. Bennett (1929–30), classical, lacking conviction, continued in a disjointed way down Davygate in the early 1950s.

St Helen's church has been threatened with demolition (1548, 1910), and over-enthusiastically restored (1857, 1875), so it has a pronouncedly Victorian feel. William Atkinson's rebuilding of the W front (1875) stuck more or less to what was there before, canted aisle walls and an open lantern on an arch sprung between the W buttresses. Much of the rest of the exterior belongs to the earlier campaign of

W.H. Dykes. Inside, the arcades are variously and confusingly 14th- and 15th-century, hardly two arches and piers the same, the result partly of demolition begun 1552–3 and reversed under Mary I. The N arcade has two delightfully detailed label stops of St Michael and Angels, and a soul being supported in a winding sheet. Dykes's roof develops one truss into a chancel arch. This was the glaziers' church; medieval glass of the 14th and 15th centuries in the W window is 'made up', though the Coronation of the Virgin and a panel of a donor and his family are clear enough. Several other windows have old roundels and heraldic glass. East window, large figures by Hardman, 1860, small figures by Wailes; reorganized. Gothic tablet to James Atkinson, d. 1839, by Hayes of Beverley. Inscription to Barbara and Elizabeth Davyes (respectively 1667–1765 and 1669–1767), in the reigns of Charles II, James II, William and Mary, Queen Anne, and the first three Georges. Architectural tablet to Joseph Buckle, d. 1760, in the vestry. Lovely, late-12th-century font bowl, arcaded, on a 15th-century capital inverted on a 13th-century base.

No. 18 Blake Street is a fine, tall house of 1789 by Peter Atkinson Senior.

The fourth side of St Helen's Square has much the best architecture; three buildings derived in differing ways from classical models. The Savings Bank, by Pritchett and Watson (1829–30), is a most distinguished design [36]; Grecian; ribbed-rusticated basement, a Corinthian colonnade swept round the corner, topped with a flourish of consoles. Soanes's influence is evident, but the handling of the Soane-ish motifs, entirely personal. Comparison with Wilkins's chilly Yorkshire Museum design is instructive. Fine, original interior. G.T. Andrews's Yorkshire Insurance Building, 1840, Italianate, is equally good – though the porch does seem an afterthought – and noble – though it has a surprised fringe of dormers [4]. These are, perhaps, the finest secular elevations in the city. Between them, Terry's, by Lewis Wade, 1922, is Baroque-Revival, with a giant order and hints of a freer style in the bronze window frames. It would do very well in Bond Street – indeed it does very well here though the Baroque detailing does not bear close examination. Its panelled interiors can still be savoured over coffee or tea.

Lendal to the City Art Gallery

Lendal was first referred to as Lendill Street, 1639, a reference to 'St Leonard's Landing'; before that it had been Aldconyngstrete. It starts between the Post Office by H. Tanner (1887), Tudorish with a nod towards Arts and Crafts, and the side of the Yorkshire Insurance Building, its architecture confidently at odds in scale with the front. The low range beyond is of 1754; the tobacconist's has a 19th-century military figure, taking snuff and popularly known as 'Napoleon'.

The Judges' Lodging is a splendidly individualistic house built for Dr Clifton Wintringham *c.* 1718–25; tall, tower-like, of only three bays, the centre one set forward, in plain brick with pilasters (but not the orders) at all the corners. The entrance is on the first floor, up a sweeping staircase, through a Venetian opening with a bust of Aesculapius on the keystone of an enormous swag. Very tall rooms, several with the orders flanking the fireplaces; Baroque vault to the basement stairs. Oval main staircase with a balustrade on Ionic columns; all remarkably little altered. It stands on the site of St Wilfrid's church and churchyard.

Nos. 10 and 12 (Lloyds Bank etc.), opposite, are almost exactly contemporary, and have original staircases and late-18th-century ceilings etc. Walter Brierley's office was (indeed still is) here. The Austin Friary, founded by 1272, stood here until 1538; scraps of riverside wall survive near Hill's Boatyard. Lendal Chapel (Congregational from 1816 to 1920) by Watson and Pritchett looks its best from the rear, since conversion to commerce; a domed apse on a huge, arcaded cube. In the yard beside it, a scrap of post-Restoration 'rusticated' brickwork.

Museum Street (probably on the sites of Finkle Street and Footless Lane) is a Victorian consequence of the building of

Lendal Bridge. There had been a ferry at St Leonard's Landing since medieval times. The Corporation mulled over the idea of a bridge from 1838 to 1860, when the foundation stone was laid of a latticed bridge designed by William Dredge. The incomplete structure fell down the following year (and was later incorporated into the Valley Bridge at Scarborough) and a new design then obtained from Thomas Page; the bridge was completed and opened in 1863. Page's Westminster Bridge Gothic, especially the lamp-posts, is immediately recognizable. It is worth descending the little staircase by Lendal Tower both for its own pretty ironwork, and the much more imposing ironwork beneath the bridge.

Lendal Tower, the Water Tower, was part of the city defences (as was the inaccessible stretch of wall to the entrance Lodge of the Museum Gardens). Its original shape was similar to the Barker Tower, on the other side of the river; its present amorphous shape is the result of adaptations to house devices to supply the city with water (John Smeaton rebuilt the engine in 1781–4), the last by G.T. Andrews *c.* 1846. Behind it is a charming garden, to ease the burden of paying one's water rates.

The Yorkshire Club is on the other side of the bridge approach. Two competitions were held for its design, Parnell of London winning the second, 1868. Brick with stone dressings and a granite-columned porch, it sits more happily in the famous view of the Minster from the walls by the Station than some of its newer neighbours on the other side of the river. G.F. Jones's slightly later Club Chambers is better not noticed.

At the corner of Lendal, excavation has revealed a Roman interval tower; clearance, the roller-coaster effect of the Assembly Rooms clerestory, neither compensating for an apparently permanent gap in the city's fabric. Thomas's Hotel survived the Victorian realignments; late-Georgian front with Art Nouveau door glazing. Rawlins Gould's Register Office (1860) is coarsely classical. The Public Library, opened 1927, is by Brierley and Rutherford, unexceptionable but dull, the elevation with unfulfilled Baroque tendencies stemming from the wedge-shaped plan of the main room. (For St Leonard's Hospital see Walk 2.)

The Assembly Rooms are in Blake Street. Weekly Assemblies had been held in the King's Manor and later in Lord Irwin's house by the Minster, but with the increasing importance of the York Season something grander seemed desirable. Wakefield gave a design but died before it could be implemented, so in 1730 Lord Burlington, 'The Mycaenas of oure age', was approached. What he produced was a version of Vitruvius's 'Egyptian Hall', based closely on a plate in Palladio's *Second Book*; Corinthian columns, 17 bays by five, against a niched wall: Composite pilasters to the clerestory. Lord Burlington's pedantic criticism of the closely spaced Doric columns of the Castle Howard Mausoleum – the noblest monument of English Baroque – parallels nicely the Duchess of Marlborough's complaint that one could not pass between the Assembly Rooms columns in a hooped skirt, which says something for the common sense of the lady, but little for the aesthetic judgement of either. This glorious and seminal interior [37] had remarkably little effect on York's architecture: it was too revolutionary, intellectual – not to say impractical. The rooms were beautifully restored in 1951, a little more festively than Burlington intended, but with the original pale green in the clerestory – so it was particularly obtuse to redecorate it in khaki 10 years later. The lesser rooms are models of extreme Palladian restraint relying entirely on porportion, except the Rotunda, which was treated to wishy-washy wall paintings by Paul Wyeth in 1951. In 1828 Pritchett and Watson replaced Burlington's front with an Ionic portico, dependable but lacking flair, and the screen walls behind the columns were interfered with later in the century.

The Corporation's new approach road to Lendal Bridge led the Dean and Chapter to apply to continue it as a processional way to the Minster, replacing old, narrow Lop Lane. So admired was the disastrous result (1859–64) that it was called Duncombe Place after its instigator, Dean Duncombe, during his lifetime. The Minster edges cornerwise into an unresolved, un-urban open space the size of – but in no other way comparable to – the Piazza di San Marco, destroying the historic huddle of old houses that set the Minster off to perfection. The Dispensary, ebullient, elaborate, red moulded brick, 1897, by Edmund Kirby of Liverpool, was intended as one of the city's permanent memorials to the Diamond Jubilee. The Probate Registry Office (H. Tanner, 1885) is much more sober-minded. The Masonic Hall, behind it, is a model of classical restraint (the moving of its main doorway on to an adjacent extension was an unfortunate mistake) – the designs were by J. Barton-Wilson of London and Brother Oates of York, carried out 1862–3. The Temple is one of the most splendid of York interiors, in Greek Corinthian, pilasters on the side walls changing to columns round the Master's chair and the porch at the opposite end. Lighting columns in the form of the five orders. Gothic chairs of 1856 are inconsequentially incorporated. Many of the other fittings are earlier than the building and there is a remarkable collection of masonic treasures. Bodley designed the South African War Memorial, 1905, which lost one of its statues when it was struck by lightning.

The Dean Court Hotel, *c.* 1864, is angular Gothic, obstinately anonymous. St Wilfrid's church, next to it, is an unpopular building. It was built 1862–4 to designs of George Goldie (who was born round the corner in St Leonard's). An impressive essay in French Gothic, it is thoughtful and alien with a tower that would dominate anywhere, but is set at an angle to the street to make sure. It is one of the few buildings that look better for having been cleaned. The formidable, burly interior is chilly despite recent recovery of some pretty painted decorations. It has escaped the worst excesses of the reformed liturgy; sumptuous sanctuary fittings; carving by Earp; stained glass by Wailes.

Red House was built, 1714, for Sir William Robinson, who was asked in 1724 to relinquish his long lease so that it might become a house for the Lord Mayor. Fortunately, he seems to have refused and the Mansion House was built instead. The windows in slightly projecting strips are characteristic of early-18th-century York houses.

In 1831 the barbican of Bootham Bar and stretches of the city and abbey walls were cleared away to improve access from the city centre to Bootham. St Leonard's Place has York's one large-scale, stuccoed, classical terrace, 1833–4, by John Harper, with railings to the architect's designs made by the Walker Ironfoundry. Much interior decoration remains among the paraphernalia of local government.

Cloistered beneath the Theatre Royal are vaulted undercrofts of St Peter's – later St Leonard's – Hospital. There has been a theatre here since 1744, perhaps enjoying its period of greatest glory between 1766 and 1803, when Tate Wilkinson was manager-lessee. Sarah Siddons, J.P. Kemble, Bernhardt, and Mrs Patrick Campbell played on its stage. It was given a new front in 1834–5, a huge, Tudor-gabled affair, by John Harper, with an arcade now ruinous in Fulford Road. The present front was designed by George Styan, the city engineer, 1879–80. All too obviously he had looked at St Wilfrid's. Shakespeare and various of his characters appear in roundels. The interior is a delightful Art Nouveau reconstruction by F.A. Tugwell of Scarborough, *c.* 1902. In 1967 Patrick Gwynne and R.A. Sefton Jenkins designed the foyer, one of the best modern buildings in the city; glass enveloping hexagonal umbrella domes interlocking round a sweeping staircase, wittily complementing Styan's ponderous Town Hall Gothic.

The De Grey Rooms, designed by G.T. Andrews, 1841–2, were built as an officers' mess; still entirely Regency; tall round-arched, pedimented windows to the elegant rooms upstairs.

Exhibition Square was created in 1879. It works on the theory that civic improvement is produced by a large Italianate building with a good deal of space in front – a theory confounded by most Italian cities, and reinforced neither by the deplorable statue to William Etty (painter, see page 164) nor the recent fountain.

The Art Gallery was built by subscription in 1879 for the Yorkshire Fine Art and Industrial Institution to designs of Edward Taylor. The loggia is pretty; the upper parts unfinished; the tile mosaics have been revealed by recent liberal-minded curators, having been covered for some years lest they should demoralize public taste.

Many of the old-master paintings in the ground-floor galleries were presented in 1955 by the late F.D. Lycett Green (1893–1959), who had collected them between 1920 and 1950 to illustrate the history of European painting of every school and period, though not necessarily by the greatest names, from a 14th-century Italian altarpiece to an 18th-century *View of Lucca* by Bernardo Bellotto. Outstanding items are Domenichio's portrait of Monseignor Agucchi, *The Roman Charity* by Baburen, *Diana and Endymion* by Burrini, *Italian Coast Scene* by Bercheni, and the *Game Stall* by Snyders, but the overall standard is consistently intriguing. Of English paintings, there are portraits by Reynolds, Kneller, Lely, Kettle, Amiconi, Soldi, and Mercier. William Etty (1787–1849), the York artist well known for his figure studies, history pictures, and portraits, has a room devoted to him, including sketchbooks and personalia. *The Election of Darius* by Sawrey Gilpin is his most ambitious painting.

Nineteenth- and 20th-century paintings on the first floor include a fine Edwardian group by Sickert, Gilman, Gore, Conder, and Tonks, presented, together with a collection of modern stoneware pottery (Bernard Leach, Hamada and Staite Murray) by Dean Milner White. The gallery also has a magnificent collection of 18th- and 19th-century topographical drawings and prints. Portraits of local notabilities (of varying artistic merit) include John Carr (bust by Nollekens), Lord Burlington, Tate Wilkinson, Peter Atkinson Senior. Stained glass by William Peckitt.

The view of the Minster from the portico has achieved classic status despite its palpably unsatisfactory foreground.

Petergate to King's Square

Petergate gets short-shift from most guidebook writers; strange since it is one of the oldest, most pleasant, and rewarding of York streets. Bootham Bar stands at its entrance; to walk into the city through the left pedestrian arch, or better still, if traffic permits, under the Bar itself, on a bright early morning is a never-failing delight. Petergate lies on and off the course of the Roman *via principalis*, its straightness happily modulated. The name is obviously derived from its proximity to the Minster; but its division into High and Low Petergate – from Bootham Bar to Stonegate and from Stonegate to King's Square respectively – though not specially ancient has survived the more obvious Victorian break at Duncombe Place, somewhat to the confusion of visitors.

High Petergate is still a place where people live. On the left it starts with a tall thin house (1782) by Peter Atkinson Senior. The range of 15th-century timber-framed houses was almost rebuilt by Temple Moore (*c.* 1905), a little mechanically for this most sensitive of architects, but no worse in that respect than much recent restoration and in the delicately detailed shop fronts a good deal better. Late-18th-century houses develop into a bleak fan-shaped layout in front of the Minster, by J.P. Pritchett, as part of Dean Cockburn's disturbance of the Close in 1838–9. The deplorable floodlights are no credit to anyone.

On the right from the Bar, 1830s houses with Soane-ish shopfronts; Nos. 3–5 a good deal older than their Georgian front with its unreliable 1763 rainwaterhead. This date is common in York because of a Corporation edict forbidding eaves that dripped into the street. No. 3 has run-through panelling of *c.* 1600 inside, 5 a good fireplace with Ionic pilasters of a century later. Nos. 7 and 9 are 16th-century jettied houses; 9, double-gabled, triple-jettied, with two-storeyed oriels, is an outstanding example. St Wilfrid's Rectory has a spacious severe elevation of the mid 18th century. The early Georgian staircase running the full height reuses late-17th-century balusters at the top, and is interfered with by a late-Georgian screen at the foot. The house probably incorporates parts of that bought by Sir Thomas Herbert in 1665 (he died here in 1681). No. 11 is Regency, keeping the medieval messuage-width; 21–3 early Georgian, with the remains of a very pretty shopfront of *c.* 1800.

Duncombe Place negotiated, looking its best where not contending with the Minster, the noble plane at the corner almost compensating for what has gone, High Petergate resumes to the right of St Michael-le-Belfrey Church (see Walk 1). No. 23 is an excellent house of 1780 with a graceful oval staircase. The following range (25–9) are much recast houses of *c.* 1700: they must always have been 'early-Georgian' at the front but still use Dutch gables at the back. In the yard behind Young's Hotel – whose claim to be Guy Fawkes's birthplace is at best doubtful – is a pretty 19th-century gable-end with busts and putti in niches. Timber-framing resumes above the Victorian shopfront of 31–3, with a quartet of urns. The gabled houses are part of the long Stonegate range. On the left, past St Michael-le-Belfrey, a big range of *c.* 1800, centre window sketchily pedimented, elegant shopfront elliptically arched with paired consoles on lion masks, ornaments like table-tennis balls depending from the cornice, has a pretty rotunda on four columns among the shop fittings. For Minerva on the corner and Minster Gates in general see Walk 4. The view back, towards Bootham Bar, is one of the most perfect in York.

Low Petergate is darker, narrower, more commercial and winding than High Petergate. No. 41, jettied, has confused panelling of *c.* 1600 inside. York Mercantile Agency's glass-gilded advertisements are lovely period pieces under a building on its last legs. The other side of the street was quickly rebuilt in the first half of the 19th century as far as the sharp set-back by Adams House, 1772, with Dean Fountayne's crest of an elephant on the rainwaterhead. Nos. 59 and 61 are timber-framed, pleasantly amended.

Grape Lane (Grapecunt Lane, 1329; origins best left unexplored) leads into a warren of lanes and alleys, Swinegate, Back Swinegate, Finkle Street, together with sundry linking passages where even seasoned inhabitants have occasionally to orientate themselves, with little to see warranting the visitor's getting lost. Lord Esher's plans for the district are in abeyance. The gap at its corner made by the demolition of half a large house of *c.* 1745 should soon be filled. No. 65, the thinnest Georgian house in the city, one bay, five storeys, has the remains of a pretty shopfront. The grand, grim, gabled row is early-16th-century, very blank in its upper reaches, with worthwhile alleys giving glimpses of the back; Precious's, doing its best to look bogus, is earlier.

York College for Girls has an elevation cumulatively odd. The original house, set back, of *c.* 1720 has an entablature with a cavalier attitude to classical discipline. Dr Hunter added a new front door in *c.* 1800; Dr Shand, wings and a porch – with Dr Hunter's door at the end of it – in 1866; he also reconstructed the rear elevation towards the new Close. Inside, a handsome staircase belongs (though somewhat adapted) to the original house. The large house next door (on columns since *c.* 1959) is far older than its 1763 rainwaterhead; older indeed than its mid-18th-century front, formed by building out a new front wall in line with the furthest-projecting jetty of the timber-framed house. The gabled back is partly associated with the 15th-century Fox Inn, demolished *c.* 1958. Inside, a 16th-century brick fireplace, a late-17th-century bulbous balustered staircase, and a school chapel with glass by Stammers, 1960. Brierley, Leckenby, and Keighley's school building (1959) is quietly modern; the shop premises next door, discordantly traditional. Between them Hornpot Lane is an ancient, unattractive alley closed in 1766 'because of very great and scandalous offences committed in the churchyard to the dishonour of God and disgust and grief of all good Christians'. It has recently been reopened for no good reason; sensible visitors will ignore its festival of fire escapes, grim brickwork, and plumbing. The name (1295) means 'horn pit'; archaeological evidence has established a medieval hornworking industry.

King's Square is triangular. Beneath it lies the Roman *Porta Principalis Sinistra*: the Palace of the Northumbrian Kings was probably here from the 7th to the 10th century (the Square first recorded as *Konungsgarthr*, 'King's Residence'). Colliergate leads out from one corner; until 1937 Christ Church or Holy Trinity filled up the end, its tower encroaching on the twist of the lane to Shambles and Newgate at the other corner. (A few ledgers and matrices of brasses remain.) Refuge House is settling in; the new building on the corner of St Andrewgate promises to be inoffensive.

Colliergate ('charcoal makers' street') continues part of this spine road of N medieval York, towards Fossgate and Walmgate, a good street in need of affection. Tall, narrow premises on the right (one much restored, timber-framed) keep to medieval site-divisions. The left side is mostly later rebuildings; No. 25 with a big Dutch-gabled end; No. 22 with vestiges of half-timbering and 'Bean's Passage'. Nos. 18 and 19 are the most remarkable, dated 1748, with a good staircase and excellent panelled saloon with chimney-piece based on a design by Batty Langley.

Sharp right at the end, past two little green-tile profiles flanking a window, down the recently-rehabilitated passage behind St Crux – leaving the horrors of Stonebow to another walk, and right again into Shambles [4], the butchers' street; narrow; not long; jetties nodding affably to one another in the middle; partly presided over by the Minster tower, it is the York street of which everyone has heard. What used to be described as the finest medieval street in Europe (it wasn't, but no matter) is now over-restored and over-commercialized. Dilapidation set in between the wars; restoration has been synonymous with rebuilding; new buildings 'in keeping' are pathetic. The best group are Nos. 7, 8, and 9, 15th-century houses that have been left alone. Many of the shops keep their butchers' stall risers, canopies, and meat hooks. From the door of No. 5 on a rainy evening the effect is still reasonably medieval. The St Margaret Clitherow shrine is a particularly nasty piece of 'restoration'. Ironically, Miss Longley's researches have shown that the Clitherow House was on the other side of the street. The interior is doubly and deeply bogus.

Little Shambles, a disintegrating but more completely medieval street, was cleared away for the new Market; this, crowded, bustling, pleasant, is one of the city's few post-war successes, though the backs of multiple stores in Parliament Street and Pavement contribute nothing to the scene. The White Rose Café is an early example of 'thorough' restoration, already achieving a certain period charm. Jubbergate has almost ceased to exist since Parliament Street was cut through it. Silver Street, first mentioned 1541, does not appear to have been connected with silversmiths. The eclectic, part-Byzantine, student decor in 'The Catacombs' should be seen while it survives.

Newgate was first mentioned in 1328 – newness in York is always relative – a little timber-framed range still partly 14th-century like Lady Row, Goodramgate, and there are more scrubbed and restored houses in Patrick Pool (which used to continue into what is now Swinegate) and Pump Court. At the corner of Patrick Pool a scrap of 15th-century masonry with a Perpendicular window, incorporated in an uninspired new building, is all that remains of the building where John Wesley preached in 1753, and which he referred to as 'the oven'.

Mansion House can be visited by writing in advance to the Lord Mayor's Personal Assistant, Guildhall, York YO1 1QL. The Guildhall is usually open Monday to Friday, Saturday and Sunday afternoons during the Summer. St Helen's and St Wilfrid's churches are usually open. Assembly Rooms open June, July, August, Monday to Friday; tel: for enquiries 59881 ext. 342. The Art Gallery opens Monday to Saturday 10.00–17.00 and Sunday 14.30–17.00.

Walk Four

Stonegate

Stonegate leads so easily out of St Helen's Square that the sense of enclosure, once one is in the street, is as unexpected as it is delightful, the more so since it links not other streets but open spaces. The Romans planned it straight, as their *via praetoria*, but their arrangements have been delicately modified so that it is no longer quite possible to see from one end to the other. It is the best of York streets, not architecturally, since it has almost nothing in it which would qualify as textbook architecture, but because there is almost nothing in it offensive to the eye: maintained rather than restored for the last 50 years; the Victorian restorations are outrageous, and enjoyable for their own sakes; keeping intact its hinterland of alleys and yards, it is the first York street to be 'pedestrianized', and in catering for visitors demeans neither itself nor them. The name may come from its medieval paving or the Roman pavement (6 ft below the present level).

Stonegate begins splendidly, on the left, with Banks's cast-iron shop front, with railway lettering, beneath a lop-sided, 18th-century gable wall (on the site of Henry Hindley, the clockmaker's house); then a series of medieval, timber-framed houses in various disguises; No. 8, Regency Gothick; No. 10 a marvellous, Victorian tiled conceit above a contemporary and elaborately bracketted shopfront. After this, Georgian and Regency recastings above the shopfronts leave the chief spectacle to the other side. However, Nos. 32 and 34 were the property of Edward Fawkes and almost certainly the birthplace of his son Guy Fawkes (1570–1606). Though he was not the leading figure in the 1605 plot to blow up King and Parliament, he is certainly the one who has caught the popular imagination.

Delights opposite start with No. 3, of *c.* 1745, recently converted into a china shop, with a festive sign and a shopfront carefully developed from the Regency doorcase. The staircase, and saloon upstairs with a charming Rococo fireplace are of the mid 18th century. The Punch Bowl seems to have crept in from Chester, and is set back from the street – a pity. Nos. 9 and 11 are early Georgian again, above the remains of a very individual Regency shopfront with latticed frieze to the bow windows. Half-timbering resumes at Kilvingtons, with one big jetty for two storeys (probably originally two, and lined up to the outer face in the 18th century), above a variety of Georgian and Regency shopfronts; much enjoyable detail includes the heart-shaped fanlight next to the disconcertingly coloured and mamilloid ship's figure-head on the corner. (Another strange feature is what appears to be a Georgian street door opening out of the back of the shop into the further recesses of the interior.)

Ebenezer Chapel, in Little Stonegate, is real architecture, by J.P. Pritchett (1851), sadly decaying. Six bays, the end ones stressed vertically, the basement horizontally; the four bays in the middle (instead of five or three) are unexpected but perfectly judged.

No. 12 Stonegate has a refined late Georgian front with pedimented centre window above a little balustrade, and nice Victorian shopfronts, unnecessarily Georgianized.

Mulberry Hall and Godfrey's are a splendid group of early-15th-century houses. (Ancient Mulberry Hall recorded as early as 1276, much the earliest reference to a mulberry tree, was probably further back from the street.) The top range of gables was added *c.* 1570 when it was the house of the Bishop of Chester, and the long, drooping bressumer, whose carving has recently been recovered from under many coats of paint, was probably added at the same time. It seems to have been in this group that George Walton, the Glasgow designer, had his short-lived York shop at the end of last century. Between the two halves of Godfrey's is the delightful alley to the Medical Society Rooms, starting among cast-iron columns of *c.* 1884, and ending with double doors beneath a huge, Victorian, half-timbered gable, and flanked by medieval wings, one of whose gable ends can be seen (r.) fossilized in later additions. The rainwaterhead of 1590 is the earliest in the city. The group is a marvellous hodge-podge of medieval, Jacobean, Georgian, Regency, and Victorian, for many years the home of the Tempest Anderson family, which added the grand 1870s dining room. The Medical Society, which has used the premises since before the First World War and owned them since just after the Second, has recently restored them impeccably under John Miller, with nothing done that was not necessary, and no feature regarded as dispensable. Inside a fine panelled room of *c.* 1600 has emerged, with a fireplace showing the beginnings of a classical overmantel, and the staircase and dining room have striking Victorian classical detailing. The garden elevation, multi-dated and multi-gabled, with a dovecote at one end, can be glimpsed by mildly trespassing off Newgate, near the site of St Benet's church.

Down another alleyway the Star Inn, whose sign spans the street, is ancient – it was certainly in existence in 1644 – pleasant, and very popular, with a view of the Minster that appears in Stonegate merely as a receding fringe of pinnacles until the last spectacular moment.

No. 31 Stonegate is late Georgian with beautiful rubbed brick arches, and an Adamesque frieze over Coffee Yard, to which it has a pretty doorcase with putti supporting swags. Coffee Yard has mostly 17th-century houses with timbered gables and heavy brick strings. It was formerly Langton Lane, named after a local family, and not always a thoroughfare. It was renamed in the 17th century when coffee houses were introduced. Auton's plumbers, which has an enterprising rainwaterhead of 1947, was the house of the Priors of St Oswald's (Nostell); the lane now passes through its timber-framed screens passage, dog-legged and pleasantly mysterious. Grape Lane Chapel, which stood near by, managed the full gamut of Nonconformity: Congregationalist (1781–94), Lady Huntington's Connexion (1794–8), Methodist New Connexion (1798–1804), Wesleyan (1804–5), Peculiar Baptist (1806–20), and Primitive Methodist (1820–51). The red 'printer's devil' on No. 33 Stonegate recalls the printing associations of Coffee Yard, though it cannot be connected with any particular printer. Thomas Gent (1692–1788), printer, writer, publisher, 'artist', producer of books on York, Ripon, Hull, was the most remarkable and eccentric of them. The upper stages of No. 33 have a charming late-Victorian adaptation, not however to be compared with the house next door. No. 35 has had an interesting history since Francis Hilyard opened his famous bookshop The Sign of the Bible in 1682. Laurence Sterne lodged for a time in Stonegate, but whether the first volumes of *Tristram Shandy* can more properly be said to have been published here (1760) under Thomas Hinxman, or at the Printing House (formerly the Bagnio or Turkish Bath) opposite St Martin's in Coney Street, is debatable. (Following the success of the first volumes publication passed rather unfairly to London.) The premises remained as a bookshop until 1873, when J.W. Knowles the glass painter acquired them, and recast the whole building to suit his taste, with splendid disregard for authenticity. The frieze of stained-glass cherubs, and the almost Art Nouveau advertisement over the side door are special delights. Much more Knowles glass and painted decoration survives inside. It is a superb period-piece, comparable in its way to Greenwood's shopfront (No. 37); late Georgian, sumptuous yet refined and of the highest quality: there can be few finer in the country.

Opposite and next to Kleiser's Court, No. 46 has another late-Georgian shopfront with an arched frieze, very pretty but a little the worse for wear. Nos. 48–58 form one of York's best medieval timber-framed ranges, where the traditional rendering has never been stripped; attractive Georgian oriels along the first floor. Behind No. 52A, in a little paved courtyard, are the remains of a Norman house of *c.* 1180, two-storeyed, stone, evidently of some size and importance; the inside of a two light window can be seen, with a waterleaf capital giving the date. It was fitted with shutters rather than with glass. No. 56 has a fine first-floor room with run-through panelling and an arcaded top of *c.* 1580. If the date of 1646 on the corner shop can be trusted it must just have escaped a by-law prohibiting overhanging upper storeys and stipulating that front elevations had to be 'built upright from the ground in brick'. On the other side of Stonegate, No. 43 has a delightful, two-tiered Georgian oriel bulging out from the jettied upper storeys; Nos. 45 and 47 have an early Georgian refronting; No. 49 is late-Georgian above the jetty and Hardcastles curves its elegant Victorian shopfront round into Low Petergate.

Stonegate meets Petergate (Walk 3) at the most aesthetically satisfactory, as well as the most ancient, road junction in York, with scarcely the tiniest detail that could be wished otherwise. Minster Gates slants slightly to the left and a slice of the Minster, full height, appears suddenly and thrillingly filling the whole end of the street. The deficiencies of Walter de Gray's transept elevation momentarily cease to matter. Minster Gates' present name recalls one of the entrances to the medieval Close. In the 18th century it was Bookbinder's Alley. Minerva, Goddess of Wisdom, sits with a myopic owl by a pile of books (not on them as a nearby plaque imperceptively records) above the corner of an elegant Regency shopfront. More good shopfronts in mid-18th-century buildings flank the entrance to Deangate.

Goodramgate to St Sampson's Square

Deangate is a disaster fulminated against elsewhere (Walk 1). It leads by a sharp right-turn at the Cross Keys to Goodramgate (see also Walk 5). The street snakes medievally across the corner of the Roman Fort, from Monk Bar, skirting the Close, then looping back to join the Roman street pattern at King's Square. The name comes from Old Norse 'Gutherungate' though the identity and even the sex of the person commemorated are uncertain. The street remains attractive because the scale of the narrow medieval messuages has been respected. It suffers from demolition, 'improvements', and formica fascias. The half-timbered group is late-15th-century, much restored, the timberwork partly exposed; the Angler's, a pleasant pub, demonstrating the aesthetic advantages of covering it up. Beside it a passage leads to a yard with a 'Wealden House' – also 15th-century, with a central, single-storeyed hall with large mullioned window and eaves deeply coved to bring them in line with those of the jettied, two-storeyed wings. Other houses are much more ancient than they appear; much-mangled 18th- and 19th-century upper floors are apt to conceal more timber framing. Hunter and Smallpage's erupts upwards into dizzy dormers like something at the seaside. The pendant arched building beyond must be among the least-loved of York's modern buildings.

Lady Row was built in 1316, to endow a chantry to the Blessed Virgin Mary in Holy Trinity church, behind; two storeyed and only one room deep, this is one of the earliest jettied ranges surviving in the country.

Holy Trinity churchyard, through an arch – probably built 1766 when Hornpot Lane was closed – with ironwork of 1815, has had its absolute rightness a little compromised; new brickwork is sadly unsympathetic; temporary educational buildings permanently impinge. But it is still the best in York as the church is the most lovable. Holy Trinity church is mentioned in 1082. This Norman church had a chancel and S chapel added *c.* 1250; one pier with crocketted capitals and arch, some of whose elaborate mouldings rise vertically from the capital intersecting those on the curve, an unusual conceit. The S arcade and aisle were extended *c.* 1330; a chantry chapel added in 1433 reused the displaced, flat-topped, reticulated windows in its outer wall and has a wide four-centred arch to the church. The N arcade is late-15th-century and may be associated with work on the chancel by the Revd John Walker who gave the E window in the 1470s. The tower is also late-15th-century, the multi-chamfers of its arches intersecting at the inside angles; a large W window. Outside, brick patching and a saddleback roof leave it picturesque but less sophisticated. The church was united with St Maurice's, but for some reason both fabrics survived and when St Maurice's, being more convenient for the new developments outside the walls, was hugely rebuilt in 1878, Holy Trinity was left alone, the only York church to escape a major Victorian restoration, so its enchanting interior survives [20]; over the billowing ledgered floor box pews tumble (work of the 17th, 18th, and 19th centuries intermingled, with a marvellous array of hinges and catches) round the 1785 pulpit. Reredos with Lords Prayer and Commandments (painted by Mr Horsley for £10 in 1721); Communion Rails of 1675, already with the characteristic York semicircular centre; Hanoverian Royal Arms; Lord Mayors Board, 1687. The plaster has been stripped from the walls but ceilings were kept, low and comfy. Over a squint in the S chapel, a shield hangs, like an afterthought. Brass to Thomas Danby, Lord Mayor (d. 1458). The E window has its original glass given by John Walker in the 1470s, a rare date for York glass: St George; St John the Baptist; the Holy Trinity; St John the Evangelist; St Christopher, over St Mary Cleopas and her family; SS Anne and Joachim and the Virgin and Child; the Coronation of the Virgin by the Trinity; Salome and Zebedee; St Ursula. The survival of the double representation of the Trinity is especially remarkable. The N aisle E window has 15th-century figures in spiky aureoles. The S aisle E window fragmentary 14th- and 15th-century figures, the S aisle chapel 14th-century heraldic glass. Outside, it is old, weatherworn stone, old tiles gently flicking this way and that, old brick patching; Victorian restoration was mercifully perfunctory; new stonework in the chancel buttresses is achingly straight.

The White Swan is ancient, truncated by road widenings of 1771; in the courtyard an old mounting block and loathsome fountain. Church Street is part ancient (Glovergail *c.* 1250 for glove-makers, later Girdlergate for girdle-makers), part improvement of 1836 when Thursday Market (St Sampson's Square) was being extended. Before that the only way through was Three Cranes Lane down Swinegate. (Ancient Swinegate is now called Little Stonegate: what is now called Swinegate was once part of Patrick Pool opposite.) During recent building work at the corner an exceptionally well-preserved section of Roman sewer was excavated, with man-hole, sluice system and inlets associated with the Baths in St Sampson's Square.

St Sampson's church was granted to Pontefract Priory in 1154. Its late-15th-century tower was battered in the siege and not restored until 1910 (C.E. Hutchinson). The rest of the church was rebuilt 1846–8 to designs by Frederick Bell, incorporating considerable parts of a late-medieval arch-braced roof with bosses. Chancel roof decoration by J.W. Knowles (1865) and two windows by Kempe and Tower (1905 and 1907). The church was closed in 1968 and in 1974, under George Pace, it was converted into an Old People's Centre, generally regarded as successful both practically and aesthetically. Partitions and separate structures within the building allow a number of simultaneous uses without destroying the impact of the interior as a whole. One panel of medieval glass in the W window. The chapel incorporates fittings from the church: benefaction boards dated and signed '1844 H.J. Rayson, Painter'; brass to William Richardson signed by Joshua Mann, engraver; and reredos incorporating painted panels designed by Bodley for All Saints, Falsgrave, Scarborough, in 1870.

St Sampson's Square, once Thursday Market, now paved and pedestrianized, is surrounded by unemphatic buildings, mostly 18th- and 19th-century, the best the late-18th-century Woolwich Office and the Arts and Crafts front of the Three Cranes with its ceramic sign. Parts of a Roman Bath, excavated 1930–1, can now be seen in the ground floor of the eponymous pub: the corner of the frigidarium (cold bath) and rather more of the caldarium (hot room) with an apse and hypocaust pillars for the central-heating system, 4th-century with stamps of the Sixth and Ninth Legions.

By the 19th century York's market facilities were strained. Parliament Street, constructed 1833–6 linking Thursday and Saturday Markets, provided greatly increased accommodation in its broad new thoroughfare. Markets continued to be held there until the mid 1950s, when they were removed to the space between Jubbergate and Shambles. The 1836 buildings were merely plain and decent, except for the Midland Bank by Robinson and Andrews, demolished

1971, a building of great dignity with a delightful domed Banking Hall. Its successor by Brierley Leckenby and Keighley is more than adequate, but the vocabulary of modern architecture seems unable to provide either the external grandeur or the internal elegance of the former building. Parliament Street denuded of market and the car park that succeeded it urgently needs imaginative urban treatment much above the level of 'shrubs-in-tubs'.

Feasegate to Coney Street

Feasegate and Davygate at right angles to one another were main exits from Thursday Market. Feasegate (perhaps from *fe-hus*, cowhouse) has been much and unmemorably rebuilt, but Dolcis and Mothercare keep a splendid cast-iron and glass facade of 1885 designed by W. Brown and proudly stamped 'THOMLINSON-WALKER IRONFOUNDERS YORK'. Nothing more satisfyingly radical has since appeared in the city. The southern bastion of Roman York lies beneath the street a little further on.

Market Street was part of Jubbergate until amputation by Parliament Street. The Tiger, The Hansom Cab, and the jettied building in Peter Lane are worth a glance; and Peter Lane (the site of St Peter the Little) should certainly be explored for the two extraordinary alleys, narrow as coffins, that link it with High Ousegate. Market Street leads to the junction of Spurriergate (left, and drab since rebuilding) and Coney Street, right, first recorded *c.* 1155 (from *Kunungr*, old Norse for 'king'). It was the spine-road of the Roman *canabae*, the settlement between the walls and the river, realigned when the Roman fortifications became irrelevant. Medieval Coney Street included what is now Spurriergate and Lendal, and ran from Ousegate to the Museum Gardens. It is now devoted to commerce rather than conservation, though not without vestiges of former dignity. Smith's new shop (1977) by Eric G. Hives and Sons is very well designed behind old houses whose back elevations and Georgian interiors hang, apparently in space, inside.

Opposite, Boots' 1900 half-timbering, by Treleaven, is the most ambitious York example of the Chester style. The Yorkshire Bank (1922) by Chorley Gribbon and Elcock is Baroque-revival, deploying quite small recessions and projections to vigorous effect. Judges' Court, down a passage, a pleasant backwater, excepting the plumbing, housed the Assizes Judges until 1806. Tall commercial premises follow, generally more interesting above than below: an elegant Art Nouveau shopfront recently successfully restored; parts of another shopfront in cast-iron; a bow in an eliptical arch and a row of gabled, timber-framed buildings, much restored. The huge street number on 25 is the only survivor of a once common (and useful) means of identifying properties.

Of Coney Street's two famous inns the Black Swan has been replaced by the British Home Stores; it stabled 100 horses in its heyday; the George, where Vanbrugh stayed, is rather more tangibly represented by a column in the Herald Office, part of the new front added in 1716.

St Martin Coney Street, or St Martin-le-Grand, is mentioned in Domesday Book. Its development was odd and complicated. The Norman church was in the NW corner. It acquired a s aisle in the 13th century, and a large chancel *c.* 1300, of which one window remains. In the 14th century the s aisle was widened to become the nave of a new church with its own s aisle. In 1437 the present sw tower was added and a splendid new w window given by Robert Semer, under whose will the rest of the church was rebuilt after 1443. So it became one of the handsomest of York churches, its buttresses topped with diagonal pinnacles tied back with gargoyles in the York manner, and with the most imposing of York clerestories. In 1862 it was restored by C.T. Newstead with a great array of pinnacles and pierced parapets. The clock was first erected in 1668 but the present bracket is 19th-century cast-iron, though the little figure of 'The Admiral' sighting along his sextant had been on the earlier clock. In the Blitz of 29 April 1942 the church was burned out, except for the s aisle and tower. In a city as over-endowed with churches as York complete rebuilding was unthinkable; George Pace's restoration (1961–8) is as ingenious as it is successful [27]. The centre of gravity moved again. The S aisle became the church, acquiring its own, narrow N aisle with a transeptal tower to house a reconstruction of Semer's W window. Vestry and parish room closed the W end of the site, the rest, laid out as a courtyard, round calcined stumps of columns, opening to Coney Street by an arch with wrought-iron grilles. The interior is a delight; colourful; almost all the fittings designed by the architect, with comfortable, traditional references abandoned only in the glass organ case (a German gift), designed to be seen through rather than seen. Frank Roper's reredos of the 'Last Supper' proved too controversial for timid members of the congregation, and was banished beneath the tower. Two 12th-century voussoirs are built into the wall N of the sanctuary. The reconstructed monument to Lady Elizabeth Sheffield (d. 1633) is not quite a success. There are brasses to Christopher Harrington, d. 1614, and Valentine Nalson, d. 1722. The magnificent early-18th-century font cover is the finest in the city, as is also the modern glass of the E window by Harry Stammers, showing the burning of the church. Five medieval clerestory windows perished in the fire; three in the S aisle survived both fire and, incredibly in this age of vandalism, some 17 years in the burned-out building. Most of the medieval glass is 15th-century, though some 14th-century fragments have been gathered together in the eastmost window. The second window has Our Lord and Lady between scenes of Corpus Christi and the Holy Family; the third, St George; the fourth, St Barbara. Under the tower and elsewhere are medieval panels on loan from various sources. But it is the St Martin window (*c.* 1437) that is the glory of the church [23], certainly the largest and arguably the finest of the city's parish church windows. Robert Semer, the donor, Chamberlain to the Chapter of York, kneels in the central light below the figure of St Martin of Tours, scenes from whose life occupy the rest of the lights.

Debenhams, towards the Mansion House, must now be regretting their lovely Victorian shopfronts, modernized away in the 1960s. Opposite, on the corner of New Street, the National Westminster Bank is by Brierley (1907). The tall ground floor has swallowed half the first-floor windows; Belcher and Pite motifs are flatly applied.

New Street and Davygate

New Street was laid out in 1746. Cumberland Row was being roofed on 23 July when the Duke of Cumberland, victor of Culloden, visited the city; a pleasant mid-Georgian range, little altered, legal offices, the corner one inaccurately rebuilt. The New Street entrance to Davygate Centre (dull) replaces Tower Cinema that in turn supplanted octagonal New Street Wesleyan Chapel of 1805, the most elegant of York's Nonconformist chapels.

Davygate takes its name from Davy Hall – house of the hereditary Lardiners of the Forest of Galtres – which in turn takes its name from David le Lardiner who held the office *c.* 1175. Davy Hall was also the name of a restaurant of the late 1890s designed by Penty and Penty, probably with help from George Walton, whose exquisite Art Nouveau ensemble was scrapped in the early 1950s. The tiny paved space just behind New Street is the churchyard given to St Helen's when the old churchyard was cleared away in 1745 to improve access to the Assembly Rooms: memorial to the parents of William Peckitt, glass painter. The Gas Office (1971) by Booth, Hancock, Johnson and Partners is enterprisingly, but not aggressively, modern, though its weathering propensities seem in doubt.

☆

Many interior features can be seen while shopping. The Norman House and Holy Trinity Goodramgate are open in daylight hours. The Roman Sewer may be visited at times (dependent on its condition) by arrangement with the York Archaeological Trust, tel. 59777. Visitors are usually welcomed at St Sampson's Old People's Centre. St Martin-le-Grand is open 10.00–17.00 Tuesday to Saturday.

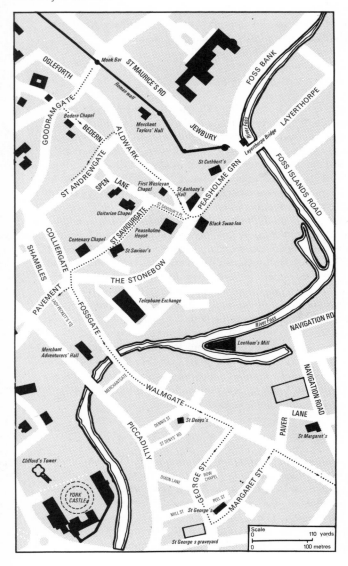

Walk Five

North-eastern York, inside the walls, is a sad, gap-toothed, battered place. Major monuments survive, in greater numbers than anywhere else in the city, but their settings, which gave them resonance, have been whittled away for road improvements, redevelopment, and bullying office blocks. Places that, concealed, were splendid, have been to their detriment tactlessly exposed. Better things are promised. St Andrewgate and Aldwark are to be rebuilt on Esher principles; opportunities to put these into practice have been disgracefully ignored elsewhere.

Goodramgate to St Andrewgate

Goodramgate starts well from Monk Bar, curving away, out of sight, beyond the projecting end of Ogleforth. Sinclair's shop, formerly the Monk Bar Chapel (United Methodists) of 1859, has the only faint claim to be Architecture; the rest, as in many of the best York streets, is simple vernacular, endlessly rebuilt, but preserving the scale of older properties and free from 'comprehensive redevelopment'. The Royal Oak and Golden Slipper are semi-detached pubs, indeterminate of boundary, timber-framed, with the remains of a carved 15th-century corner post.

Dr Gee suggests that the prominent projection above the National Trust shop is one end of the bridge built in 1396 to connect the Close with the Bedern, the College of Vicars Choral founded *c.* 1252. Bedern ('prayerhouse') was a common name for such establishments, as at Beverley, Ripon, and Lincoln. Originally there were 36 vicars, assisting and occasionally deputizing for the canons. Inflation cut the numbers in 1420, and they dwindled further after the Reformation, but the College was not dissolved until 1936, though its buildings had long since been demolished or put to other uses. The vicars had separate houses, but shared chapel, hall, kitchen, and buttery. The dunghill was uncomfortably close to the well. The original lintel survives over the entrance from Goodramgate. Most of the mid-14th-century chapel was demolished in 1961, having leant drunkenly but picturesquely over the street for many years. What remains has an old door to the street, reused earlier material, like the Norman corbel over the altar, aumbries, and a pretty little archway. The contemporary hall is even more spectral, its interior surviving almost without benefit of an exterior, its original scissors roof with collars. Excavation of the site is in progress preparatory to very promising Esher housing. St Peter's School used the College from 1644 to 1730, when it moved to St Andrew's church (possibly the St Andrew's church mentioned in Domesday Book), closed *c.* 1550, but turned to such – and other less suitable – uses instead of being demolished. It was at one time a brothel; it is now happily a Mission Room. Much-mangled medieval masonry, a Perpendicular window, a blocked chancel arch, a 15th-century roof, the timber framework of a former bell turret, and 18th-century wall benches.

See p. 196

St Andrewgate has been cleared almost from end to end; even in the last year, old buildings have been bulldozed with indecent haste. What remains is being conserved; what is promised is very good. No. 20 was Thomas Atkinson's own house, the door and central window treated as a single composition under an arch, a bullseye and enormous swag in the pediment. Small wonder he died insolvent. Nos. 34–8 were built as a fire-engine house *c.* 1854, hence the Tuscan colonnade.

Aldwark to Peasholme Green

Aldwark has the tattered remnants of gentility. The name means 'old fortification', presumably Roman since the name seems Anglo-Saxon.

Misdirected zeal has exposed the Merchant Taylors' Hall, instead of leaving it a little courtyard behind a row of cottages. The charter of the present Company is of 1662, but the medieval gild of the tailors was probably founded in the 14th century and was certainly in existence by 1415. The Hall was built by the Gild of St John the Baptist, a religious and trade fraternity dominated by the tailors. After the Reformation the religious associations were quietly forgotten. The bleak, brick exterior is a recasting of *c.* 1672 and *c.* 1715, to which latter date belong the flimsy porch and Wren-ish pedimented window at one end of the Hall. The opposite end and, more impressively, the interior proclaim the timbered origins of the building. The early-15th-century arch-braced roof trusses have been strengthened with later tie-beams and there are remains of the screens passage and service rooms. The big fireplace with curve-topped over-mantel should be *c.* 1715. In the Small Parlour, stained glass by Henry Gyles shows Queen Anne (cracked), supported by three brown cherubs over the Company's arms, and is misleadingly inscribed 'This Company had been dignified in the year 1679 by having in their Fraternity eight Kings, eleven Dukes, thirty Earles and forty-four Lords', which must refer to the London Company. The Company's Almshouse, 1730, cozy and tiny, stands next door. Beside the Aldwark gates Oliver Sheldon House has a handsomely asymmetrical front of 1732 with tall windows and a massively blocked and pedimented doorway, but a 17th-century ceiling inside. Other period features were imported when the building was admirably restored for the York Civic Trust, by Francis Johnson (1969). Beyond, behind an early-18th-century garden wall architecturally treated, the site of St Helen-on-the-Walls, demolished *c.* 1550, has been excavated – St Helen was the mother of Constantine, proclaimed Emperor in Eboracum in 306 – and another promising new housing scheme has just been started. Regency houses occupy the other side of the street, and at the far end, beyond much that is better ignored, a squarish plain building was York's first – and for many years only – Wesleyan Chapel. The site was acquired in February 1859;

the building opened on 15 July, John Wesley officiating.

Aldwark leads to Peasholme Green ('low lying ground by a river'), from which Haymarket opened diagonally, leading in turn to Hungate ('street of the dogs'). The low lying ground was known in medieval times as 'The Marsh', an area of floodable ground gradually reclaimed for building, but always remaining a poor district. In Rowntree's survey of 1901 it figured as one of the worst slums in the city. Its parish church of St John the Baptist was closed as early as 1523 and demolished soon afterwards. Post-war clearance and re-development has left a dishevelled open space, new buildings intent on vacuous individuality ignoring one another, and, on the fringes of the district, a few old buildings surprised at their own survival.

St Anthony's Hall and St Cuthbert's Church keep each other company. In 1446 Henry VI granted a charter of incorporation to a religious and social gild, which, though officially in honour of God, the Blessed Virgin Mary, and St Martin-the-Confessor, soon became associated with St Anthony. Building started at once and the chapel was consecrated in 1453; its entrance was in Aldwark flanked by two niches. The western end of the hall above must have been constructed at the same time, but with its axis the other way. The much larger eastern part of the building was added *c.* 1485–1500. The gild came under the supervision of the Corporation, escaped suppression in 1547, and was not dissolved until 1627. The buildings became a storehouse, a hospital, a house of correction, from 1705 to 1946 the Blue Coat School, and in 1953 The Borthwick Institute of Historical Research. The lower walls are medieval stonework; the upper parts were rebuilt in brick in 1655, with big windows under brick pediments. Inside, the earlier part of the Hall has a king-post roof, originally ceiled; the later part a fine arch-braced roof whose bosses are Wolstenholme replacements of originals cannibalized to restore the Guildhall roof in the mid 19th century. Other medieval roofs remain in the aisles, now walled off, but in this half of the building originally open. The earlier aisles were always screened off.

St Cuthbert's church, mentioned in Domesday Book, survived suppression in 1547; All Saints, Peasholme, on the opposite side of the Green was closed in 1586 and pulled down for the sake of its building materials.

St Cuthbert's stands in a pleasant churchyard, above the street, below the walls. Mid-15th-century ashlar with a thin late-15th-century tower, and fossilized in the E wall the gable end of a much earlier building, possibly pre-Conquest, certainly of Roman materials. Fifteenth-century door to the porch. Cozy, single-cell interior, the E window pushed off centre by the ancient gable, the altar on a high platform over a quadrant-vaulted crypt no longer accessible, the mid-15th-century roofs alternating arched-braces with vestigial hammer-beams, with a double truss midway, probably where the work of two donors met; medieval glass, heraldic and fragmentary; 17th-century pulpit and altar-table; Mayoral boards, hatchments, commandment and benefaction boards, and two intensely black panels on which may be dimly traced the outlines of Moses and Aaron; Cartouche to Charles Mitley, carver (d. 1758), and a cast-iron font painted green. The church was saved from demolition in 1547 by the intervention of Sir Martin Bowes, who had been Lord Mayor of London, gave York its Sword of State, and whose family lived at what is now the Black Swan, on the other side of Peasholme Green, where other inhabitants included Henrietta Thompson, General Wolfe's mother, who spent her childhood here. The Black Swan is late-16th-century timber-framed with a late-17th-century brick wing behind. Much later 17th-century work inside, massive staircase, and panelled rooms with painted overmantels, dark, vaguely biblical, doubtless subjects for inexhaustible speculation during opening hours. The building copes manfully with its dismal surroundings, which, together with the Stonebow, successor to Hungate, the wise visitor will do his best to ignore.

St Saviour's Place to Pavement

St Saviour's Place leads uphill to the junction of Spen Lane (Ipsingail in the 12th century – 'Lane with aspen trees') and

St Saviourgate, buildings elaborately conserved alternating with others decaying by vacant plots. Peasholme House (1752) is four-square Georgian with no frills, obviously related stylistically to contemporary houses in Micklegate. Restoration for York Civic Trust has rid the front of humiliating adjuncts. Simple panelled interiors and an Ionic staircase screen contrast with the gorgeous floral rococo ceiling imported from Bishophill House. No. 14 was built in 1780 for the Minister of the chapel in Aldwark; a pretty house, already with a front garden. In Spen Lane the Spiritualist National Mission Church is a pinched, polychromatic house with Hornsea fish-scale tiles. For a hundred yards St Saviourgate – originally Ketmongergate ('the flesh-sellers street') – is one of York's handsomest Georgian streets; that it manages to hold its own against three terrible new buildings that have invaded it is little short of miraculous. It is also a Nonconformist stronghold and J.P. Pritchett's Salem Chapel (1839), noble portico topped by a curly pediment, formed an ideal culmination to the street. Hilary House is its tactless successor. Mistaken enthusiasm pre-viewed Stonebow House in the *Architectural Review* (January 1963, p. 8). Georgian St Saviourgate developed early; there are houses dated 1735, 1739, and 1740. No. 24, a very fine house, is a little later, but earlier than its 1763 rainwaterhead, and much earlier than its pretty late-18th-century doorcase. More of these were inserted when Nos. 16–22 (a terrace of *c.* 1745) were recast at the end of the 18th century. Lady Hewley's Almshouse is Tudor, 1840, by J.P. Pritchett with an heraldic panel and inscription from the original Almshouse, in Tanner Moat, founded in 1700. The Hewley family lived in St Saviourgate.

St Saviour's church, less imposing than its Nonconformist neighbours, dates back at least to *c.* 1090, but was almost wholly rebuilt in stiff Perpendicular by R.H. Sharp, 1844–5. Large 15th-century E window, its stained glass now in All Saints', Pavement; eastern aisle windows of the late 14th century, with curvilinear elements among the Perpendicular ones; 15th-century tower; spacious aisled interior used as a store; monument to Thomas Atkinson, architect, d. 1798.

The Unitarian church [35], the earliest of York's surviving Nonconformist churches, was built for the Presbyterians in 1692–3, Lady Hewley being a principal contributor. Cruciform, brick with a low central tower, it has delightful Walker railings to the street (1852) and a pleasant though unsympathetically decorated interior; Georgian pulpit; monuments by Skelton and C. Fisher, and one by Regnart to Mrs Sandercock (d. 1790), with anchor, sarcophagus, urn, and a whole library of books; in the vestry, portrait of the Revd Charles Wellbeloved, minister, antiquarian, and Director of Manchester College, 1803–40.

The Masonic Hall was built as a Mechanics Institute, 1845, by J.B. and W. Atkinson; in an individualistic classical style with rounded-headed windows in rectangular frames and a tight little clerestory along the top. The painted decoration of the Temple is Egyptian, by Brother T.B. Whytehead (1908–9, R.C.H.M.), like a setting for the Magic Flute. Marble busts of Victoria and Albert view the decor, he stoically, she somewhat askance.

Centenary Chapel, by James Simpson of Leeds, 1840, is in grey brick with a giant Ionic portico to the street. The splendid interior has round-ended galleries on cast-iron columns, beneath the vast, compartmented ceiling. The gallery seating banks spectacularly up the curved back wall. Even the engraved, flashed glass and lincrusta dado are Greek Revival. The recent colour scheme is unsubtle but patriotic. Cast-iron parish-boundary plates in the yards around.

'Whitna' and 'whatna', dialect words meaning 'what kind of a', may account for Whipmawhopmagate, York's longest street name for its shortest street. It was bounded on one side by a church with an equally puzzling name, St Crux; however its dedicatee was not an unknown saint but the Holy Cross. First mentioned in Domesday Book, and perhaps the finest of York's medieval churches, it was finally demolished in 1887 after six years of indecision. The Parish Room built on the site incorporates a fragment of medieval wall, a traceried door, a Knowles window of 1863, hatchments, a pedimented overdoor of 1671, several post-medieval brasses and a

striking collection of monuments; Sir Robert Watter, d.
1612, in a deep recess, framed by columns on bulbous
heraldic plinths and topped by ill-matched putti, the Watters
lie stiffly below children kneeling, or sleeping in domed and
curtained cots, and allegorical persons the worse for damp;
Sir Tancred Robinson, d. 1754, by Richard Ayray, a putto
seated uncomfortably on a trophy; Henry Waite, d. 1780, by
Fisher, whose exquisite decoration surrounds a profile bust
so unflattering that it must be a portrait.

Pavement was one of York's principal medieval streets,
extending from the churchyard of St Crux to the churchyard of All Saints', Pavement (Walk 6), below which stood,
from 1672 to 1813, the Market Cross – 'of the Ionic order but
ill executed'.* It was apparently one of the first city streets to
be paved, hence the name, but its original name was
Marketskire, 'market district'; markets on Tuesdays, Thurs-
days, and Saturdays were reduced to Saturdays only by 1776.
It was the site of the pillory and place of execution of
Thomas Percy, Earl of Northumberland in 1572. It was a
street of merchants' houses but its glory is much diminished.
Parliament Street, preserving civic decencies, was broken
through in 1833–6; Piccadilly tried hard just before the First
World War and failed miserably after it; Stonebow, opened
in the 1950s with the unfulfilled ambition of relieving traffic,
is deplorable.

What remains is centred on the Herbert House. Christopher Herbert bought property here in 1557. His great-
grandson Sir Thomas Herbert, who attended Charles I
during his captivity and at his execution, was probably born
in a house in Lady Peckitt's Yard, a splendid alleyway
(named after the wife of John Peckitt, Lord Mayor, 1702),
narrow, dropping steeply (for York) past a timber range of
c. 1580, to a late 17th-century house straddling the exit, with
decorative brickwork in oval, bullnosed panels, windows
with arched central lights anticipating Norman Shaw, and a
magnificent modillion cornice. (Aesthetic disillusionment
follows quickly for those who pass beneath.) The house on to

* Francis Drake, *Eboracum* (1736; facs. 1978), p. 292.

Pavement (despite its claim to be Sir Thomas Herbert's birthplace) was not built until *c.* 1620, elaborately timbered at the front but brick at the back, an arrangement indicative of conservative tastes. Over-enthusiastic restoration of 1926 stripped the plaster and altered the shapes of the windows. Fine contemporary panelling inside. Roger Jaques, Lord Mayor, entertained Charles I here in 1639 when Thomas Widdrington, Recorder and one of the first historians of the city received a Knighthood. (His *Analecta Eboracensia* was refused when offered to the Corporation for publication, and he forbad his heirs to publish it in perpetuity. It eventually appeared in 1897.) Over Lloyds Bank are the remains of a two-bay house of *c.* 1700, recognizably classical. A cast-iron shopfront, the tall thin Golden Fleece, and its bogus-half-timbered neighbour may also be enjoyed.

Fossgate to Walmgate Bar

Fossgate is going up in the world a little too late: too many gaps have been inappropriately filled or acquired an air of permanence. Nos. 11 and 12 are terra-cotta, 1898; No. 15 has a shell-hooded door; Macdonalds has a vast Venetian arch in Doulton-ware, built as a cinema front in 1911 by W.H. Whincup. In a lane behind, a Dutch gable of the late 17th century and a scrap of masonry that may be part of the Carmelite Friary moved here in 1295. Behind a fierce glazed-brick facade the Blue Bell has a charming inner bar.

Beneath the Company's arms on a rebuilt Dutch gable and flanked by pleasant pastiche shopfronts is the passage leading to the Merchant Adventurers' Hall. This religious gild of Our Lord and the Blessed Virgin, founded in the late 14th century, came to dominate the city's commerce, under its other hat as the mercers' gild. Land was acquired off Fossgate in 1356 and a Royal Licence the following year. A hospital was founded in 1373, the chapel restored 1411, and a Royal Charter granted in 1430. The existing buildings probably date from just after 1357, with a forebuilding to Fossgate added after Queen Elizabeth's new Charter of

1581, when the Company became the Merchant Adventurers. The ground floor is brick and stone with cusped lancets in the older parts; the upper floors half-timbered, variously windowed, many original openings replaced by large sash windows. The 16th-century building has vine-carved bargeboards. Tudor tracery from the chapel E window does duty as an ornament in the little garden strangely and pleasantly divorced from the realities of Piccadilly by a high wall. The entrance is to the upper floor. Two-aisled Hall [31] with timber 'arcade' and king-post roof trusses with struts below the tie beams. Inscriptions here and elsewhere catalogue numerous 'repairs and beautifications'. Sixteenth- and 17th-century panelling and benches; a portrait of George I given 1722; early-Georgian Sheriff's seat, like a reredos with niches; interesting topographical drawings; elaborate early-17th-century fireplace in the Governor's Room from a house in Pavement. The basement, which held the hospital, is also double aisled, some of the wall posts standing on stone responds that may be part of an earlier building. The late-16th-century arched-brick structure supports the great fireplace above. The Chapel is a delight, entered under a low, four-centred arch with remains of 15th-century screen-work. Benches facing each other across the brick floor and pulpit and Masters' seat flanking balustered communion rails are late 17th century. Charming patterned glass with blue borders.

On the opposite side of Fossgate, Straker's Passage, dog-legged and seedy, leads past the early 1970s glass-house, brick-towered extensions to the Telephone Exchange, designed by Leeds Polytechnic – much more lively than the original dimly genteel 1955 building – to a little quay by the River Foss with marvellous views downstream to Castlegate spire over Foss Bridge and upstream to Leetham's Mill [52], the proudest industrial building in the city, and one of its major monuments, moored like a great ship between the Foss and Wormald's Cut, built 1895–6 to designs of W.G. Penty. The battlements and cylindrical turret may be concessions to the city's history; little else is. Sheer scale, ranges of windows in tall recesses, gables shaped or cut off at unexpected angles, and all the splendid geometry of hoists. The back of Walmgate is also seen, not wholly inspiring.

Foss Bridge is a charming balustraded hump-backed design of 1811 by Peter Atkinson Junior, replacing one rebuilt in 1403, which by 1586 was, as Camden described it, so built over that you could not tell you were on it. Stubbs's grimly Venetian palazzo, 1878, faces the pleasantly old-fashioned front of Dorothy Wilson's Hospital, built 1812 'for the maintenance of ten poor Women as also for the Instruction of English, Reading, Writing of 20 poor Boys for ever'.

The Red Lion, in Merchantgate, does its best to look bogus, but isn't. Piccadilly is best ignored; between the garages and office blocks the Castle displays its worst aspect (Walk 6).

Walmgate, once a major medieval street, pursues a dispiriting and unsteady course to Walmgate Bar. Gaps proliferate. (The name is probably derived from a woman called Walba.) Some of the surviving buildings are tended carefully, like the excellent Victorian Rope Shop; others decay. No. 70, unremarkable outside, has ambitious interiors of the very early 18th century; using orders and arch-topped panels.

St Denys's, a foundation of the late 12th century, is a short church and wide. Once much bigger, it was damaged in the siege of 1644, the spire removed in 1778, nave and tower demolished in 1802, and the present w end built in 1847 (Thomas Pickersgill, Architect). The reset, late-12th-century doorway has lost most of its original jambs, but the arch has chevron, beakhead, and a wavy leaf pattern. There are traces of a 13th-century lancet in the w end of the n aisle. Most of the existing building is of *c.* 1330–40 with reticulated tracery and thin, close-set buttresses. The curvilinear e window of the n aisle exhibits premonitions of the Perpendicular style. Cream-washed interior of two enormous bays, originally three, the nave mid-way in height between the aisles but narrower than either. Fragmentary interiors have a special visual magic all their own. Dorothy Wilson's monument (d. 1717), in the shape of a Georgian doorway, recounts her charities at length. Dorothea Hughes' Jacobean monument, and Fisher's tablet to Mr Hotham (d. 1806) have suffered from amateur embellishments. The medieval glass is of unusual interest and beauty. Clockwise from the NW corner, window 1 has two early-13th-century panels, rather too fragmentary for identification, on a grisaille ground, the earliest glass in any of the parish churches, and an early-14th-century St John the Baptist, in series with the next two windows; 2, the Virgin and St Margaret above charming donors, under excellent canopies, Crucifixion in the tracery; 3, Our Lord between St Thomas and St John the Evangelist, a most beautiful window, the borders and canopies a delight, the green glass a welcome change from the all too prevalent blue and red of later York glass; 4, a Jesse tree of the mid 14th century, the twining stems tolerably intact but the figures mere jumbles; 5, the E window tracery has been rebuilt (1979) but its glass is still in store; 6 and 7, fragmentary 15th-century glass including in the S window a splendidly crowned Virgin, her blue robe held by angels and the Holy Ghost alighting, angels playing medieval instruments and a disgruntled cherub emerging from a muddle. Enthusiasts may note the next window, by Clutterbuck, and the two W windows in Powell's Pressed Quarries. Under the church is a vault of the Earls of Northumberland; the 3rd Earl, mortally wounded at Towton (1461), was buried there.

See p. 196

Opposite the church in Walmgate stood Percy's Inn, the Earls of Northumberlands' mansion. Behind it was the original Walker foundry. Soon after his appointment as 'Ironfounder to Queen Victoria' in 1847 John Walker moved his premises to the Victoria Foundry opposite the end of George Street. His best-known works are the Kew Gardens Gates of 1845–6 and the magnificent railings of the British Museum (1851). York has many charming examples of his work. By the 1880s the firm was known as Thomlinson-Walker. Medieval churches of St George, St Mary, St Stephen, and St Peter-le-Willows in the Walmgate–Fishergate area have all vanished. The Cattle Market, served by 17 inns in 1826, was held here and overflowed in linear fashion as far as Petergate. Its reestablishment outside the walls in 1827 must have come as a relief. Haberdashers' Hall stood on the corner of George Street, whose pleasant early-Victorian terraced housing leads round the corner to St George's church (R.C.) by J.A. and C. Hansom (1847–9): the three-gabled, bell-turretted exterior has been joylessly repaired in cement. Attractive interior. Liturgical reform has left the pretty, prickly fittings alone. Hardman E window possibly designed by A.W.N. Pugin. Barnett glass in the side chapel the colours of jellies. In the churchyard opposite, the only gravestone left upright (in a concrete plot) commemorates Richard Palmer alias Richard Turpin, 'notorious highwayman and horse stealer, executed at Tyburn, April 7th, 1739'. The fictitious romances associated with this squalid thief seem indestructable. Pleasant recent housing towards Fishergate Postern. Walmgate regained has two timber-framed houses, Bowes Morrell House, probably late-14th-century, and a Penty and Penty building of the late 1890s in Norman Shaw style about to be restored as part of a promising housing scheme.

'TO ST MARGARET'S CHURCH' is announced in excellent lettering over Walker iron gates in the middle of nothing. The churchyard used to be a delicious surprise, the path between cottages, turning away down an avenue past the church, now piteously and pointlessly opened up, with seats to view the shopping precinct opposite.

St Margeret's church is first mentioned *c.* 1180; the brick tower is of 1684; the rest was almost rebuilt by Thomas Pickersgill in 1851–2. It is used as a theatrical store. The magnificent, but fast-decaying porch [10] is late-12th-century, brought here after the siege from St Nicholas's church. It has beasts, foliage, masks, the signs of the zodiac, and the inner order set deeply back beyond walls with little niches.

Dismal recent housing round Hope Street unforgivably ignores the chance to put 'Esher' into action, compounds the ragged spaces of earlier schemes, and reduces Walmgate Bar to insignificance.

The city walls provide a convenient and complementary return route (Walk 8, pp. 237–40).

☆

Access to Bedern Hall and Chapel will be dependant on the use finally found for them. The Merchant Taylors' Hall is open May to September, but is much used for functions: enquiries should be made at Bernard Thorpe and Partners, tel. 55452. St Anthony's Hall is open Monday to Friday, tel. 59861. ext. 274. St Cuthbert's is open intermittently; vicarage, 86 East Parade, tel. 24190. Black Swan, opening hours. The Chapels are locked, but accessible on Sunday mornings. St Saviour's and St Margaret's churches are both used as stores and closed to the public; the key to St Denys's church is available locally; St George's is usually open. The Merchant Adventurers' Hall is open Monday to Saturday.

Addenda

Restoration at Bedern Hall (p. 184) has revealed one idiosyncratic window and part of a pretty fan-vaulted recess.

Fifteenth-century stained glass reinstated in St Denys's E window (p. 194) has a fragmentary crucifixion and St Denys holding his head.

Walk Six

York Castle

William the Conqueror's twin castles were built 1068-9, facing each other across the Ouse, defending the city from downstream attack. They were not popular. They were both destroyed in the Danish insurrection of 1069, and both immediately rebuilt. The castle on the NE bank was the more strategically important, between the Rivers Ouse and Foss. William dammed the latter to provide both better defences for his motte-and-bailey castle with its timber palisades, and the King's Fishpool, which was to become an important part of the city's defences; the dam, constantly repaired and altered, was not demolished until 1856. The miserable incident of the Jewish massacre in 1190 (see p. 28) has recently been commemorated. York Castle was fortress, royal palace, mint (until 1546), prison (until 1929), and courts of justice.

In *c.* 1244 Henry III decided to rebuild in stone; a new keep on William's mound, Hall, Chapel, and Offices, surrounded by a stone wall with bastions and two gatehouses. The work took about 20 years; the master mason was Henry de Rayns and the carpenter Master Simon.

By the mid 14th century the castle was decidedly tatty and the King lodged with the Franciscans. A long history of dilapidation, dismantlings, and rebuildings followed; the oddest incident when Robert Redhead, the gaoler, started to demolish the keep in 1596, by now known as Clifford's Tower, and was only prevented by protests from the citizens who felt it to be 'an exceeding ornament to the city'.

In 1642 the castle was repaired for the King including the new forebuilding of Clifford's Tower, which continued in

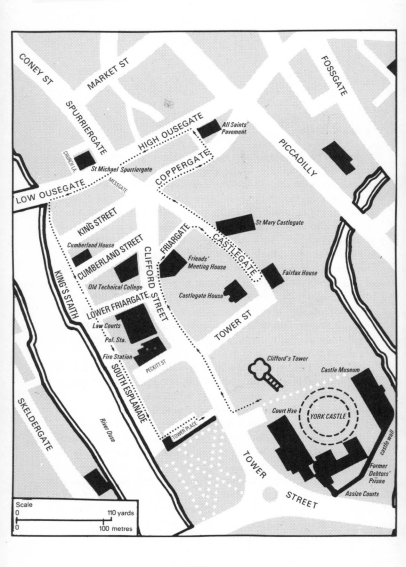

use until gutted in 1684 after a salute on St George's Day: by this time it was held in less esteem and known as the 'Minced Pie'.

In 1701–5 the Debtor's Prison was erected; in 1773–7, the new Assize Courts replacing the 17th-century Grand Jury House; in 1780, the Female Prison. The oval lawn, known as the 'Eye of Yorkshire' was a late-18th-century creation. County elections were held in the castle until 1831; North Riding elections until 1882. Accessions were proclaimed: executions carried out (Dick Turpin, 1739, Eugene Aram, 1759, the Luddites, 1812; the Peterloo Rioters were tried here, 1820). The walls and gates were much altered; the keep became Mr Wand's garden ornament.

Plans were submitted in the 1820s for a grand new prison by Atkinson and Sharp, and by Robert Wallace, who had the novel idea of retaining Clifford's Tower but removing the motte. In 1825 a design by Robinson and Andrews was selected, and built 1826–35. It had a cylindrical Governor's House with radiating cell blocks, surrounded by walls and gates of gloomy grandeur, known as 'Sydney Smith's hardest joke' from that excellent wit's having been on the committee. Prison, wall, and gatehouse were demolished in 1935 to make way for an abortive scheme for council offices. Vacant sites in York are apt to acquire a permanence not always accorded to its historical monuments.

The medieval Castle was roughly lozenge-shaped with gatehouses near the sharper corners, surrounded by a high wall, a moat, and partly it seems by an outer wall. Clifford's Tower [29], the keep – known in medieval times as 'the great tower' – stood separately, surrounded by its own extension of the moat. A substantial stretch of Henry III's curtain wall survives behind the Debtor's Prison, its big round towers bluntly finished off with a coping, together with the recently excavated and rather shapeless remains of what may have been the 'Great Gate', mostly demolished in 1735; however, the 'Great Gate' may have been that which faced down Castlegate.

Clifford's Tower, Henry III's quatrefoil keep (1245–62) is tolerably intact, though settlement has diminished its original metropolitan elegance, as have the informalities of the 1642–3 forebuilding, with off-centre heraldry and cozy roof. The massive, battered plinth was both strategic and structural. Segmental turrets corbelled out between the larger lobes housed garderobes. The jambs of the original entrance are inside the forebuilding. The ashlar interior has the upper walls set back, deep arched embrasures narrow to slits below, and rather more accommodating windows upstairs. Twin staircases lead to the Chapel on the first floor of the forebuilding – half 13th-century wall arcading and half rebuilding of 1642 – and the wall-walk, no longer quite so hair-raising as once it was. The view is varied: the trees and towers on Bishophill, the riverbanks downstream almost suggesting open country, the Castle courtyard below, and the marvellous conjunction of Castlegate and Pavement churches with the Minster compare favourably with seedy views in other directions. The trim and treeless motte was restored to its original shape in 1935.

The Debtor's Prison (1701–5) was probably designed by William Wakefield. U-shaped, Baroque, already Vanbrughian and monumental, its banded-pilastered centrepiece and segmentally pedimented wings contrast oddly with its thin surprised bell turret.

John Carr's Assize Courts (1773–7) – though plans had been prepared some years previously – have a grand Adamesque Ionic elevation with recessed portico, and end pavilions, a façade for nothing but the circulation space. The courtrooms emerge as a couple of skylights: the 18th-century was not interested in functional expression. Peter Atkinson Junior and his partners Matthew Phillips and R.H. Sharp (1818–21) designed the long, rendered range behind, not quite on the same axis, and in *c*. 1870 Gould and Fisher added the High Sheriff's Luncheon Room and County Committee Room (very respectable ashlar classical) on yet another axis. In the late 1830s Robinson and Andrews designed the stone screen in the Entrance Hall, premonitory of station ticket offices. Carr's courtrooms remain superb despite alterations; circular domes on twelve columns set in a square at the ends of rectangular rooms, an arrangement recalling Thomas Atkinson's Bar Convent Chapel (Walk 16) though not so subtly handled. Highly individual versions of the Corinthian order are associated in the Crown Court with something resembling a Doric Triglyph, and in the Civil Court with exquisite plaster decoration to the dome [41].

The centre of the Female Prison (1780) was 'designed' by Thomas Wilkinson and John Prince to match the middle of the Law Courts, the work 'supervised' by Carr, but the end pavilions were not added until 1802 by Peter Atkinson Senior. The two prisons now house the Castle Museum; the new glass entrance between them does not play at 'styles'.

The Castle Museum

Dr Kirk's collection of everything he saw passing out of use as he went about his practice was formed between the 1890s and the 1930s, by which time it had outgrown the Memorial Hall at Pickering and was offered to York. The Female Prison was adapted to house it, 1935–8; the Debtor's Prison opened as an extension in 1952. The collection continues to grow hugely. The contrast with the Yorkshire Museum is immediately apparent. Clinical information is not dispensed: the cases are crowded and enormous fun.

Rowntrees' fire engine, gorgeously emblazoned, faces armour; Victorian Parlour, piano and gloom, stuffed cat, birds and fruit under glass domes; Moorland Cottage, gloom again, stuffed dog, patchwork, and painting of a prize bull; Georgian Room, livable; Tudor room (largely Jacobean), heavy with rich late-17th-century provincial furniture.

Equipment for chemists and vets, measuring and weighing; chatelains, truncheons, and card cases; china of all sorts; glass pipes, pot pipes, silhouettes and scent bottles, miniatures and memorial cards; firescreens in beaded velvet; lace and pins. Argaud and colza lamps, model ships and windmills; a case marked 'Oats'; globular wool weight, sets of measures like the Tower of Babel, a chamber-pot with lizards, a Gothick organ. A gallery of grates and fireplaces, Georgian to Victorian, rural and sophisticated, marble and painted wood. Keys, jelly moulds, and knitting sticks; the chat of pensioners remembering their youth; farm implements in a barn and 'Pat the Giant', the largest ox ever bred in the country. Then the street with a glass sky. A tudor house from Stamford, 'Ebeneezer Ellerker' Victorian Gothic, the rest mainly Georgian, Pewterer, Coppersmith, Wine and Spirit Merchant, Tallow factory with faint authentic smell. A replica of the Duke of Windsor's christening cake; a padded cell, frayed. Shops commemorating local businesses; William Alexander, Joseph Terry, Henry Hindley, T. Cooke. A fire, with rescue, illuminated by a 2p piece.

In the Debtor's Prison: Royal weddings, samplers, dolls'-house furniture in brass. Jet, plumes, fans, bustles and corsets, clothes for school, the sands, weddings, Queen Victoria, war. Outside, by the Foss, in need of trees, Raindale Mill, raw rubble stonework, but the rumble, clack, and swirl marvellously authentic. Flour can be bought, hygienically stone-ground elsewhere. Edwardian street, motor bodies, drapes, electrical engineers; the William IV Hotel ('Good beds for cyclists'); Metropolitan drinking fountain. In the cells, workshops for cutler, combmaker, brushmaker, smith, printer, tanner, and engraver. Mantraps. The condemned cell with cast-iron bed and stone privy.

Researches on regional characteristics of chimney corners, gingerbread moulds, mousetraps will be published.

Tower Street to Clifford Street

Tower Street maintains a perverse but historic right-angled turn round Clifford's Tower. Peckitt Street commemorates William Peckitt, glass painter; pleasant 1840s development facing the Byzantine side of the Fire Station, 1856, by J.B. and W. Atkinson, originally Trinity Chapel, preferable to the utilitarian front.

Clifford Street was cut through an unsalubrious trio of lanes in 1880–2: Kergate, Thursgail, and Hertergate, later known respectively as First, Middle, and Far Water Lanes. South-west towards the river stood the Franciscan Friary (*c.* 1230–1538) where Edward II and Edward III held parliament and Richard II stayed in preference to the Castle.

The foundation stone of the Law Courts and Police Station was laid in 1890 by the Duke of Clarence, whose bust is in the entrance hall (which has a glowing tilework fireplace). The architect was Huon A. Matear; the style, eclectically forbidding with much indefinably historical ornament. In the gable, carving of Richard II giving the first Civic Sword to Mayor William Selby. The side of the building enjoys its freedom from symmetrical restraint; the back is marvellous townscape from the bridges and the other side of the river.

The York Institute of Arts and Sciences, by W.G. Penty, 1883, is in Waterhousian brick and terracotta; Romanesque, topped by a faience arcade and pepper pots. The S.S. Empire (wrestling) was opened in 1902 as York New Grand Opera House, designed by John Briggs. Its original decorations survive, vulgarized, unlikely to be visited by many readers.

On the other side of Clifford Street the Rechabite Buildings are at least partly – probably wholly – by Penty, 1883. Low parti-coloured brick with terra-cotta parapet and ventilators from the 'Wizard of Oz'; high, lushly moulded brick and terra-cotta over excellent cast-ironwork.

The Friends Meeting House, in inventive if unattractive Low-Countries-Renaissance style, is by W.H. Thorpe, Leeds, 1884. Behind, the delicately understated Meeting House (1816–19) by Watson and Pritchett had simple scrubbed benches and balustraded galleries on cast-iron columns, one of York's best interiors. Ingenuities of the original heating system undermined the foundations: demolition was inevitable.

Castlegate to Coppergate

Friargate leads furtively to Castlegate, originally part of Nessgate, largely Georgian, run-down but recoverable. It was the main route until Clifford Street was cut through, leading to one of the Castle Gates, then out of the city by the cranky course of Tower Street. Sir Walter Scott stayed in the street with William Alexander. Of the minor houses, No. 11 has a grand doorcase whose scale is pompously reflected in the 1951 Festival Flats. Two great Georgian houses, both by John Carr, flank the Castle end of the street.

Fairfax House was built for Charles, Viscount Halifax, *c.* 1755–65. The elevation is a mere wraith; pediment pruned of its ornament, window surrounds severly cut back, ironwork gone, and the original doorcase replaced by a miserable successor. Inside, it has the finest plasterwork, the grandest staircase, and some of the richest woodwork in the city. The plasterwork varies from the Palladian coved and coffered ceiling of one of the upstairs Saloons to the delightful flower-trails of the other. The entrance hall leads – between rooms with more exquisite ceilings – to the staircase at right-angles; Palladian compartmenting under the landing but a charming oval figure-panel on the wall, ironwork by Maurice Tobin, Corinthian Venetian window, great Rococo wall brackets, presumably for busts, lovely doorcases on the landing, and a great coved and trophied ceiling. The condition of these glorious interiors is a disgrace to the city. At least the ripping out of walls and fireplaces happened before their qualities were appreciated; the tasteless horrors to which the present tenants have subjected them for two decades did not.

The low building with entertaining chimneys, just before the Castle wastelands, was Robinson and Andrews's York office. Behind, unregarded, a funny weatherboarded building on Gothic brackets.

Castlegate House [42], 1762–3, was designed by Carr for Peter Johnson, Recorder of York; much more up to date (and much better looked after) than Fairfax House opposite. Windows under arches, with little balustrades beneath, were a favourite Carr motif, so were the tall – in this case four–storeyed – canted bays of the garden front. Handsome staircase behind a screen of columns. Doorcases and the Saloon ceiling show the move towards the Adam style.

St Mary Castlegate, like several other York churches, has

had a convoluted development, but nowhere else has the process been so oddly arrested as here. An inscribed foundation stone of the early 11th century (discovered at Butterfield's restoration of 1868–70) says that the church, called a 'Mynster', was founded by Efrard Grim and Aese, but cross fragments of a century earlier and said to come from St Mary's are in the Yorkshire Museum. If anything remains of the 11th-century church (if indeed the inscription refers to St Mary's at all), it is the rough stonework flanking the chancel arch, S of which, on the E face, is a Norman window head. The lower jambs of an arch N of the chancel are also early 12th century. The N nave arcade includes material of the mid 12th century (a scalloped capital) and the S arcade of the early 13th (nailhead capitals). If Butterfield's restoration is reliable there was a large chapel N of the chancel by the 1340s. It was in the 15th century that work became curiously disorganized. Most of the chancel was rebuilt (but the tall narrow moulded arches are probably 16th-century cut through previously blank walls); so were the aisle walls, the windows with battlemented transomes; so was the chancel arch and the W arch of the N chapel, but this cuts across behind the E respond of the nave arcade left apparently irresolvably in space. The massive W tower and spire were probably built outside the old W wall and the westmost bays of the arcade widened to link up the old and new work; the transition from square to octagon in the tower does not attempt any subtleties. There are remains of other medieval structures W of the N aisle and E of the S chapel. Early-14th-century glass has three saints, three charming crowned heads, and a panel of fleurs-de-lis. A few minor 18th-century monuments remain. Butterfield designed the furniture, which was dispersed when the building was converted into the Heritage Centre, now called 'The York Story', in 1974–5. The architects were George Pace and Ronald Sims; the designer James Gardner. It has proved a curious venture. The drawings, models, paintings are pretty enough; the attempts at 'period' pathetic; the scholarship not infallible; the more sophisticated electronic elements unreliable. Recording the architectural development of the city with scarcely a single *real* architectural or historical object in sight, where so much was readily available, and putting design and theme before evidence leaves it an enjoyable misconception.

Coppergate (Coopers or a reference to Danish copper furnaces) is largely Edwardian. Habitat is half 1908, with faience ladies holding up an oriel, half *c.* 1902 by Hornsey and Monkman with peacock panels. The Three Tuns has a lovely, wayward timbered front and nice, old-fashioned interior. Excavation by York Archaeological Trust before re-development on Nos. 16–22 Coppergate located several Viking-age timber buildings on the street frontage, standing up to 6 ft in height and amongst the best surviving domestic building from anywhere in the Viking world. Their layout on narrow property running back from the street towards the River Foss influenced all subsequent property boundaries up to the present day. It is hoped eventually to re-erect the buildings in a museum near by, incorporating as many as possible of the original timbers. More Victorianized and Victorian half-timbering towards Pavement, a facing on the remains of medieval buildings.

High Ousegate to Tower Place

All Saints' church Pavement is mentioned in Domesday Book. Early evidences are an Anglo-Scandinavian graveslab with Jellinge-type ornament of the early 10th century, and a group of unusually fine early-12th-century glazed tiles, found when the vestry was demolished and now in the Yorkshire Museum. It is one of the most unified churches in York, rebuilt in the last quarter of the 14th century and intended to have a semi-cruciform plan with a crossing but 'transepts' not projecting beyond the aisles. This may have been abandoned in favour of a W tower in the early 15th century; the 15th-century clerestory ignores the 'crossing'. The tower is the distinguishing feature outside, bluntly square to roof level, elegantly open and octagonal above, with the same kind of attenuated cresting as the E end of the

Minster. Subtlety of transition between the two stages is not attempted (John Shaw improved on this when he modified the design for St Dunstan-in-the-West, Fleet Street, 1833) and the design was probably based – like Castlegate and North Street spires – on the Friars' churches. The chancel was removed in 1782; the E wall rebuilt 1887 by Fisher and Hepper. Door knocker, probably 13th-century, a lion swallowing what is persistently described as a 'woman' though this person has a beard. The fine pulpit on a chalice base was made by Nicholas Hall in 1634. Four good windows by Kempe; enthusiasts will enjoy searching for wheatsheaves or, in the case of the E window, the arms of Cardinal Kempe. Monument to Tate Wilkinson (see Theatre Royal, Walk 3); several medieval brasses and a half length 17th-century figure brass without inscription. Fittings from St Crux and St Saviour's have been incorporated: a 15th-century lectern from the former, the desk largely original; several sets of benefaction and mayoral boards and Royal Arms. The late-14th-century glass in the W window is from St Saviour's church; small saints and a series of Passion panels, the 'nailing' and 'deposition' especially good; the Ascension has a pair of feet disappearing into the canopy. Lenses found in the tower lend credence to the pleasant story of a lantern to guide travellers at night through the Forest of Galtres. The charger on which St John the Baptist's head was given to Salome is said to have been here until *c.* 1386.

High Ousegate is a hump-backed street, starting with Barclays Bank by Edmund Kirby of Liverpool, 1901, granite, faience and brick in shades of pink, impervious to decay. Its original riot of dormers and turrets has been trimmed. Two remarkable houses follow, battered and confusingly dated 1762 and 1758, they belong to the rebuilding of Ousegate in the very early 18th century after a fire in 1694; centrepieces with giant orders and distinctly Mannerist window surrounds, originally above rusticated ground floors. The upper part of a house of 1743 is much tamer. Habitat has an ebullient front of *c.* 1902 by Hornsey and Monkman, with exceptionally elegant Art Nouveau shopfront, slim uprights, bevelled glass and dull-mirrored ceilings to the arcades. The Midland Bank at the corner is by J.B. and W. Atkinson with subtly varied stonework textures, and the Coach and Horses on the other side of Nessgate is – at least in part – by Bromet and Thorman of Tadcaster (1910), architects responsible for some undervalued but very original Gothic–Art Nouveau furniture of just before the First World War (Tadcaster and Bramham churches).

St Michael Spurriergate is four-square and dull outside, the S wall rebuilt and the E set back in 1821, the N side rebuilt in 1867–8, the tower taken down (1965–70) after the foundations had been found not so much inadequate as non-existent. Some old stonework and a 15th-century door survive in the W wall, and a pretty, gilded clock face towards Low Ousegate. Beautiful interior, restored by George Pace [25] and cleared of all clutter. The arcades of *c.* 1180, doubled in height in the 15th century using old arches and waterleaf capitals, which were copied for the W tower piers, dive inconsequentially into the E wall. At the W end the tower arch soars above the flat ceiling, which tilts up to accommodate it. The reredos is early-18th-century with sumptuous carved communion rails, and the NE porch is another outstanding 18th-century piece with added, oval Royal Arms. Mayoral boards of George II and George III; a glass topped box of pewter flagons and dishes; a glass fronted case with Charles II stamped-leather altar frontal. Chalice brass to William Langton, d. 1466, one of only four in Yorkshire. Brass to William Shaw, d. 1681, signed by Joshua Mann. Monuments include John Wood, d. 1704, flat, architectural in coloured marble; Katherine Coppinger, d. 1763, with serpentine front; William Hutchinson, d. 1772, one of Fisher's finest works, a sarcophagus with urn and putto, exquisite detail, yet strongly architectural.

There is medieval stained glass in seven windows, three fragmentary; and some of the lights have flashed, engraved panels of the early 19th century, one in the N aisle E window signed John Barnett. Most of the 15th-century glass is in the S aisle. From the W: eight panels including St Margaret and Noah with more green glass than is usual in York; a Jesse-tree, figures on red and blue backgrounds, King David with a harp; the Orders of Angels, Angels and Archangels share a panel; the E window has a large figure of St John the Baptist and a reconstructed panel of 'a woman clothed with the sun', above the fall of Lucifer, remarkable for the jewels of coloured glass 'annealed' to the borders of St John's robe and the vesica, a rare and highly sophisticated medieval technique.

William Fairfax lived in Low Ousegate in the 13th century; it was widened in the 18th century and again at the rebuilding of Ouse Bridge, 1810–20 (Walk 7). The best things are Chennel's wine shop, the Wine Lodge off a little court behind, and two cast-iron cats climbing a building opposite.

Steps from Ouse Bridge lead to King's Staithe, the centre of the city's medieval, maritime commerce which died away with the coming of larger vessels in the 16th century and the establishment of Hull's pre-eminence. It has the best of York's riverside, cobbles, ramps, hefty nautical ironwork (recent victim of Civic Trust's gilt complex), a warehouse with iron palisade above amorphous medieval corbels. The King's Arms, dated 1898 but older, has a simpering portrait of Richard III. King Street, formerly Kergate, has gloomy Victorian grandeur and good floorscape.

Cumberland House, very early-18th-century, built for Alderman William Cornwall, has strong top and inter-mediate cornices, the central windows linked into a stone, vertical feature (as at Middlethorpe Hall, Walk 15), a basement, and door (pedimented on magnificent consoles) in Cumberland Street as a protection against flooding. Good contemporary interiors.

The Police Station, early-Victorian Friar's Terrace, and the later South Esplanade are above the massively buttressed river wall of the Franciscan Friary, built *c.* 1290. At the end is the 'Davy Tower' – from which a chain could be stretched to the Crane Tower – the upper part of which is a Summer House of *c.* 1735. The wall turns at right angles, becoming the least intimidating part of the city's defences, interesting as retaining its narrow wall walk. Behind is Tower Place [44], a charming Regency enclave, bow windows, pretty doorcases and gardens, and the intermittent threat of flooding.

Beyond Skeldergate Bridge (Walk 7) is St George's Field, named after the Templars' Chapel of St George, now an unhappy patch of tarmacadam where every citizen once had the right to walk, dry linen, and shoot with bow and arrow. The New Walk was first set out in 1730–4 and extended downstream in 1739 after the building of the first 'Blue Bridge'. John Carr's Pikeing Well, 1756, is a rough stone grotto with a fringe of Norman (and possibly Roman) antiquities. Back towards the city, along St George's Field, when the pantechnicons are not too thick, York's finest medieval skyline marvellously unravels itself.

Clifford's Tower, The Castle Museum, and Debtors' Prison are open daily. (See leaflet in Tourist Office for times.) The only easy way of access to the Assize Courts is to attend a trial. The York Story is open weekdays 10.00–17.00, Sundays, 13.00–17.00. Those with strong stomachs and nerve can see the staircase of Fairfax House. All Saints' Pavement is usually open; St Michael Spurriergate intermittently so.

Walk Seven

Skeldergate Bridge to Bishophill Senior

The foundation stone of Skeldergate Bridge was laid in 1878, after only five years of civic deliberation. Learning from their initial mistakes at Lendal Bridge, the Corporation obtained designs from Thomas Page, which were later modified by his son George. Its ironwork is more elegant, less adventurous than Lendal Bridge, with three river spans – one of the narrower ones opening to admit ships to the staithes upstream, others to the riverside walks on either side. The pretty toll-house is a great improvement on the Lendal ones and the far-flung outworks stretching into Clifford Street and Skeldergate are much grander. The bridge was opened in 1881. It is visually the best river-crossing in York, aligned on the turret of the Debtor's Prison with good views both upstream past the staithes to Ouse Bridge and downstream along the New Walk.

Skeldergate is the saddest of York streets. In 1945 it was still handsome though undeniably tatty. Since then John Carr's own house, damaged during the war, the 16th-century Plumbers' Arms, a 17th-century Dutch-gabled warehouse, and several Georgian houses have been de-molished, a fate likely to have overtaken Albion Chapel by the time this book is published. Minor demolitions and set-backs for road improvement have left the street open from end to dispiriting end, each preceded by ineffective protest and succeeded by equally ineffective attempts to tidy-up the mess. The name may derive from *skialdari* ('shieldmaker') or from *skelde* or shelf from its position above the river, though neither derivation is entirely convincing.

A few good things remain. The Bonding Warehouse

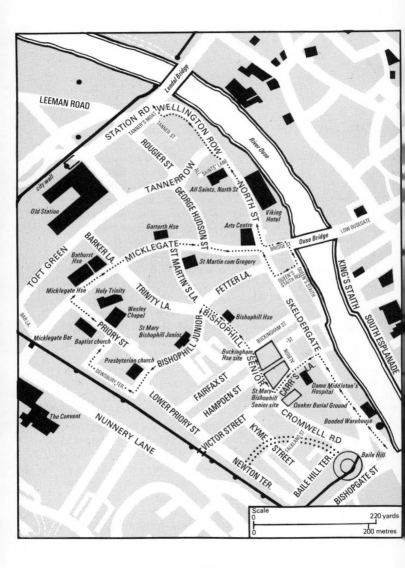

(1875) by George Styan, the city surveyor, is a splendid piece in restrained, polychromatic brickwork; tough, but with a few festive touches along the skyline. John Henry Cattley's saw-mill, of 1839, is real 'Functional Tradition'; big arched openings at the bottom, bullseyes at the top. No. 56 is a grand house of *c.*1775, possibly by Carr; big pediment with urns; Doric doorcase with idiosyncratic details like octagonal panels; detached cornices float over first-floor windows (cf. No. 47 Bootham, by Carr). The carriage entrance knocked through one side is hardly sensitive. The saloon has a charming contemporary ceiling, asymmetrical trails composed into a symmetrical whole.

Middleton's Hospital, founded 1659, originally stood on the street – its 'ghost' is seen on the side wall of No. 56 – but it was rebuilt, severely classical, behind a terrace, to Peter Atkinson Junior's designs, 1827–9. The statue of its founder, Mrs Middleton – with Puritan hat – probably comes from the earlier building. The Joseph Terry Almshouse (1899) is a delightful Arts and Crafts design by Penty and Penty; canted bays, little sloping buttresses, and beautifully detailed ironwork to the street.

Beyond the expensively ineffective sub-station (on the site of John Carr's house) are, while it survives, the gaunt carcase of Albion Chapel, 1816, designed by the Revd John Nelson; the Cock and Bottle dismally enshrining bits of its splendid predecessor, the Plumbers' Arms – where pleasant legend has it that the Duke of Buckingham conducted his chemical experiments – and the ravaged backs of riverside warehouses.

Skeldergate has associations both with *Robinson Crusoe* and with Wilkie Collins's *No Name.*

Carr's Lane, formerly one of several Kirk Lanes, renamed because of its association with the architect, was the most magical of York alleys, a strip of paving through cobbles, tight between high brick walls, trees high up behind a fence in Bishophill churchyard, a little cottage growing out of the wall at a kink in the path; uphill to the Golden Ball, a Cecil Aldin pub, or downhill to the Lawcourts skyline across the river it was a total delight. The fence has been smartened up;

the trees are fewer, the walls lower; the little cottage has been replaced by well-meant flats. The magic has irretrievably gone.

St Mary, Bishophill Senior, one of the most ancient of the city churches, was first mentioned *c.* 1190, but excavation has revealed a much earlier Christian site and the name may imply an earlier foundation than the neighbouring Bishophill Junior. The church had work ranging from the 10th to the 15th century, a brick tower of 1659, and extensive restoration by J.B. and W. Atkinson (1859–60, only 16 years before losing its parish to St Clement's). The wreck was demolished in 1963; what could be was incorporated in Holy Redeemer, Acomb. John Flaxman was baptized here (1755). The graves of Peter Atkinson Senior, architect, and Richard Chicken, one of the models for Mr Micawber, have vanished.

On the other side of Carr's Lane, one passed, until recently, through a cottage garden into a Quaker burial ground of exquisite serenity, surrounded by lime trees and old walls, and furnished with little round-topped grave-stones, commemorating, among others, John Woolman, friend of Benjamin Franklin and early advocate for the abolition of slavery, members of the Tuke family, and Lindley Murray, grammarian. Good intentions have been as fatal as any bulldozer. It must have seemed humane to build old-people's flats, give them a terrace and some flower beds, and tidy away unwelcome reminders of mortality. One of the most moving sights in York has gone, and we are left with a little green patch not quite big enough.

Bishophill lies on level, 'high' ground between Micklegate and the walls. After pages of complaint it comes as a pleasant change. Victorian terraced streets, respected by their owners, are enhanced by cheerful colour schemes; post-war development is no better than elsewhere, but there is less of it. Its earliest recorded name was Bichill, meaning 'bitch hill' for no obvious reason; the alternative Bishophill (from the mid 13th century) seems to be connected with land owner-ship by the Archbishops.

Cromwell Road was formerly narrower and called Gaol Lane. The Gaol designed by Peter Atkinson Junior (1802–7), on the site of the Old Baile, was demolished in 1880. Victor Street (late-17th-century Old Rectory, dilapidated, with pilasters and a coved cornice) was called Lounlithgate in the Middle Ages, from the Lounlith ('hidden gate'), a small postern in the walls, whose remains were uncovered when Victoria Bar was opened (1838) to serve the growing suburbs in Nunnery Lane.

Bishophill Senior, the street, runs along the crest of the ridge above the river, turning sharp left into Bishophill Junior. At the corner of Buckingham Street (mid-19th-century houses, classically restrained) stood one of York's grandest 17th-century houses, Fairfax or Buckingham House, built by Thomas Fairfax, whose daughter married George Villiers, Duke of Buckingham, in 1657. Though demolished in the early 18th century, its high, multi-gabled skyline is familiar in early views of the city.

The old houses in Bishophill are sadly neglected. Bishophill House, early-18th-century, four-bay, had two extra bays and a grand Ionic doorcase added *c.* 1740. The saloon (*c.* 1765) had the most sumptuous of York's Rococo ceilings (now in Peasholme House) and a bow overlooking the river, semi-circular, stark, with bronze sashes, like something by Le Corbusier.

Fetter Lane ('Felt Lane', 1344), St Martin's Lane, still with some townscape quality, and Trinity Lane join untidily. Trinity Lane has been ravaged. No. 29 survives, a tall 17th-century building, altered, with an Arts and Crafts wing added by Penty and Penty *c.* 1895, which has tall dormers at the back ending in pom-poms. Tuke House, where William and Esther Tuke started their boarding school for girls, for which Lindley Murray wrote his *Grammar*, was demolished in 1961.

Bishophill Junior to Priory Street

Where Bishophill Junior and Senior meet stands Cooke, Troughton, and Simms factory, by Brierley, 1916, combining Arts and Crafts and Functional Tradition elements, carefully detailed, black brick below, red above, large windows with thin relieving arches, trapezoidal gables.

St Mary, Bishophill Junior, below the road in a crescent-shaped churchyard, displays its antiquity more publicly than any other York church [7]. The base of the tower is 10th-century, built fairly regularly of Roman *saxa-quadrata* below a band of less regular limestone, gritstone, and herringbone masonry. The top stage, later, but still pre-Conquest, is in large gritstone bocks with very characteristic two-light belfry windows with balusters, strip pilasters, and enclosing arches. The tower probably formed the 'nave' of the original church, and traces of the 'chancel' can be seen inside flanking the equally characteristic arch. The church suffered 'an unintelligent and destructive restoration externally', according to the *Ecclesiologist*, 1861; the architects were J.B. and W. Atkinson; the effects are still apparent. The interior has fared much better; low, comfortable, spreading, its country atmosphere is unexpected. The tower arch is one of the best of pre-Conquest arches. The N arcade is standard mid-12th-century work; the chancel, 13th-century (one lancet), extended eastwards *c.* 1300, and the S arcade is a remarkable creation of *c.* 1330, the arches richly moulded with deep hollows, but wide, low, and almost triangular in outline. The chancel chapel is contemporary with this (very thin column) and the nave roof is 15th-century with modern bosses. There are several pieces of Anglian cross-shaft, medieval bells awaiting rehanging, a medieval font with a cover of *c.* 1700, a Royal Arms of 1793, two splendid chancel chairs, and a little 15th-century glass showing St Michael, the Virgin in Glory, and two Archbishops. The reredos and other fittings are by Temple Moore, their electric-blue decor, one must hope, temporary.

Holy Trinity Priory, Micklegate, was granted to Leonard Beckwith in 1542. Its site remained open ground until sold for building in the 1850s. G.T. Andrews produced a scheme for houses round an oval garden, 'Priory Gardens', but a street must have seemed more economical and Priory Street was the result. Nos. 8 and 10, and 31 and 38, are recognizably in Andrews's style, and are shown on Whittock's *View of York*,

1858, as is also Dewsbury Terrace, a charming backwater, lovingly maintained, its small railed gardens facing the walls. Dewsbury Cottages are humbler, with a sidelong view of the turrets on Micklegate Bar. Other houses are later and less attractive.

Like St Saviourgate, Priory Street became a centre of Nonconformity. The Presbyterians have the dullest chapel (1879, by T.B. Thompson, Hull), grey brick, pilastered. It has lost its tower, like the Baptist Chapel, by William Peachey of Darlington (1868), a building with an unpromisingly coarse exterior – though Mr Peachey's watercolour in the vestry makes it appear quite attractive – but a charming cast-iron Gothic interior, with roses among the gallery cusps. The Wesleyan Chapel (1854), chapel cottages, and original school (1858) are by James Simpson of Leeds, like Centenary Chapel, and the change in style from Grecian to Italianate is instructive. It is much the most handsome of the group; dark brick, plenty of stone dressings, the aedicules to the upper windows Michelangelesque, especially in sharp perspective. The interior keeps to the pattern of Centenary but without its flair and delicacy. Chapel cottages were for the head-master and the chapel keeper, with a nice social distinction between the door-surrounds. T. Monkman and Sons' school extension (1905) is a worthwhile, Arts and Crafts design. Beyond the Chapel, Hodgson Fowler's scholarly W front of Holy Trinity Priory (1902–3) edges uneasily into this Nonconformist scene. The 13th-century Priory Gatehouse stood at the end of the street until 1854.

Micklegate

Apart from the county families whose town houses are among its glories, Micklegate had associations with many interesting York personalities. The families of both Charles Watson, the naturalist, and J.A. Hansom, architect, founder of the *Builder*, and designer of the Hansom Cab, lived at 114. Edmund and Henry Gyles, glass painters, both lived at 68. J.B. and W. Atkinson had their offices just below St

Martin-cum-Gregory churchyard, and both Peter Atkinson Junior and Hargrove the historian lived at 38. Micklegate (*Myglagata*, 'the great street', recorded from the 12th century), the handsomest of York streets but not the best (see Stonegate), runs in a long, swinging S curve steeply sloping in the middle stretch, where setts make a welcome change from tarmacadam. Visitors should try walking it in both directions; the experiences are quite different. It passes through the Roman *colonia*, though not on a Roman alignment since it links Micklegate Bar to Ouse Bridge and not the abandoned Roman crossing near the Guildhall. The ends of the street have suffered but the middle remains – one trusts – inviolably splendid.

Micklegate Bar presides at the top, its rather too regular back by Peter Atkinson Junior, 1827, then Victorian and Georgian elevations, as often in York hiding earlier work, and a few recent intruders. Shops keep interesting features, like the Rococo ceiling of 136. The pebble-dashed, 18th-century Coach and Horses compares favourably with its neighbours. No. 118 is one of the best of York's smaller Georgian houses. Sir William St Quintin, whose town house it was, described it as 'a very neat, convenient dwelling house'; it was built in the early 1740s for Robert Bower. Tall, narrow brick front with almost no dressings, and a nice reminder that not all Georgian doors were six-panelled and plain (the ground floor was reinstated in 1968). Excellent contemporary interiors; scrolly pedimented fireplace over-mantels with a painting by Adam Willaerts on the ground floor and a later 18th-century classical relief on the first floor; staircase with a marble floor in the basement.

The Nag's Head is 16th-century, half-timbered, refronted in the 18th century but keeping the old gable to the street. Nos. 94 and 96 were redeveloped in the 1840s; the Falcon was formerly a grander hostelry occupying the whole site. No. 92 has a discreet elevation of *c.* 1800, only a twirl of ironwork for ornament.

Micklegate House is the grandest house in the street, and the grandest of a group of mid-18th-century houses apt to be attributed to John Carr, for want of someone better, though there must have been architects working in York between William Etty's death in 1734 and Carr's first works in the early fifties. Nos. 53 and 55 Micklegate and 54, Peasholme House, and 39–45 Bootham all belong to this group. They have features in common; the big modillion cornices, bands at first-floor and first-floor cill levels, and a special sort of 'rustication' of longer blocks set slightly forward of shorter blocks. Micklegate House has a standard Corinthian door-case, set against a rusticated wall. The building is not quite symmetrical; the rustication interferes with the window arches at one end. The iron railings are swept round the steps to end in integral lamp brackets flanking the doorway. The interior has been sadly maltreated, but the planning must always have been curiously untidy for so ambitious a house. The staircase has the best remaining plasterwork, three sorts of balusters in rotation, and a heavy window surround. The best fireplace, a beautifully taut design, is now in the Treasurer's House. In the Library are two small stained-glass panels, signed by William Peckitt, of 'Rover', a greyhound, and 'Dick', a spaniel on a cushion.

Bathurst House (No. 86) is early-18th-century, with tall windows, the middle set slightly forward. The door is late-18th-century and the top storey was added in the 1820s, reusing the cornice and very handsome rainwaterhead. The curious hall doorcases have very flat elements and little consoles set against the walls and seem more likely to belong to the original house than to the Regency alterations, as suggested by the R.C.H.M. Staircase with double spiral balusters and a classical window surround, one column made longer than the other to get over a change in level – what would Lord Burlington have said?

The opposite side of the street presents earlier developments, Nos. 85–9 form a timber-framed range of *c.* 1500, twice jettied with battlemented bressumers. Stripping the traditional York rendering, and the replacement of old windows with modern casements, has left them mechanical in appearance. They were probably built for letting as butchers' shops by Holy Trinity Priory. Victorian shopfronts and a cast-iron Doric prop fortunately survive. No. 83 has a tiny Regency front, lovely crisp detail to the door; grinning lions' masks.

Holy Trinity Churchyard, at shoulder height to the street, is filled with trees and interesting lumps of masonry. The stocks are just inside the gate. The church, of pre-Conquest origin, was given by Ralph Paynel to Marmoutier, the Benedictine Abbey near Tours, in 1089. Parish rights continued to exist and there was a church of St Nicholas closely linked to the monastic church, which may simply have been its nave under another dedication. A substantial 11th-century church was badly damaged in the fire of 1137 – when it was described as 'Holy Trinity in the Suburbs', and rebuilt between *c.* 1180 and the middle of the 13th century. In 1453 the parishioners of St Nicholas were allowed to build their tower adjacent to the monastic W front, economically reusing some Norman windows – an early example of constructive conservation. Monks and parishioners were evidently on amicable terms; indeed, after the Monks had been ejected in 1536, their neighbours took the opportunity offered by the Pilgrimage of Grace to reinstate them. However, the Monks bowed to the inevitable in 1538 and the church became fully parochial instead of monastic. The tower fell, bringing down the chancel in February 1552, the clerestory was removed, the roof lowered, and a series of other prunings left nothing of the medieval exterior standing except St Nicholas's tower, and the N arcade was filled up with windows of the strangest approximation to 14th-century tracery. Pruning was followed by restoration in 1850 (J.B. and W. Atkinson), 1886, chancel (Fisher and Hepper), and 1902–5 (Hodgson Fowler), when the W front and porch were rebuilt, leaving the whole so full of loose ends that the only wonder is that it does not look worse. The massive early-Norman central tower piers are better seen outside than in. What is memorable inside is the masculine nobility of the 13th-century arcade. The triforium survives at the W end and the tower has fossilized a scrap of the clerestory on its outer wall. The arches are separated by slim shafts sharpened like pencils. The 16th-century roof incorporates earlier timber work.

In the porch are two 15th-century wooden bosses and an exquisite 12th-century capital: St Nicholas Chapel has a fragment of 11th-century carving, a waterleaf capital, a double-coped graveslab, and a 15th-century carving of the Trinity found in Delft in 1952, but said to have belonged to the church. The font and cover are from St Saviour's, the cover one of the best of the York group, dated 1717 on the upper tier and 1794 on the lower. Delightful cast-iron traceried safe; Hodgson Fowler reredos; Kempe glass in the E and W windows. Among many tablets the best perhaps are Elizabeth Anne, d.1760, and Elizabeth Scarisbrick, d. 1794, by Thomas Atkinson; the most interesting to Dr John Burton, author of *Monasticon Eboracensis*, immortalized as Dr Slop in *Tristram Shandy*, 'about four feet and a half perpendicular height, with a breadth of back and sesquiped-ality of belly, which might have done honour to a sergeant in the horse-guards' – a large scroll firmly anchored by a couple of books and an urn almost obliterating its Gothic back-ground.

At the corner of Trinity Lane is, behind a splendidly strategic chestnut, the Rectory (Brierley, *c.* 1898), with a wide variety of windows just under control; and round the corner 'Jacob's Well', a timber-framed house, inconsequen-tially finished off with a storey of white-washed brick. Isabel Warde, last Prioress of Clementhorpe, lived there after the Dissolution, and gave it to Holy Trinity church. It was the Jacob's Well Inn in the 19th century, and bought again for the church in 1904–5, when it was restored under the direction of Harvey Brook, who installed here almost the only survivor (from Davygate) of the late-medieval bracketed canopies that were once a common feature of the city's houses. (There is another in the Yorkshire Museum.)

Barker Lane was Gregory Lane until the 16th century, from a church of St Gregory made redundant in 1549. It leads to Toft Green, more interesting historically than aesthetically – except for the railway buildings. The line of the Roman road passed between it and Micklegate and extensive Roman remains were found when the Old Station was built. The open space was known both as the King's

Tofts (from a pre-Conquest Royal Palace) and Pageant Green, since it was here that the waggons and properties of the Corpus Christi Pageant Plays were kept in the 15th and 16th centuries. Next to Toft Green stood the Dominican Friary (Blackfriars) from 1227 to 1538.

After Nos. 78–84 Micklegate – a terrace by Peter Atkinson Junior, 1822 – both sides of the street have minor 18th- and 19th-century elevations, many of them concealing earlier work: Spelman's has pretty Regency bows above the shop-front; 75, connexions with the Cave family of artists; 67, an unreliable rainwaterhead of 1763; 57–9, with pretty Adamesque doorcases of *c.* 1783 (flanking a centre rather unhappily reconstructed in 1947), their exquisite detail clogged with dark-'blue' paint, is York's Labour Party's headquarters.

At this point in the street two grand Georgian houses face one another; 53 and 55 are of the early 1750s; Garforth House (No. 54) was being finished in 1757. Nos. 53 and 55 are the more obviously related to Micklegate House. Originally the elevation was symmetrical with a grand, orthodox Doric doorcase, which was doubled up, probably when the house was subdivided *c.* 1873, when the upper rooms were redecorated. The ground-floor room has original panelling and a Kentian, pedimented overmantel with some individual touches of detail. The staircase is one of the most memorable in York [40], Rococo decoration to the ceiling and walls all within geometrical framework and a splendid swag full width over the window. The landing is a *tour de force*, a Venetian opening under fragments of pediments leading into a vaulted lobby beyond; it is a composition of almost Mannerist concentration and energy, even overcoming the unspeakable vulgarity of its present colour scheme.

Garforth House, opposite, was the town house of the Garforths of Wigganthorpe Hall – where Carr was to work in the 1780s; there is a tradition that Carr designed it, but no positive evidence. The repertoire of features from Micklegate House is better handled here – with a full Doric entablature for the pediment, though the door surround still collides with the rustication; it was originally balanced by a servants' door whose spectral pediment can still be traced on the brickwork. The brick is a beautiful deep colour on the front, a lighter-coloured brick being used, as was often the case, for the back elevation (which may be studied from the upper stages of a neighbouring car park). The interior is beautifully maintained; panelled downstairs with rather linear treatment to the door and fireplace surrounds (cf. the Micklegate House fireplace in the Treasurer's House); staircase with Rococo Decoration concentrated round the Venetian window, and on the ceiling, free within a geometrical framework. The saloon ceiling has an ovalish centre within a rectangular frame, but this geometrical basis has melted away among the Rococo twiddles, leaving the exquisite result irresistably reminiscent of a superior iced cake; by contrast the door surrounds are among the most nobly classical in York.

No. 50 has an early-Victorian shopfront of solid merit, spreading over the first floor in a flat colonnade. Nos. 42–8 were built in 1747, when a Mithraic altar stone was found on the site.

Grey brick and polychromatic Victorian buildings overlook the pleasant chestnuts and old table tombs of St Martin-cum-Gregory churchyard.

St Martin-cum-Gregory, originally St Martin's, is one of the most interesting and attractive of York's churches, now the Diocesan Youth Office; its interior has been emptied of unnecessary fittings, without loss. Less restored than usual outside its varied textures of stone and old brickwork are as delightful as the cleared, whitewashed interior, its chancel grandly paved with ledger stones. It narrowly escaped destruction in the parochial reorganization of 1548 and was united with St Gregory's in 1549. Eleventh-century masonry survives at the E and W ends of the present nave arcades, and there are two fragments of Anglian cross built into the tower wall. Aisles were added early in the 13th century with arcades each of two wide bays. The N aisle was rebuilt *c.* 1340 (reticulated windows) projecting W from the old nave, suggesting there was already a tower; at the same time aisles

were built N (over an undercroft) and S of the chancel – the S
aisle E window probably belongs to one of these, but is not
necessarily *in situ.* In the second quarter of the 15th century
almost the whole of the chancel and its aisles was rebuilt to a
unified scheme, closely buttressed (a little richer on the N,
where it showed, than on the S, where it did not), and the S
aisle of the nave was rebuilt in line incorporating an older
porch at the W end. The N porch, 1655, is still Gothic; but the
brick tower of *c.* 1677 had a balustrade until the Atkinsons
restored it away in 1844–5, otherwise leaving well alone. The
S chapel roof is 15th-century; the nave roof, 16th; the
arrangements of the Rood-loft staircase can be seen better
than elsewhere in York. There are a series of interesting
stone shelves round the walls.

The 18th-century fittings are outstanding: reredos of
c. 1750 by Bernard Dickinson, Joiner, high pedimented
centre on Ionic pilasters between smaller pediments on
swept-back panels to fit them into the narrow spaces; altar
rails, 1753, with the characteristic York semi-circular middle
projection; early-18th-century brass chandelier; font cover;
poor box, and superb bread shelves, a columned and
pedimented niche with curved shelves on little triplets of
brackets; benefaction boards; leather fire buckets of 1794;
inscribed pulpit of 1636; Royal Arms of William and Mary.

Among the monuments, a Roman tombstone has two very
worn figures (another worn figure by the tower arch may
also be Roman); apart from two cartouches, the dilapidated
wall tablets are quite eclipsed by the splendid series of
chancel ledger stones: Susannah Beilby, d. 1664, with arms
and interesting lettering; Mary Peckitt, d. 1826, in the
middle of Henry Cattall's inscription of 1460; Mrs Bathurst,
d. 1724, with her coat of arms in a recess.

Many of the windows have medieval glass, much of it
fragmentary, but still worth the closest inspection; note
especially the two tiny, late-15th-century panels of the
Betrayal, and David and Goliath in a S chancel window. The
most complete medieval window is the E window of the S
aisle, of *c.* 1340, though even here the central panel of St
Martin dividing his cloak with a beggar is an interpolation

from a N aisle window. The side lights probably represent the Virgin and St John, part of a Crucifixion group, on backgrounds powdered with fleur-de-lis under excellent canopies, with censing angels in the tracery lights. North aisle E window has 14th-century panels of Our Lord and St Thomas. In the N aisle figures of St John Baptist and St Catherine of *c.* 1335 (restored by J.W. Knowles in 1899) flank very different glass. There was a considerable revival of interest in the making of stained glass in the late 17th and 18th centuries, and the two most notable York glass painters of the period, Henry Gyles (1645–1709) and William Peckitt (1731–95), are both buried here, Gyles in the churchyard, Peckitt in the chancel. Peckitt's memorial to his two daughters, signed and dated 1792, contrasting strangely with its 14th-century neighbours, shows Hope in a brown scarf, by an orange urn, pointing upwards to a child, who in turn points to some of father's roundels in the tracery. Mrs Peckitt was not to be outdone; in another window, another orange urn is inscribed to Peckitt's memory 'designed and executed by his afflicted widow, 1796'; the side lights are filled with geometrical patterns made up from Peckitt's experiments in producing coloured glass.

In the next window E one of the quarries is scratched with the inscription 'I hope this may be a place for true protestants to resort to and never to be ruled by Papists. God Bless King George ye 2d and Billy of Cumberland Whome God long preserve', and another, 'Our Noble Duke Great Georges Son who Beat ye Rebels near Culloden the 16th Day of April 1746'.

The bottom of Micklegate has suffered sadly. The Co-operative Stores is not a success, straight, horizontal, unsympathetic, replacing curving, vertical, irregular timber-framed houses. One would like to think that it could not happen now. The other side of the street has fared better, but the loss, even if it does prove temporary, of the Queen's Hotel is very hard to bear.

Cromwell Hotel has an excellent mid-Victorian pub elevation and Art Nouveau shopfront set on to an older house. (A particularly luscious ceiling rose in the first-floor room.) The Crown has strangely blank architecture to its upper storeys.

The Queen's Hotel site remains forlorn. Its promised reconstruction is awaited with increasing pessimism. The two houses were built for Henry Thompson and Alderman Richard Thompson and were finished *c.* 1727. Shops and an hotel front, both nicely old fashioned, took up the ground floor, below two long ranges of not quite even windows. One house had been much redecorated but kept the dome of the staircase well, dissociated in the attic, a marvellous space beneath a great bracketed cornice. The Queen's Hotel kept much original panelling culminating in the superb saloon [38], a room of remarkable splendour; Corinthian pilasters, flanking the piled-up friezes and panellings of the overmantel, articulating the wall panelling, and supporting a sumptuous entablature.

St John's church was closed in 1934, restored by York Civic Trust, became in turn the Institute of Advanced Architectural Studies, and York Arts Centre. Partitioning for architectural education and the paraphernalia of Drama have confused its interior. The church was first mentioned in 1194. Its core is the base of a late-12th-century tower attached to the end of a slightly earlier nave; the Norman W window and the heads of two others remain. A S aisle was added in the 13th century (part of one pillar) and a N aisle in two stages in the 14th, the eastmost arch associated with a chantry founded by Richard de Toller in 1320, the others much later in the century. In the mid 15th century the S aisle was widened and rebuilt and a new wall reconstructed on a slanting line to the W of the old tower, which was blown down in 1552; the half-timbered belfry (1646) is a rare example of church building under the Parliamentarians. The E wall was rebuilt when North Street was widened in 1850 (George Fowler Jones, architect) and the S wall largely renewed by J.B. and W. Atkinson, 1866. There are four medieval bells and two 17th-century ones; indents for brasses and a 15th-century table tomb. (The medieval glass was moved to the Minster in 1939; the late-15th-century lectern is at Upper Poppleton.)

Lanes off Skeldergate or the steps from Ouse Bridge lead to Queen's Staithe, built 1660 by Alderman Topham, and reconstructed *c.* 1810 to deal with the coal trade. Cobbled with massive stone revettments to the river it still deals with barges rather than pleasure boats. Some riverside buildings have been rehabilitated a little too genteelly. 'T. H. Wood', with vast brick gable and iron-latticed windows, and 'Varvill's', a towering confection of arches (J.B. and W. Atkinson, 1849), deserve a little better.

Old Ouse Bridge and St William's Chapel, subjects of countless paintings and engravings, must have been among the city's most picturesque features. A wooden bridge collapsed in 1154 under the crowds welcoming the return of William Fitzherbert as Archbishop; his prayers proved prophylactic and no one was killed. William was canonized in 1227 and the chapel on the new stone bridge was rededicated to him the following year. (There are some remains of the chapel, which stood on the side of Boyes Store, in the Yorkshire Museum). In 1565 two of the arches were destroyed by melting ice piled against the piers and the famous single arch with its 81 ft span, as structurally daring as it was picturesque, was built in their stead, with the help of Thomas Harper of London. At the end of the 18th century the advantages of rebuilding or widening were canvassed, and on the advice of Thomas Harrison of Chester it was decided to rebuild. Peter Atkinson Junior, having already won a competition for widening the bridge, was appointed designer. The new bridge was built 1810–20, the old bridge retained while half the new one, split lengthways, was built alongside; the division can still be seen beneath. It is a spare, elegant design, niches on the piers between elliptical arches; a long gently curving parapet without balustrades.

Bridge Street is short and apart from the 1911 faience of Boyes Store uneventful. Like Low Ousegate on the other side of the river it was widened at the rebuilding of Ouse Bridge. Minor buildings of the 1820s remain on the downstream side.

North Street to Lendal Bridge

North Street has been North Street since the late 12th century, though what exactly it was north of is a matter for speculation. Narrow, dark, furtive, a muddle of warehouses, little yards, alleys to the waterside (one of which was Dublinstones – *Divelinstaynes* – commemorating Anglo-Scandinavian commerce with Dublin), a dealer in Baroque picture frames, a ceiling admired by Queen Mary; it was the untidy epitome of a riverside street. It was swept away in the 1960s (the ceiling found a home in the King's Manor), to be replaced by a riverside walk, which has the merit of having made everyone think twice about putting one on the other side of the river; a fussy garden and the painfully solid Viking Hotel, which dominates so many views without contributing to any.

Father Shaw was incumbent of All Saints, North Street, from 1904 to 1950. During that time the church acquired a confusion of little altars, images, candlesticks and old carpets, pictures and devotional objects of every description, altogether too much, and it was dark and rather grubby; but it was the most moving church interior in York; a church to bring you to your knees. By 1975 the structure was giving cause for concern and there was a real danger of the church closing. York Civic Trust offered to restore the structure but also dealt with the interior, tidying and redecorating, and this work was carried out in what seems to have been unnecessary haste, especially where it came to dealing with the conflicting opinions of experts on medieval painted decoration. Some visitors may enjoy the result; the author no longer feels it necessary to speak in a hushed whisper.

Development was complex. The R.C.H.M traces it back to an aisleless cell, given a S aisle in the late 12th century, developing a cruciform plan in the early 13th (one late-12th-century column S of nave; two early-13th-century ones in N arcade, one incorporating a Roman gritstone column; in SE corner of the chancel is a fragment of 13th-century arcading). The E end was reconstructed, 1320–40, new chapels with reticulated windows flanking the chancel. In the

early 15th century the aisles were widened and the arcades
further amended, then in the middle of the century the very
elegant tower and spire were built on amazingly slender
piers inside; and the whole church lengthened westwards by
two bays. The growth pattern recalls St Mary's, Castlegate.
The chancel and chapels have much the best of York's
surviving medieval church roofs, all 15th-century with
arched braces on very short hammer beams with angels; the
N aisle has the best carving; the chancel, the controversial
new colour scheme.

Monuments include brasses to William Stockton, d. 1471,
and Robert Colynson, d. 1458 (both mayors), Thomas Clerk,
d. 1482 (with evangelical symbols), Thomas Askwith, d.
1609, and Thomas Atkinson, Tanner, d. 1642, a half-length
figure praying; numerous 13th- and 14th-century sepul-
chral slabs and 18th-century ledgers; cartouche to William
Etty, architect, d. 1708.

Fittings include an alabaster of the Resurrection, a
misericord of a pelican in her piety, and a limestone head
and shoulders of a woman, all 15th-century; a pulpit of 1675
with painted panels, benefaction boards, and mayoral board
of 1723. The possible remains of Mr Etty's reredos were
removed at the restoration. The chancel screens by Edwin
Ridsdale Tate, 1906, show real medieval flair in adapting
their tracery patterns to irregular arch forms.

The church has some of the finest medieval glass in the
city. Wailes restored the E windows in 1844, somewhat
drastically; the 1965 restoration of one window in the S aisle
has been quite as aggressive. The windows are dealt with
anticlockwise, starting in the S aisle (several are not in their
original positions) and most of the glass is of the early 15th
century. *1* St James, the Virgin, and a priest saying Mass, an
exquisite panel, the head amazingly perfect. *2* The 'Nine
Orders of Angels'. Before restoration this was a muddle of
glorious fragments. Speculation on its subject ended with
the discovery in the Bodleian of a drawing (1640) by Henry
Johnston, and the window was reconstructed with much new
plain glass; honest, but one feels ungrateful; some of the
colours set the teeth on edge. Incidental joys, exquisite heads

and a robe in the left light, remain. *3* St Michael and St John the Evangelist over figures of donors. *4* South aisle E window, mid-14th-century glass, much restored, small canopied subject panels against quarries, Crucifixion group with the Virgin and St John, above the 'Agony in the Garden' and Donors. *5* The E window, moved from the N aisle, was given by members of the Blackburn family who kneel flanking the Trinity, beneath large figures of St John the Baptist, St Anne, and the Virgin and St Christopher. Wailes glass in the tracery. *6* North aisle E window, formerly the E window. Early-14th-century panels of the life of Christ (of which the Adoration of the Magi and the Resurrection are the least restored) under more adventurous canopies than those in the S aisle. *7* One of the most fascinating and least attractive of York windows, donors crowded beneath panels representing the last 15 days of the world, the most terrifying of prospects represented with the utter simplicity that must have attended the original presentation of the Mystery Plays. Aesthetics were clearly subservient to the narrative based on the 14th-century poem 'The Pricke of Conscience'. The window almost certainly by John Thornton of Coventry. *8* The six Corporal Acts of Mercy, but neither the canopies nor the donor panels belong with the beautiful and very well preserved subject panels, the bearded gentleman dispensing charity with just a touch of irony in his expression. *9* Large figures of Our Lord, St Thomas the Apostle, and perhaps St Thomas Becket; delightful canopies with little figures playing among the crockets, the prophets in niches in the borders. *10* Heraldic glass and more canopies.

At the W end of the church, the Anchorage, by Ridsdale Tate (*c.* 1910), is part of Father Shaw's improvements; half-timbered at the front, shuttered concrete at the back.

All Saints' Cottages are late-15th-century, the gable end to North Street, timber-framed; a good carved corner post with brattishing and roses. Beyond a little Regency house is more timber-framing with another carved post on the corner of Tanner Row, where the Old Rectory is again half-timbered

(17th-century staircase with carved newels imported at a restoration of 1937).

Wellington Row commands a good view of the riverside opposite. Lendal Bridge, the Yorkshire Club, Lendal Chapel, the Council Offices and Guildhall, owing more to E.G. Mawbey (1888–9) than Robert Couper (1447–8), the 'Venetian' building beyond the Herald Printing Works, and the new back of W.H. Smith's all contribute happily.

In Tanner's Moat the two Moorish arches are the remains of Botterills Horse Repository (W.G. Penty, *c.* 1880), whose vital ugliness was infinitely preferable to its horrid successor looming in Rougier Street. It was suggested that it was the ugliest building in Europe but there was then less competition.

The city walls provide a convenient return route.

☆

St Mary Bishophill Junior is locked (key at the Old Rectory, Tanner Row, tel. 54316). Variations in service time allow all the Priory Street Chapels to be visited on Sunday morning. Holy Trinity church is usually open and the key for St Martin-cum-Gregory can be obtained at the Rectory, tel. 23798. The Arts Centre (St John's church) can usually be visited. All Saints' church is open. None of the Micklegate houses is open, but a polite enquiry at some of the larger ones is always worthwhile.

Walk Eight

Eboracum was the archetypal Roman city, regular and rectangular. Its defences evolved in five stages. Cerialis's earthworks of *c.* AD 71–4; the superior Agricolan earthworks *c.* AD 84 with timber foundations and palisades, which obliterated and replaced them; and the Trajanic, stone-fronted ramparts and gates (107–8); these have largely to be taken on trust, archaeological evidence remaining below ground. In *c.* 197, under Severus and Caracalla, the walls and towers were rebuilt; and further work, especially along the SW, river front, with massive polygonal corner towers, was carried out under Constantius Caesar, *c.* 296. Visible remains are substantially Severan at the E corner and Constantian at the W corner. (See Walk 2.)

The Roman walls, patched and repaired, remained as the city's defences until the late 9th century, when they were buried beneath Danish earthern ramparts, and certainly by this time the city was extended and defended SE of the Roman fortress towards the Foss. The defences of the Colonia on the Micklegate side of the river were similarly buried.

From St Leonard's Hospital to the Merchant Taylors' Hall the medieval walls follow the course, and a little over half the length of the Roman walls.

After 1066 further extensions took place: two castles flanked and defended the downstream approaches to the city; the ramparts were extended NE as far as the King's Fishpool; the extensive Walmgate suburb was probably enclosed at the same time. Stone gates – called 'Bars' – were built, not of any great height, but wooden palisades were not replaced in stone until 1250–70, all after Henry III's example at the Castle. St Mary's Abbey walls, built 1266 but only truly *defensive* from 1318, are dealt with in Walk 2. Barbicans, added to the gates *c.* 1320–30, followed proximate Scottish wars. The Walmgate walls were built – or rebuilt – after 1345. Repairs and strengthenings followed rebellions of 1489 and 1569, more extensively the siege of 1644, and finally to meet the threat of the 1745 rebellion. But by the end of the 18th century the future of the walls was in doubt, in 1799 the Corporation determining to demolish them. Three of the barbicans, three of the posterns, and several stretches of wall were demolished, but early conservationists subscribed towards restoration, which was completed in 1889. They are now excellently maintained and much appreciated. The famous daffodils are pretty for several weeks and untidy for several months.

The York system of walls on top of earthern ramparts is unique in England; accompanying moats have largely disappeared, and the walls themselves never approach in grandeur what remains at Oxford and Canterbury, nor, however, do they degenerate into a roadside public footpath as do parts of the Chester walls.

The experience of walking along the walls, however crowded they may be, is preferable to walking beside them; the views are better and their unremitting coexistence with York's inner ring road is less apparent. The best place to start the circuit is the Barker Tower at the Station end of Lendal Bridge, which gives a good beginning, a dullish middle, and a glorious end to the walk. For anyone merely wishing to sample the walls' delights Monk Bar to Bootham Bar must be regarded as pre-eminent, a walk where the sensible reader will ignore the book and enjoy the view.

Barker Tower to Skeldergate Postern

Barker Tower is an ashlar cylinder with a mossy conical roof, little windows in original battlements beneath the eaves, the swelling base surrounded by riverside steps, overshadowed by Lendal Bridge. First mentioned in 1376, it supported one end of the defensive chain across the river to Lendal Tower.

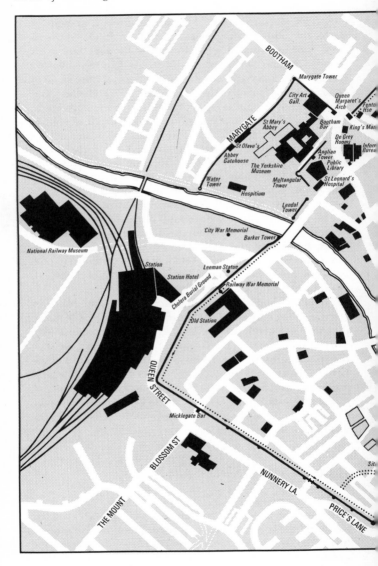

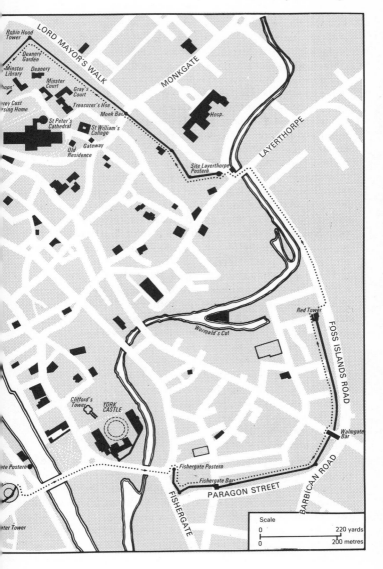

Robin Hood
Tower

Deanery
Garden

Minster
Library   Deanery

hops

rey Cust
rsing Home

Minster
Court

Gray's
Court

Treasurer's Hse

St Peter's
Cathedral

Monk Bar

St William's
College

Gateway

Old
Residence

LORD MAYOR'S WALK

MONKGATE

Hosp.

LAYERTHORPE

Site Layerthorpe
Postern

Wormald's Cut

Red Tower

FOSS ISLANDS ROAD

Clifford's
Tower

YORK
CASTLE

Walmgate
Bar

te Postern

Fishergate Postern

Fishergate Bar

BARBICAN ROAD

ter Tower

FISHERGATE

PARAGON STREET

Scale

0   220 yards

0   200 metres

235

The walls maintain their integrity despite numerous breaches in the interests of transport: the 1840 coalyard arch replacing North Street Postern, arches of 1876, rebuilt 1965–6, and 1874 giving road access to the new station, and much more impressive arches of 1839–40 and 1845 giving rail access to the Old Station – only people suffering from vertigo should desist from this stretch – railway architecture can be reviewed aerially; the Minster prospect is a classic of countless calendars. Musket loops are followed by battlements as the wall climbs. The Tower of the Tofts, at the corner, is probably that shot down by the Scots (1644) and rebuilt as a 'platt forme for a peece of Ordnance'. The SW stretch of the walls is long and straight, the walls and bank high, approaching Micklegate Bar at top-storey level, but side-stepping it so that the pleasant continuation among trees is seen ahead, apparently inaccessible, but reached by a passage through the Bar, with a good view down Micklegate on the way across.

The outer arch and passage walls of the Bar are early-12th-century, using Roman gritstone and sarcophagi. There may have been additions of the 13th century, but the royal arms suggests a late-14th-century date for the upper parts, with tall bartizans corbelled out from the flanking buttresses [28]. It was the favourite place for displaying decapitated heads: Hotspur, 1403; the Duke of York, 1460; Northumberland, 1572. Not badly damaged during the 1644 siege, restoration of 1737 is commemorated by the arms of Sir John Lister Kaye; the barbican was demolished in 1826 – despite Sir Walter Scott's offer to walk from Edinburgh to York to save it – and the inner face tidily rebuilt by Peter Atkinson Junior in 1827.

The wall continues with glimpses of the Convent garden outside and Dewsbury Terrace inside. The semi-circular bastions are late-13th-century, supplemented by the half-hexagonal ones when found to be too far apart. Victoria Bar was 'Erected by Public Subscription under the direction of the City Commissioners. AD 1838. GEORGE HUDSON ESQRE. LORD MAYOR'. It was cut through to accommodate new developments both inside and outside the walls, and remains were found of the medieval 'Lounlith' or hidden gate. Beyond the Victoria Bar Chapel, 1880 in polychromatic brick, by W. Peachey, and beside Newton Terrace, the walk passes delightfully through the treetops with glimpses of marvellous skyline towards the city, and indeed away from it to Scarcroft Road School. The dip in the internal bank indicates the point of departure of the missing half of the Old Baile ramparts, the surviving half bears the wall on a cranky course, past the corner tower, probably the Biche Daughter Tower rebuilt 1645, to the mound of the Old Baile itself, one of William I's twin castles, built 1068–9, destroyed and immediately rebuilt. By the 14th century it was in the hands of the Archbishops who were in dispute with the Corporation about responsibilities for its defence until it changed hands in 1466. It has been planted with trees since 1722 and the mound top has the best winter view over the city, more of its good features and fewer of its bad ones on display than usual. The wall descends to an unconvincing polygonal tower (1878) replacing Skeldergate Postern (demolished 1807). The Crane Tower, demolished 1878, could have chains slung across the river in times of emergency to the Davy Tower (see Walk 6).

Both Skeldergate Bridge (Walk 7) and Castle Mills Bridge have to be crossed – the latter with attractive locks below – before the walls are regained. The Castle and a succession of dams filled the defensive gap (Walk 6).

Fishergate Postern to Red Tower

Fishergate Postern has a 14th-century arch with portcullis slot, and a tower of 1504–7, one of the most pleasing objects on the wall: tall, ashlar, buttresses sliding away from the corners (in one of which a garderobe originally issued into the moat), little windows in the battlements below the pretty 17th-century roof like a Sussex farmhouse. The offset corner tower, like the wall, is of *c.* 1345; the contract survives; the stone litter bin has no regard for texture.

Housing inside the walls is successively pleasant, dim,

feebly aggressive, and feebly Georgian. Outside, the pyramidal Swimming Pool by the City Architect's Department (1974–6, project architect Richard Sawyer) has a service building of interesting form. The Cattle Market was held here from 1827–1970.

Fishergate Bar does not conform. It is low with a central arch and flanking passages. Mentioned in 1315 though largely 15th-century, it was blocked after damage in 1489 and became a House of Correction with loathsome conditions. It was reopened in 1827.

Walmgate Bar keeps its barbican, splendidly in the way, portcullis and 15th-century gates. The arch behind the portcullis groove is 12th-century; the rest of the structure 14th, with bartizans to tower and barbican, much repaired after damage in 1489 and 1644, when it received the full attention of the besieging Parliamentarians. The little house inside, lived in until recently, is supposed to date from 1584–6, but the superimposed orders seem more likely to belong to repairs after 1646. John Browne, the antiquary, was born in the house in 1793.

The wall beyond has high plinths with foundation arches showing, low banks giving up altogether near the Red Tower, and cross-bow slits with little finialled gablets, a rare concession to military decoration. Little scrubby trees come as a welcome change to bare banks. Red Tower was built in 1490; on a promontory in the Fishpool; of brick, which incensed the city masons and provoked the murder of John Patrick, a bricklayer. It was a cowhouse in 1800 and restored in 1857, by George Fowler Jones, who gave it an attractive roof with dormers.

Foss Islands Road's attractions are esoteric. The Fishpond of the Foss formed in 1068 (noted for bream and pike) did not finally disappear until the Foss Navigation Company chanelled the river in 1792 and the Corporation, from 1853, replaced the footpath subject to flooding by a road (likewise subject to flooding). Initiates will enjoy the Coke House; the railway landscape behind the hoardings, becoming a canal in times of flood; the remains of camouflage on the Electricity Works chimney; a nature reserve, replacing a cooling tower.

The Dutch-gabled end of Leetham's Mill is more memorable than the mangled back of the County Hospital.

Layerthorpe Bridge and an uninviting road junction have next to be negotiated. Old Layerthorpe Bridge and Postern – picturesque subjects of numerous watercolours – have gone, the bridge has been 'improved', the Postern cleared away, 1829–30.

Layerthorpe Tower to Bootham Bar

Layerthorpe Tower is a deliciously amorphous rebuilding after 1644, perched on a buttress squinched one side, corbelled the other. The wall here is built on arches, moulded medieval masonry piled inconsequentially below; pretty gardens of St Anthony's Hall and fine views of the Minster over promised and promising new housing. This stretch of wall has been indulged with improvements, romantic rather than authentic: battlements behind which no man could hide, merlons through which he could not fire, and bartizans in which he could not stand. Happily, no authenticizing hand has removed them. The line is irregular as far as the Merchant Taylors' Hall (Walk 5) along the Norman extension of the ramparts to the Fishpool; and the wall has been heightened in parts (the original profile is visible outside). The oval tower in the corner has toy battlements; the upper part of the next tower replaced a summer house, and the small arched openings beyond were lavatories for the guards.

Beyond the Merchant Taylor's Hall, the wall follows the Roman alignment. The complex history of the fortifications can be studied in the lane and grassy space inside the wall, before Monk Bar is reached. A substantial stretch of late-3rd-century Severan wall, together with an interval tower and the E corner of the Roman fortress are exposed. The corner has a rectangular tower at 45° inside the quadrant curve; where this turns away from the medieval wall, the Severan wall stands almost to its full height from plinth to projecting string course, once level with the wall walk. Trajanic foundations, hidden below, are on a slightly different alignment. The clay hump in the middle of the tower is all most of us are likely to see of Agricola's ramparts.

Monk Bar is 14th-century heightened in the 15th (replacing the Norman Gate further along), the most advanced piece of medieval military architecture surviving in the city. Outside notice the Plantagenet arms, the doors for the barbican (demolished 1826), and the high-level gallery whose floor had holes, now blocked, through which missiles could be dropped. The inner face of the Bar, the only medieval one to survive, has a puzzling gallery over the arch. Inside, straight flights of stairs in alternating flanking walls, and stone vaulting to all but the top floor, made the building defensible upwards as well as outwards – though the ultimate point of this stratagem escapes the author. The portcullis survives in working order.

Monk Bar to Bootham Bar is one of the most perfect urban walks in England – every step a delight – but one only available since 1887–9, when the wall walk on arches was added, together with the enormous Robin Hood's Tower at the angle. Buildings on the left, close-in at first, recede in stages, opening up the view of lovely gardens behind Gray's Court, whose gallery door is like a bookcase on a flight of steps, a glimpse down Chapter House Street, the back of Treasurer's House and the Minster magnificent above. Opposite Chapter House Street a dip in the outer bank represents the Roman *porta decumana* and its Norman successor and further N Andrews's College of Ripon and York, St John Buildings appear agreeably through the trees. The terrace behind the Minster Court houses must have been a delightful place in which to meditate before the tourists came.

The Deanery and its garden are no happier at the back than at the front, but with all that is best in the Minster superbly displayed beyond the Minster Library, changing perspective and becoming more dominant with every step, few will cavil at small insufficiencies in the foreground. Round towers are 13th-century, polygonal ones later. Outside the walls beyond a precious jungle of trees, backs of

Gillygate houses, more important than their fronts, await sensitive restoration.

Bootham Bar stands on the site of the Roman *porta principalis dextra*. Its interior (smelly) is the only one to which the public has access; the portcullis (fixed) can be inspected at close quarters. The late-11th-century outer arch has the oldest masonry in the fortifications. The upper part of the front is mid-14th-century, much altered and restored, the Stuart arms added in the late 17th century. (The Bar narrowly escaped destruction in 1831 when a section of wall was demolished to make way for St Leonard's Place; the amputated section is dealt with in Walk 2.) The inside face was rebuilt in 1835 (Peter Atkinson Junior, architect) replacing a classical front of 1719, which had a niche with a statue of Ebraucus, legendary founder of the city.

☆

The walls are open daily till dusk, but may be closed in bad weather. Walmgate Bar, a book shop, is sometimes accessible.

Walk Nine
The Station Area

(The area covered by this Walk is shown on the map for Walk 8, pp. 234–5.)

Railway York is grouped conveniently but unchronologically round the south-western corner of the walled city; Old Station, North-Eastern Railway Company Headquarters, and Hudson House inside the walls; New Station, Scarborough Bridge to the N, and the National Railway Museum to the NW, approached through the tunnel carrying Leeman Road grimly beneath the tracks, outside the walls, themselves pierced with various Victorian means of access. Towards Poppleton Road, carriage works and sidings extend vast and uninviting over an area the size of the old walled city.

To save the reader unnecessary to-ings and fro-ings among the traffic this account is geographical rather than chronological and deals with the various buildings in the order shown above.

The Old Station

York was not quite in the forefront of the railway age, though certainly at the centre of subsequent developments. The Stockton and Darlington Railway opened in 1825. A railway to York was first mooted in 1832, with the fortunately mistaken supposition that the cheap transport of coal to the city could bring with it an economic and industrial boom similar to that being enjoyed by Leeds and Bradford. The York and North Midland Railway was formed in 1835, and in 1836 it was authorized to build the line to Normanton, completed in 1840.

The first station was a temporary affair between Queen Street Bridge and Holgate Bridge – opened on 29 May 1839 with a journey to South Milford – because the projected arch, the first of five through the walls, could not be completed in time.

The permanent station was to be inside the walls – another miscalculation – on a site bounded by Toft Green, known as Friar's Gardens from association with the Dominican Friary. T. and J. Backhouse, Nurserymen, had to vacate their lease, and the House of Correction (1814) and Lady Hewley's Almshouse (1700) were cleared away to make room for it. The architect for this joint project of the York and North Midland, and Great North of England Railway Companies was G.T. Andrews, with Thomas Cabrey as consultant. Plans for the Booking Halls, Waiting Rooms, and Offices were submitted in 1839 and for the double train shed and Refreshment Rooms in 1840. The station opened – late – on 4 January 1841. The main contractors were Holroyd and Walker, Sheffield; the columns by Thompson, Ironfounder, York and the roof by Bingley of Leeds.

Andrews and Cabrey were also responsible for the first arch through the walls (1839) giving access for the lines, and followed one by one by the Barker Tower for the Coal Depot in 1840, and another near the corner of the walls giving access from warehouses inside to the main lines outside.

George Hudson, 'The Railway King', masterminded the project. He had something of genius, if not of an over-scrupulous kind, leaving his mark as one of the creators of the national railway system. The only approach to the station from the city was over Ouse Bridge and along either North Street or Barker Lane. When, in 1843, a new link to Micklegate was constructed it was called Hudson Street. Hudson's opposition to the new East Coast route from London to York proved ineffective. It was the beginning of his downfall. He was found to have 'manipulated' funds. Though he continued to perform his Parliamentary duties for another decade, by 1859 he was an outcast, living in Calais. Hudson Street was re-named Railway Street, by public demand. It was again re-named George Hudson

Street, in 1971, to commemorate the centenary of his death.

The number of platforms was soon doubled, and in 1845 when the Scarborough Line was opened, a new platform had to be added fronting the walls. A hundred trains a day were passing in and out through Andrews's arch. Confusion and complaints resulted.

In 1851 Andrews's plan for an hotel were submitted, built across the head of the platforms, facing the city. It was opened 22 February 1853. Queen Victoria used it on her one, half-hour visit to York on 13 September 1854.

Andrews's station buildings are in his Italianate mode, the Hotel of positively Georgian restraint. The original station faces Toft Green, across a forecourt with excellent cast-iron gates of *c.* 1850. Not quite symmetrical, brick (grey until recently) with stone dressings, it has none of the Baroque touches of Paragon Station, Hull. The walls behind the colonnades flanking the arcaded Booking Hall have been brought forward leaving the elevation rather lacking in shadow. The Refreshment Room (in local red brick, because it was out of sight when first built) was on the arrival platform for the benefit of through-train passengers.

The whole station remained intact until 1965–6 when almost all the train sheds were demolished. Though it had lacked the spectacle of Euston, it was certainly one of the finest of early railway ensembles, and the demolition of the sheds without apparently even considering their use as a covered car park, let alone their potential as a Railway Museum, is one of the saddest episodes of post-war vandalism in the city.

North Eastern Railway Company Headquarters and Hudson House

By the end of the century the North Eastern Railway Company had outgrown Andrews's station offices, even though they had also taken over the old hotel. A new site was bought opposite, and the new Headquarters Building to the designs of Horace Field erected 1900–6 in stone from

Portland and bricks from Sudbury. Baroque middle, Hampton Court wings and Amsterdam gables, and sash windows; the late-Norman-Shaw style handled with skill and enthusiasm. It is less formal at the back, experimenting with mullioned and transomed windows where these suit better the internal arrangements, but with a return to general symmetry high up, where it tells from a distance. The staircase tower at the corner of Tanner Row perfectly resolves the difficult angle between the streets. The surviving interiors show all the same care for detail.

Field's offices and Andrews's hotel, facing one another, linked by charming Edwardian ironwork, give York its one street of Metropolitan grandeur. (Affronted post-war offices in Rougier Street demonstrate the decline in architectural standards.) Both buildings have recently been cleaned; the Old Station has changed dour grey for a charming cream, flushed with pink; it will take a little more time to get used to the deep, rich orange of the N.E.R. building.

Hudson House (1967–8), between Andrews's station and the angle of the city wall, the new headquarters building of British Rail, Eastern Region, is one of the most successful of York's new buildings, designed by S. Hardy, of British Rail's architectural staff, disciplined and making good use of lift-shafts to vary the skyline; 'pre-cast' units faced with granite chippings are not the most seductive of materials. It is built over the site of the tracks leading to the old Station.

Station Road and Station Avenue

The N.E.R. War Memorial (1922), at the top of Station Rise, is one of Lutyens's more ponderous designs: an obelisk perched on inscribed Portland Stone walls, around the War Stone, its verticals delicately tapered, its horizontals imperceptibly curved. The upper of the two arches in the walls near by was cut through in 1874, the lower in 1876 (rebuilt 1965–6), both to give access to the new station from Lendal Bridge.

The open space between Station Hotel, walls, and Yorkshire Museum across the river could be one of the great urban landscapes of England. Instead it is parcelled off into little parks-development plots, spiced with road signs. Its three memorials are respectively funny, dignified, and moving: Alderman Leeman (Milburn, 1855, bad) fingers a button admonitorily at railway passengers; Lutyens's City War Memorial (1924) uses his standard cross; the Cholera Burial Ground for victims of the epidemic of 1832 has happily survived several attempts to clear it away, poignant without sentimentality.

The New Station

In 1865 Alderman Leeman* reported to an enthusiastic city council that the Railway Company (by now the North Eastern Railway Company) had decided to build a new station outside the city walls. The mounting chaos of the old Station had become insupportable; the new Station was to be designed as a through station on the grandest scale, obviating all the reversing that had been previously necessary, though the great curve proved to have its own administrative problems. Parliamentary powers were obtained the following year, but attacks on the Company's probity, echoing the Hudson scandal, led to postponement of any action until 1871, when work started to the designs of Thomas Prosser, followed in 1874 by Benjamin Burleigh and in 1876 by William Peachey. The main contractors were Messrs Lucas Bros. of Lowestoft and London, after industrial troubles caused Mr Keswick of York to give up the contract. The new station was opened on 25 June 1877 after the usual succession of set-backs and delays. The Hotel, Peachey's unaided effort, was opened 20 May 1878.

The Prosser–Burleigh–Peachey designs suffer from conflict of aim between architecture and engineering, for, where the architecture outside is graceless, in unappealing yellow Scarborough brick (though the Hotel does manage an

---

* Chairman of the Company, M.P., and Lord Mayor three times.

effective skyline), the engineering inside is superb architecture [50]. The glorious curved train shed with its radiating ribbed roof on Corinthian columns, 800 ft long, did not meet with universal approval: 'a very splendid monument of extravagance', lamented a shareholder. The great arched screens that formed tympana at the ends of the shed have been replaced by what look like segments of inefficiently designed bicycle wheels; one original end remains by the pretty, twice-domed tea room in Station Square. The platforms were extended on a smaller scale in 1900 and 1909, but still with pretty detailing, which is more than can be said for the bridge of 1904, or the extra platforms added in 1938.

The best feature inside the Hotel is the grand central staircase, running full height, which must be preserved from the ministrations of Fire Officers; enthusiasts will enjoy the Railway Mania Bar, and those qualified should inspect the grey and white marble splendours of the 'Gents'.

Scarborough Railway Bridge, the only rail–river crossing in the city, was built in 1845 with the footway originally between the tracks. It was constructed in 14 weeks. The arched abutments survived the reconstruction of 1874 when the footpath was moved to its present, less alarming position.

The National Railway Museum

The Railway Museum was opened on 27 September 1975 by H.R.H. the Duke of Edinburgh. Its collections, including that vast part which the public does not see, are the most important, historically, in any railway museum in the world. It is the first National Museum outside London, combining material from the British Transport Museum at Clapham with that of the old L.N.E.R. Museum started in York in 1928. It achieves a metropolitan scale, but its atmosphere in no way resembles its metropolitan counterparts. On a busy day it is more like a battleground for enthusiasts. Its attendants are, however, called 'Warders'.

The building is the old York North Motive Power Depot

ingeniously adapted by British Rail's own architects. The engines – some having had operations to reveal their intestinal arrangements – and rolling stock are kept on the lower level, centred on two turntables; the gallery houses smaller items and there is space for special exhibitions. The railways' architectural heritage is sadly under-represented though almost the first thing one sees is the giant statue of George Stephenson from Euston Hall.

Any selection is necessarily personal. The oldest locomotive is 'Agenoria', 1829, by Foster, Rastrick and Co; 'Copper-nob', 1846, with domed firebox; 'Boxhill', 1880; 'Gladstone', 1882, splendidly decorated as for the Jubilee; 'Hardwicke', 1892; George Jackson Churchward's majestic heavy freight locomotive, 2818, 1905; 'Mallard', holder of the world speed record for steam traction, 1938; 'Evening Star', 1960, last steam locomotive built for British Railways. Among the rolling stock the Royal Saloons provide a different kind of delight. Queen Victoria's Saloon started life as twins in 1869, economically recast as one in 1895, classical outside with touches of Gothic within. Edward VII's Saloon, 1903, is a much more masculine affair, with modifications of taste to suit Queen Mary; the Duke of Sutherland's Private Saloon, 1900, is scarcely less splendid, especially the metalwork and door furniture.

The 'Weatherhill Engine', 1833, grandly sculptural, like Anthony Caro, is the most impressive object in the Museum. The real sculptured *feel* of many of the exhibits – quite missing from the Italian memorial to George Stephenson – is remarkable. The 'Swannington Incline Engine', 1833, attempts the Greek Revival. 'Gaunless Bridge', by George Stephenson, 1823–5, decorates function gently, like a Windsor Chair.

Early Railway lettering is a joy; so are the working models. On the gallery, relics of railway steamers and paddle boats, timetables, tickets, truncheons, bills, cutlery, a clock in the guise of a railway carriage; moulds for Thermit welds like angular Henry Moores; awards for courage and resource, commemorative shovels, *Handbook of Inspired Thoughts for Station Waiting Rooms*, Travelling Charts with architectural details, menus and wine lists, cutlery, tea urns and china. A model of Euston Station, and the clock from the Great Hall are no great recompense for the loss of Hardwick's masterpiece.

☆

Most of what there is to be seen of the old Station can be seen from the walls. The new station is always open. An excuse should be found for visiting the staircase of the Station Hotel. The National Railway Museum is open weekdays 10.00–18.00, Sundays 14.30–18.00.

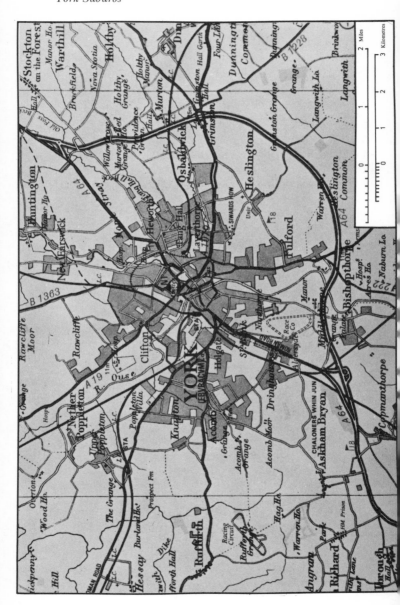

The Suburbs

The Suburbs of York are its secret delights. Roman cemeteries and medieval suburbs spread far beyond the walls, but early work is sparse – the 1644 siege saw to that; though excavation has revealed much, there is not a great deal that the reader can see. From the mid 18th century onwards, however, they became at least as rewarding as the centre of the city and, at their best, more consistent. Nowhere in central York can one walk such pleasant miles as from Bootham Bar to Clifton Green, or from Micklegate Bar to Dringhouses; though the traffic is heavy they are blessedly free from the detritus of tourism.

Early-19th-century York was surrounded by villages, on and off the main roads. Clifton, Heworth, Fulford, Dringhouses, and Acomb were near enough to encourage linking developments that had style and their inhabitants have been sensitive enough to maintain it. Further away, Skelton, Wigginton, Haxby and Huntington, Osbaldwick, Dunnington, Bishopthorpe, and the Poppletons have been engulfed, but not obliterated, by their own suburban growth, New Earswick is a model village, and Heslington remained an estate village until it became a University village.

That Bootham and Clifton form the handsomest approach
to York will be seriously disputed only by inhabitants of the
Mount. The varied architectural excellence compensates for
any natural deficiencies and one can walk from Bootham Bar
to the city boundary – and it is an experience best enjoyed on
foot, preferably on a Sunday afternoon – with nothing worse
to look at than a couple of garages and a vacant plot.
Bootham is Old Norse meaning 'at the booths', perhaps
movable merchants' stalls before the Conquest.

Its original Roman straightness gently modified, the road
has been the setting for numerous military comings and
goings: Archbishop Thurstan going to victory at the Battle
of the Standard (1138); Edward II retreating from Byland
(1322); Queen Philippa leaving to defeat the Scots at Nevilles
Cross (1346); Lambert Simnel unsuccessfully trying to get
into the city in 1487. Cleared during the siege, it was the
scene of two of its more dramatic events: Prince Rupert's
entry into the city – that he was allowed to get in seems more
remarkable than his subsequent defeat at Marston Moor –
and the destruction of St Mary's Tower.

Bootham starts with a set piece: the Bar and Minster
towers, better seen, though less easily appreciated, in their
tight urban setting than across the dreary wastes of Exhibition Square. No. 24 has a good cast-iron shopfront.
Opposite, enough of the Abbey Precinct wall has been
exposed, to the detriment of the street (opening out the
space where enclosure was needed), revealing the back
of the Art Gallery, ugly as only a building devoted to the arts
can be. The wall starts with an arch and postern tower (stone
outside, brick within) of 1497 (the arch popularly known as
Queen Margaret's Arch from the long-held misconception

that it was cut through for Margaret Tudor in 1503). The Abbey wall is higher than the city wall, since, though it had a ditch – long a bone of contention between city and monastery – it had no bank. The lower part is the boundary wall of 1266. The upper part, and the round and square towers, were added after 1318, when the Abbey was given a licence to crenellate. The different masonry of the two periods is even now very evident. St Mary's tower is a circular corner tower added in the late 14th century, which, after the Dissolution, became a repository for the records of Yorkshire monasteries. On 16 June 1644 the besiegers successfully mined it – with disastrous consequences to the records – and attacked the King's Manor before the garrison could be rallied to drive them out. The tower was rebuilt on a smaller scale – the clumsy joint can still be seen – using material from Lord Sheffield's range at the King's Manor.

Marygate (left) is a delightful street, starting between walls, dropping steeply, curving gently down to the river, past Georgian and Victorian buildings, with the added charms unusual in York of starting down a street at someone else's chimney level. Marygate Lane promises well, but leads only to a car park, since the demolition of a little knot of terraced streets. Almery Garth, Little Garth, and the houses fronting Marygate are Georgian in Victorian fancy dress. The Bay Horse (1894), tile-hung and half-timbered, is by Penty and Penty. Opposite, the Abbey Wall has been revealed by the demolition of old cottages, the stonework supplemented with new where the exposure proved disappointing. The water tower, hexagonal inside, but circular outside, was another addition after 1318. St Olave's church (really St Olaf) recalls the Palace of the Earls of Northumbria, which stood nearby, but church and Abbey Gatehouse are so linked that they are more sensibly dealt with under the Museum Gardens (Walk 2). No. 29, tall narrow Georgian with a pretty doorway, and a terraced garden above the remains of the Abbey Almonry, is the only house to survive on this side. Past the square tower with cross-bow slits an attempt has been made to reproduce the shutters that once filled the crenellations: the rebates for the mechanism survive on the Abbey wall but nowhere else on the city fortifications.

Eighteenth-century Bootham developed as the most desirable of city suburbs; houses for the County families; speculations for letting in the Season. The NE side evolved first; York's handsomest range of Georgian buildings. The SW side followed in the 1840s. Before the railways came there may even have been a view.

Wandesford House was opened in 1743 for 'ten poor maiden gentlewomen'; windows in tall arched recesses of the kind favoured in Beverley and on stable blocks; big pediment with a bust of the foundress, Mary Wandesford; door added in 1968 under the misapprehension that the original was inadequate. Nos. 39–45 formed a mauled terrace of *c.* 1748, with features in common with the houses in Micklegate attributed to Carr. Carr certainly designed No. 47 (1753) with an accomplished, restrained front, cornices floated above the windows and no embarrassment about putting the door on one side. Panelled ground-floor room, rococo staircase ceiling, and excellent fireplace in the first-floor saloon. No. 49 is 17th-century heightened and recast in the 18th. No. 51 is the finest late-Georgian house in the city [43], built *c.* 1800 for Sir Richard Vanden Bempde Johnstone, by Peter Atkinson Senior; a noble, spacious elevation, all the openings with stone surrounds, Doric portico to the door, Ionic window surround above, the triple central features growing narrower with each storey. The delicate ironwork of the balcony survived the war effort; much more has been reinstated. Interiors of scrupulous simplicity round an entrance hall with a Doric screen to the branching staircase beyond. Nos. 53 and 55 share a Greek Doric portico (early-19th-century), and No. 61 has an Ionic doorcase and charming balconies of *c.* 1840. Most of this group belongs to Bootham School, a Quaker foundation moved to York from Scarborough in 1822, taken over by the York Friends' Quarterly Meeting in 1828, and established in Bootham 1846. Behind the Georgian houses is a restrained Arts and Crafts block of *c.* 1902 by Fred Rowntree. Trevor Dannatt's Hall of 1966 is one of the least compromising and most successful of modern York buildings. Copper and shuttered concrete handled delicately yet strongly; a sculptural presence defining a space to frame the distant view of the Minster. The Science Block by Fletcher Ross and Hickling (1976) is both tamer and more obtrusive.

The other side of Bootham did not develop until the 1840s. No. 54, Bootham Lodge, and Penn House show the gradual coarsening of classical detailing in that decade. No. 54 has a good staircase with screens of columns to the hall and first-floor landing. W.H. Auden, poet, was born here in 1907. Penn House has a squat Ionic portico fronting St Mary's, a road nicely aligned on the gritstone gate piers of Bootham Park Hospital opposite, one of the little bits of planning only discovered by walking aimlessly about.

Bootham Park, opened in 1777, was one of the first mental hospitals in the country, though the early shortcomings of its patients' treatment led 20 years later to the foundation of the Retreat (Walk 13). John Carr designed Bootham Park, producing a fine elevation whose Roman Doric portico was originally crowned by a cupola. It misses absolute distinction by the not uncommon 18th-century practice of suppressing the lower parts of the entablature along the wings, giving a slightly mean, institutional appearance to the upper edge of the design. The Victorians would not have made that mistake. The arched windows in larger arched recesses are a favourite Carr feature. Little remains of Carr's interior but the Victorian Adamesque decoration of the tower-like hall is entertaining. The Chapel by Gould, 1865, in stone doing its best to look like brick. The hospital grounds are splendidly spacious. The case for their preservation was passionately and rightly argued when it was threatened by the ring-road proposals; new, disfiguring hard tennis courts have not produced a murmur of protest. Along Bootham are railings between gritstone monolithic piers, a characteristic York feature. The Scarborough line is managed unobtrusively.

Record House was one of the sights of York when first built for Mrs Aston, *c.* 1827, A beautifully spare, stone elevation with a central bow, behind Walker railings and Soane-ish gritstone piers. The architect has not been established, though Pritchett or the Atkinsons seem probable. Opposite, Ingram's Hospital (flats since 1958) built by Sir Arthur Ingram *c.* 1630–2, damaged in the siege and restored *c.* 1649. Long wings still with Tudorish detail but a Dutch gable over what was once a chapel behind the central tower. The late-12th-century doorway with developed dog tooth was brought from Holy Trinity, Micklegate; an early example of conservation.

Bootham changes name to Clifton, and urban townscape changes subtly to suburban, with a less rigid adherence to the street line, real front gardens, trees taking over as a primary element and a greater variety of architectural style. The earlier houses are still on the right. The White House is early-18th-century embedded in a much larger late-18th-century house, hence the disconcerting window pattern. Nos. 14 and 16 are an odd pair of *c.* 1800 with an overall pediment. (St Peter's Grove has dark-red houses of the 1880s with terracotta sunflowers and East Lodge, 1896, now Savage's Hotel, by Brierley, vernacular breaking into Tudor round the porch.) St Peter's School footbridge was designed by C.R. Thorpe in 1966. Opposite, Bootham Grange, No. 11, and Burton Cottage just beyond the school, are all in the greyish brick favoured in the 1840s. Bootham Grange is the most imposing with giant pilastos, but the other two are more attractive.

St Peter's School claims to be one of the most ancient in the country, descendent of the School founded in 627 by James the Deacon; though even its most ardent apologists must agree that the connexion has been tenuous at times. The School of York of which Alcuin was both the most famous pupil and master was certainly established in the 7th century under Egbert and then Aethelbert. In 1069 its library was destroyed by fire, but the following year Archbishop Thomas ratified the position of schoolmaster. Its premises had to be moved at the end of the 13th century when the Minster nave was rebuilt. Its close connexion with St Mary's Abbey meant that the school ceased to function at the Dissolution. In 1546 Archbishop Holgate founded his Grammar School. In 1557 the Dean and Chapter refounded their school under royal licence, first in the Hospital of St Mary, Horsefair, after 1644 in the Bedern, and from 1833 in a new school in the close (now the Choir School). The Proprietary School in Clifton opened in 1838, but by 1844, though it had pupils, it had no funds, whereas the Minster School had funds but no pupils. Amalgamation was arranged and the Clifton buildings were made over to the Dean and Chapter.

The first buildings were by John Harper; Gothic, much more attractively handled than Pritchett's stiff efforts in the Close; the centrepiece with tall openwork turrets suggests a nodding acquaintance with St Augustine, Canterbury. School House and the little lodge, in grey brick, were added *c.* 1844; the apsidal Decorated chapel by J.B. and W. Atkinson in 1861. In the Drama Centre (originally Gymnasium) by Francis Bedford (1894–5) rough stonework contrasts oddly with Arts and Crafts Gothic doorways of exquisite refinement. Brierley did some discreet infilling behind School House, and the Science Block with interesting fenestration *c.* 1902. The big Tudor block with central gatehouse is by Penty and Thompson, 1927. Architectural discipline having evaporated, post-war additions were thinly traditional until 1960 and have been thinly modern since. The feeblest of all, set centrally and devastatingly on the river front, is partly and inevitably devoted to art.

Burton Stone Lane developed quickly after the sale of the De Gray Estate in 1836, William Bellerby building terraced houses on either side of the entrance to his joiner's yard. The Burton Stone is a cross base with unexplained additional sockets. The Burton Stone Inn is by Brierley (1896), though more in the style of Penty, and Burton Stone Lane has more minor Brierley at Lumley Barracks, 1911, severely Georgian, and St Luke's church, 1900–2, Gothic, bleakly unfinished outside but with an impressive barrel-vaulted interior.

Clifton continues Georgian opposite Clifton Methodist church, Edward Taylor trying his hand at Gothic in 1909, the spire bad architecture but marvellous townscape. No. 66 is a mid-17th-century recasting of an earlier house, much restored, but the best example remaining in the city of the brick-rusticated and Dutch-gabled style of just after the Restoration.

The Avenue is largely the creation of the 1890s and Penty and Penty. Their delightful, tile-hung terrace (Nos. 2–9) might come from Bedford Park; Rosenlain (No. 22) is a little later, more 'modern', with tall pilastered chimneys and rendered upper storey. W.G. Penty lived in the sharply gabled, 1880s house at the Clifton end, which he called Brantwood, doubtless in homage to Ruskin. The Pentys also designed the delightful Grey Mare with its shell-hooded doorway, on Clifton Green, beyond traces of old Clifton village it is worth noting vestiges of timber framing in No. 88.

Clifton Green is one of York's chief delights [51]: a Victorian village green, white fenced, amply treed, with a splendid horse-trough under a canopy, small houses of the 1830s and 40s – No. 16 a delightful Gothic cottage worthy of Pugin – grander ones of the 70s and 80s, grandest of all St James's Terrace in grey brick with bays and bumpy gables, and a heavy-going but effective church by George Fowler Jones, 1866–7. The church school (1877) and vicarage (1879–80) are unexpectedly by J.L. Pearson; the school, simple Gothic, the vicarage a very competent effort in Norman Shaw style, with which local architects were not to catch-up for another 15 years. Towards Water End the John Burrill Almshouses are by Ward and Leckenby, 1931; traditional forms lovingly handled.

Ouselea in Shipton Road is a co-operative housing scheme by Michael Butterworth (1972), a little too formidable to the road, beautifully landscaped behind, almost a desirable place to live. Perhaps Barry Parker's pleasant housing of 1936 in Galtres Grove (off Malton Way) will be found to have more permanent virtues.

☆

Some of the interiors of Bootham School may be seen on written application to 47 Bootham. A public footpath crosses the grounds of St Peter's School. Clifton church is open.

Walk Eleven
Bootham Bar to New Earswick

Between the Scarborough Line and the road to Hull dullish suburbs spread from Regency beginnings near the walls, round gas and electricity works, Brierley schools, a proliferation of hospitals, Rowntree's factory, and the villages of Heworth – near enough to have promoted early linking development, an axis of seemliness along the Malton Road – and Osbaldwick. The other scattered objects of interest can all be seen on two sallies, NE from Bootham Bar to Earswick, and NE from Monk Bar to Osbaldwick.

Gillygate (from St Giles's church, demolished after 1547) is an ancient street outside the walls; cleared in 1644; rebuilt; largely late-18th- and 19th-century; an example of conservation through planning blight, since the buildings below the walls, reprieved after 30 years threatened demolition on unconvincing pretexts, remain a continuous, if at present dusty, pleasure, awaiting sensitive repair. Nos. 3 and 5 were built (1797) by Thomas Wolstenholme, maker of composition ornaments, much of whose delicate decoration survives inside. The front with its highly individual window pattern is mangled but still enjoyable. Joseph Halfpenny, engraver, lives in Nos. 18–20. No. 28, one of a pair of 1769, has a candlesnuffer on its handsome doorcase, and a Gothick staircase ceiling contemporary with Atkinson's work at Bishopthorpe. Other minor pleasures await a touch of paint. E.J. Sherwood's utterly joyless Salvation Army Barracks (1882–3) suggests that General Booth's attitude to music did not extend to architecture.

Regency Clarence Street, once Horsefair, has degenerated into a car park with a view of the Minster. The site of St Mary's Hospital, adapted after 1557 as one of the houses of St Peter's School, was recently excavated.

Lord Mayors' Walk, SE, was laid out and planted with Elms in 1718, an early civic improvement, still handsome despite its scruffy entrance; the walls, with the Minster diagonally above, facing the College of Ripon and York St John. This started as the Diocesan Training College for Schoolmasters (opened 1845) and the Yeoman School (1846), later Archbishop Holgate's Grammar School. The College, much the grander of the two, with gatehouse, tall chimneys, and projecting wings, and presumably the school, were designed by G.T. Andrews in smooth Tudory style. The old chapel, *c.* 1858, is now a drama centre. The new chapel (1964), the one interesting post-war building, was designed by George Pace. The plan is Y-shaped for flexibility, with the sanctuary at the fork; brick with slit windows; four monopitched roofs rising outwards with an oratory beyond the narthex with its own little monopitch rising inwards; exposed steelwork inside, and simple furnishings; one of Mr Pace's tougher buildings.

St John's Street, NE, nicely aligned on the Minster, leads to the Groves, part of the sadly battered 1820–50 development along the N side of the city. In Penleys Grove Street (from Paynlathes Crofts) are villas and houses by J.B. and W. Atkinson, the best Nos. 29 and 31, with pretty glazing and ironwork. Eldon Street and Brownlow Street have artisan dwellings of the 1840s. Park Grove School (1895) by Brierley has dramatic contrasts of scale at the ends and long restrained teaching ranges flanking the high hall. The brickwork detailing is a delight. The roofscape has been emasculated. St Thomas's church by George Fowler Jones (1853–4) is in gritty lancet style, and Groves Chapel (1883) by W.J. Morley, Bradford, has a coarse classical loggia. Nice 1840s cast-ironwork survives in what remains of Union Terrace and along the edge of the hospital site. Lord Llewellyn Davies's new hospital (opened 1976) seems not so much to have had surgery as to be undergoing it; sections of the architecture are cut away to reveal troublesome parts, while life-support systems are housed in boxes on the roof. Past reception with an alarming carpet and desk like an air terminal, intimidating circulation spaces lead to comfortable wards. It is all more frightening for the visitor than the patient.

Haxby Road School is Brierley again (1904), similar to Poppleton Road School, better preserved and with angular dormers, but cluttered by later buildings. Rowntrees Factory is on such a scale that architecture was apparently beyond contemplation.

Haxby Road continues N past more factories, playing fields, thin countryside, the remains of Foss Navigation at Lock Cottage, a nature reserve ('no admittance') to New Earswick, which everyone should visit. Rowntrees started their new village in 1902. The community was to be managed by a Trust and Village Council, the houses not sold but rented, and their occupants by no means confined to Rowntree's employees. The architect was (Sir) Raymond Unwin. Beginnings were modest, just 28 houses around Station Road. Early N expansion along Sycamore and Chestnut Avenues kept to a simple Voysey–Lutyens vernacular; small groups, short terraces, occasional individual houses; brick and rendering, plenty of gables and gardens, existing trees supplemented by imaginative planting; through rooms gave more flexible planning; upstairs bathrooms and outside stores were incorporated; many features which have become clichés were imaginatively invented here. Main roads were straight, minor roads curved with the houses arranged to enclose a space. The Folk Hall (1905–6) is the community centre: dog-legged in plan, rendered with bits of half-timbering, and carrying an enormous roof punctuated by dormers. (The interior was reconstructed and the Swimming Pool added, 1968, by Robert Matthew, Johnson Marshall and Partners.) The Green is not a success, too large for the buildings round it, the school altered, the shops unexciting; the absence of a church to give a focus is felt. (The little church by Leslie Moore is just outside the village.) Barry Parker, Unwin's partner, became architect in 1919, and designed the N extension of the village, an exercise in cul-de-sacs, terraces, and groups full of tiny variations; windows of different sizes wittily disposed, unified by the forgotten expedient of a standard size of pane. Individual houses are engagingly odd. Much of Parker's work survives unsullied by 'improvements'.

Post-war additions were kept under control by Louis de Soissons and C.W.C. Needham, but recently individualist architects have been employed for particular projects with unhappy results. Modernization of the oldest parts of the village has removed chimneys and ruined Unwin's intricate planning by substituting communal open spaces for his big front gardens, leaving little exposed strips for the all-too-often inadequate husbandry of individual owners.

☆

College of Ripon and York St John, enquire at the porter's office. St Thomas's church is locked.

Monk Bar has the best setting of any of the city gates: a tight little open space – happily now secure from threats of clearance – which it dominates completely. The Bay Horse has an 1830s front, stables in the moat, and a domed ice house on the ramparts. Old St Maurice's church was replaced by a much larger building by Fisher and Hepper (1875), in turn demolished in 1967. The site is pleasantly maintained, keeping old gravestones. The Norman doorway is now at James the Deacon, Acomb, while the famous late-12th-century window with germinal tracery (a bullseye above two round-headed openings) is inaccessible in the basement of the Hospitium.* St Maurice's Road leads SE to Jewbury (site of the Jewish cemetery) and Rockingham House, an austere design of 1792 with prominent bow windows.

Monkgate has provided endless speculation as to which monastery engendered its name. Until the 12th-century it ran further N towards the Roman *porta decumana* and the Minster, and was called Monk's Street after the pre-Conquest community serving the Minster; realigned, it retained its old, out-of-date name. It remains handsome despite demolitions; one side minor Regency – No. 37 probably by G.T. Andrews, 1848; No. 58 the nicest, set back – the other grander, starting with the County Hospital. This was originally established in 1740 and rebuilt 1849–51 to designs of J.B. and W. Atkinson, the most imposing of York's Victorian buildings [49]; 15 bays and 3 storeys above a rusticated basement, all the openings with stone surrounds, the middle ones emphasized, the rest a model of classical

---

* A similar window can be seen in the ticket office at Kirkham Priory.

restraint. For once comparisons with the Farnese Palace seem justified. A Georgian and Victorian range follows. No. 38 is very early 18th-century with projecting middle bay and angular fanlight. From 1803 to 1811 it housed Manchester College, after the Revd Charles Wellbeloved (a notable York antiquarian whose home it was) had been appointed its director, and it was much enlarged at the time. George Hudson, the Railway King, built No. 42 for himself and adapted 44, a house of *c.* 1725, giving it an interesting cast-iron staircase. No. 44 exemplifies the dangers of replacing glazing bars. Nos. 62–6 are early-Victorian classical, and round the corner in Foss Bank, forlorn lodges in Soane-ish grey brick are relics of York's first gas works, established *c.* 1823.

In Huntington Road, N, Grove Terrace gives its name and 1824 date in massive letters over the middle house. (St Mary's Hospital – the Grange, built as a workhouse *c.* 1845 by the Atkinsons – is dispiriting and grim. By the Foss, but further out, the Fever Hospital, 1881, is a funny, happy building with cast-iron verandahs and a clock tower. There is a pleasant ramble along the far river bank through willows and a narrow quiet park.)

Heworth Green, NE, starts with a traffic island and a bridge. Downstream the gas works once provided an industrial landscape of some grandeur, on which the present scruffy car park is no improvement. Heworth Croft (*c.* 1842) is probably by the Atkinsons. No. 26 is a year or two earlier. No. 45 is entertainingly Victorian, dated 1861, now a nunnery, with initials of Queen and Consort. (Mill Lane leads to Layerthorpe, first mentioned *c.* 1080, whose antiquity has to be taken on trust. St Mary's church was destroyed after 1547. Regency streets have been bulldozed since the war. The railway bridge is the perfect place for viewing the collected worst of York's modern townscape.) Heworth Green was originally one-sided, its 1840s and 1850s houses had a view over the Stray until inter-war developments removed it. The range, never regular, has been much altered but still has plenty of enjoyable detail, especially ironwork. From the road junction Malton Road crosses Monk Stray, with its golf course, N: good Minster views and Herdsman's Cottage, *c.* 1840, straight from the pages of Loudon; Stockton Lane, NE, has a cube-shaped manor house (*c.* 1830) with remains of a Gothic porch, a ramshackle coach house to delight Ian Nairn, and a cottage with a nice Georgian doorcase. Heworth Road leads uneventfully E to Heworth church by G.F. Jones, 1868–9. Early English with tracery cut from slabs and a tower contorting upwards into a spire through bits of pyramid and slope. Jones's favourite semi-cruciform plan. Polychromatic vicarage behind. East Parade was started in the 1830s; the earlier houses have narrow gardens, the later, more substantial ones. It was aligned on the Minster, which suffered an eclipse with the building of the gas works, now only partial behind the one remaining gasholder. East, past Edward Taylor's Methodist Chapel (1890) with a prettier, miniature version of the parish church spire, Heworth's village origins can still be sensed. Behind, Tang Hall Beck regularly floods its little strip of countryside.

Between Heworth and Hull Road are vast housing estates, at first roads with thrilling names like Fourth and Fifth Avenues, then Constantine, Alcuin, Etty, and Flaxman are unflatteringly commemorated. St Aelred's church (R.C.) by Stephen Simpson (1956) has the distinction of being the first York church to dispense with the 'styles' – prematurely it seems. Far more interesting is St Hilda's in Tang Hall Lane, by Cecil Leckenby (1934); unfinished but a strong, strange design; Gothic owing something to Temple Moore, with lancet windows and a multiplicity of offsets. Temporary W front of great charm; a Mid-West weatherboarded house with an enormous gable disconcertingly above. Excellent vaulted interior with passage aisles. Stained glass by H. Harvey (1955–71). Seventeenth-century font cover from St John, Micklegate, which moves sideways along a little track.

Behind the Magnet in Osbaldwick Lane, Campbell Court is a satisfyingly simple housing scheme for elderly people, 1954, by the University Design Unit. Osbaldwick – a pre-Conquest name meaning the dwelling of Osbald – being off the main road, stays rural despite development and has a

real village green. The moated castle site has been built over.
The church was restored in 1877 by J.O. Scott. It was a
single-cell building with bell turret and twin lancets. Its
curious fate is not apparent from the Green. It has been
stretched to an L-shape with corner octagonal sanctuary,
and aisles defined by steel columns belonging to one
aesthetic with plaster saucer domes of quite another. Pulpit
(a grand 17th-century piece), altar, and font provide a
tenuous diagonal axis. Monument to Mary Ward, founder of
the Institute of the Blessed Virgin Mary, the educational
activities of which are now world-wide:

> To love the poore, persever in the same, live, dy and
> Rise with them was all the ayme of Mary Ward who
> having lived 60 years and 8 days dyed 20 of Jan 1645

in lettering of endearing incompetence.

Heworth church, Heworth Vicarage, Melrosegate, tel.
54160 and St Hilda's church, St Hilda's Vicarage, Tang Hall,
tel. 23150 are apt to be locked. Osbaldwick church is open.

Lawrence Street, originally part of Walmgate, is broad, curving, tree-lined, cobble-verged; has little houses, an imposing church, and Walmgate Bar as climax; all of which raises expectations far too high. It is as though it were attempting to be gracious and failing very badly. Concentrated activity during the siege of 1644 removed the ancient street (not to mention much of Walmgate Bar) and there is little to enjoy in what has replaced it. St Nicholas's Leper Hospital and St Edward the Martyr's church were both suppressed *c.* 1548. St Nicholas's church was never rebuilt after the siege, though Fairfax had its splendid Norman door rebuilt at St Margaret's, Walmgate (Walk 5). St Lawrence's tower is the only relic of pre-siege Lawrence Street. Its Norman base has another reset, late-Norman door carved with conventional foliage, interlace, and monsters, and an Early English lancet, while the top stage (15th-century) has recently had its pretty battlements restored away. The chancel is outlined in grass and gravestones. Sir John Vanbrugh married Henrietta Maria Yarburgh here on 14 January 1719. The previous Christmas Day he had written to the Duke of Newcastle, 'tis so bloody cold, I have almost a mind to Marry to keep myself warm'. The Rigg monument by Plows, marvellously ripe in a railed enclosure full of ivy, commemorates six children killed in a boating accident of 1830. The enormous new church, built 1881 to designs by J.G. Hall of Canterbury, is a retardataire performance with a spire of 1893 harking back to the Commissioners' churches of the 1830s. It has lancets, Kentish rag, heavy French detailing of unsettled style, and a towering, narrow interior. The 15th-century font with three tiers of minute carvings repays the closest of inspection.

The Ellen Wilson Almshouse (1894), by A.S. Ellis of Westminster, combines Gothic and Jacobean elements. The Church Hall, a Wrenish design of 1935, is by Ward and Leckenby. A chequerboard shopfront, a couple of decent pubs, the economically Georgian Working Men's Club, and the good Regency front of No. 93 are worth a glance. Behind a formidable wall the Convent of Poor Clares (1872–5) by George Goldie is in bald, Italianate brick, with black bands instead of mouldings.

Heslington Road is S of Lawrence Street, parallel, approached along Regent Street, and more rewarding. It rises up the moraine, which then curves away eastwards to Siward's Howe, its highest point with a conspicuous and military-looking water tower. Fairfax House, 1925 and 1933 by Chapman and Jenkinson of Sheffield, is an exercise in pediments, mansard roofs, and bullseye-windows; Lutyens would have made it more enjoyable. Behind it is one of York's oddities, Belle View House (or its ground floor), now converted into a swimming pool; fort-like with corner turrets and little Gothic canopies to the windows, it was built for Mr Plows the sculptor to house himself and his collection, but only some grand Corinthian capitals from Carlton House remain. Wilkins is supposed to have brought them to York for use in the Yorkshire Museum. The Herdsman's Cottage (*c.* 1840) is by the up and downhill approach to Walmgate Stray. Immediately beyond, Laurel Beeches was built in 1909 for the superintendent of the Retreat. It shows Brierley at his best, formal behind, informal at the front, designed to take every advantage of the sloping site with its stepped approach, steep roofs, and mixture of leaded and sash windows. The Retreat was opened in 1796 by the Society of Friends, for the humane treatment of the mentally sick, 19 years after the County Asylum (Bootham Park), with whose swaggering elevation the solid simplicity of John Bevan's design is in marked contrast. Lamel Hill with a 'Chinese' summer house was used by Lord Fairfax as a gun battery during the siege.

Till only a few years ago the old lane SE to Heslington seemed to lead direct from city to countryside; now it leads (pedestrians only) to the University, which is a rather different matter. Motorists have to use the new University Road.

York University was established temporarily in various city buildings in 1960. Plans for development were approved in 1962, and the first new buildings were opened three years later. Heslington Hall became the administrative centre and its mature parkland became the setting for the new buildings. The Architects are Robert Matthew, Johnson Marshall and Partners, with Andrew Derbyshire as architect in charge. The University was planned as a series of separate colleges. The buildings were designed on a modular construction system, which allowed a good deal of flexibility, and initially a certain amount of fun. The idea of magnifying the fishpond into a lake threading through the whole site was brilliant; it produces most of the best effects [56]. The earliest of the new buildings are also the happiest, but they have the best setting; some of the more monumental buildings ape their informality with curious results. Later buildings, pruned by inflation of unnecessary frills, are set in the bleakest parts of the landscape. Between the colleges linking covered walkways give the whole place a curious impression of being spatially inside-out, and obliterate so much of what lies ahead that it can only properly be comprehended when one is going somewhere else.

An anti-clockwise tour round the lake can conveniently start at the Lyons Concert Hall (1968), which has a pleasant interior (with a Grant Degens and Bradbeer organ) and a perversely shapeless exterior whose underlying symmetry only becomes apparent from a long way off. Tall, thin sculpture by Barbara Hepworth. The Biology Laboratories (1968) are low and flat-roofed with an utterly joyless clock tower. The extensions to Wentworth (1972, extended 1975) use brick, though they do their best to disguise the fact, and some monopitched roofs have crept into the architects' vocabulary latterly. Goodricke (1968) is the most box-like of the colleges, the most interesting object being the heating calorifier in a glass case in the courtyard. The Physics Laboratory (1967), a large glass box with the structure sticking through at the ends, and feeble variations in the glazing patterns, is the least happy building in the campus. The Central Hall (1968) is the one building making no attempt to avoid monumentality. Semi-octagonal, the raked seating steps and cantilevers out about the foyer and brick terraces, to a walkway round the top, whose aluminium trim wraps round and down the flat side of the building, which is centred on the lift tower. Structural loose-ends are tied up in a skeletal turret above the roof. Vanbrugh College by the lake, and Alcuin on the hill above are of 1967, already showing a marked decline in the exuberance of the design. Langwith and Derwent Colleges, the first of the colleges (both 1965), are much the most enjoyable, stretching the resources of the structural system in the little oriels and glass spires, and the imagination of the designer in the intricate planning of courtyards. Jerky concrete bridges cross University Road. The Bowes Morrell Library (1966) is monumental in size and conception, but, lest it should be too intimidating, bits of the pattern are left out and white panels are put in here and there, so the building looks as though repairs are permanently in progress. Good interior with galleries round a central staircase and smokers relegated to the topmost tier. The umbrella-shaped Water Tower, behind the Chemistry Laboratories (1965), is the most successful vertical element on the site; the triple Boiler House Chimney the most prominent.

Heslington Hall, at the E end of the campus, was built for Thomas Eynns, Secretary of the Council of the North, and finished *c.* 1568. It was sold to the Hesketh family in 1601; survived the siege; passed to the Yarburgh family in 1708 and had its gardens formally laid out. Yarburgh Graeme rebuilt or extensively recast it (1852–5) to designs by P.C. Hardwick. Alterations of 1876 and 1903 removed some of the more extreme elements of Hardwick's design, and there were alterations under Dr Feilden before the University moved in. Hardwick's entrance front follows Eynns's house very closely (the original front door is in the kitchen garden), and Eynn's pendant ceiling still remains in the Hall, where Dr Feilden's staircase is a curious contrast to the feeble wooden screen at the top. Hardwick's ceilings in the reception rooms have jagged geometrical patterns. The two flanking towers on the garden side are also part of Eynns's house. In the gardens, the University has contributed a formal pond and a Henry Moore, and the 18th century a delightful two-storey gazebo and the marvellous trimmed yews, like rows of tall unfashionable hats.

The Village had a typical estate church by J.B. and W Atkinson, 1857–8, early-14th-century in style, not large, steep-roofed, with a broach spire, set by itself to look well from the Hall. In 1966 George G. Pace and Ronald G. Sims designed an extension, turning the axis at right angles, a series of interlocking octagons providing vestries and meeting rooms beyond the new N sanctuary. Outside, the roof forms seem to have given a little trouble, but inside it is an unqualified success with a slatted roof unifying the whole, sweeping down then up into dormers, which prevent any sense of oppressive lowness. Characteristic fittings make much use of wrought iron. Atkinson's chancel is used as a weekday chapel.

Heslington is the most rewarding of York villages since it remains a real 'estate village'. The University has provided it with banks (whose design seems inimical to the village aesthetic), a few large houses (mostly discreet), and an excellent new housing estate. In Back Lane the cottage-like village school of 1795 faces the rather grander Gothic building of 1856 (is it by Hardwick or the Atkinsons?) and 1940s council housing compares favourably with flaccid Georgian in Lloyd's Close. Main Street has trees down one side, wide grass verges, and is full of nice individual touches: Laburnum Cottage with a Chinese Chippendale porch; Almshouses (1903) in late-17th-century style, probably by Brierley; Manor House and Little Hall, both Georgian; behind the village shop, Wesleyan Chapel (1884) with Tudor glazing bars; the street then turns at right angles SE towards Fulford, past walls and stables to another pleasant group: the Lodge with pretty glazing and cast ironwork; Almshouses founded by Sir Thomas Hesketh in 1605 and rebuilt by Henry Yarburgh in 1795; and More House, mid-18th-century, whose three-storey bays leave just enough space for the door. Behind it the University Design Unit has produced an excellent estate for the Holmfield Housing Society (1969–71); houses in brick and pantiles, in simple unfussy shapes, echoing old village buildings and giving overall a real sense of place. The brickwork however seems sadly impermanent.

Both St Lawrence's church, Vicarage, 11 Newland Park Close, tel. 24916 and Heslington church, Vicarage in village, tel. 59389 are usually locked. The University Grounds are open but for access to the buildings tel. 59861. Frequent concerts, films, plays, etc.

Walk Fourteen
Fulford

Fulford developed early and pleasantly, and since it quickly took up all the available space between the river on one side and the East Moor on the other and was cut off from the city by the development of the Cavalry Barracks from 1795 and the Infantry Barracks from 1874, it remains pleasant with its own distinct identity. Between Barracks and city Victorian predominates. There had been a little, tentative development along the riverside in the early 19th century, but when the cemetery was laid out, E of the main road, in 1836, it was said to have 'very commanding views – and from its secluded position it is not likely to be encroached upon by new buildings'.*

The Battle of Fulford, the first and least remembered of the three decisive battles of Autumn 1066, was fought on 20 September: Morker, Earl of Northumberland, and Edwin, Earl of Mercia, were defeated by Harold Hardrada and Tostig. The city capitulated and the probability that Hardrada would become King must have seemed high; but success was short-lived and only five days later they were defeated by the arm of Harold Godwinson at Stamford Bridge. The survivors could man only 24 of the 315 ships that had brought the invading army to Riccall. By 28 September William of Normandy's expected invasion had become reality and Harold Godwinson marched south again, to be defeated at Hastings on 14 October. Archbishop Aeldred of York officiated both at Godwinson's hallowing early in 1066 and William's coronation on Christmas Day.

Fishergate – 'the street of the Fishermen', recorded from *c*.1080 – starts at Fishergate Postern, though the name was

---

* *Yorkshire Gazette*, 8 April 1837.

formerly and more logically that of the street (now Fawcett Street) leading to Fishergate Bar. The Mason's Arms has a splendid Gothic fireplace of *c.* 1830 from the Castle Gatehouse; Oxtoby's decorators shop has a delightfully old-fashioned front: behind these the Glassworks looms. The Festival Flats (1951) have weathered decently, but seem scarcely festive. No. 29 is good late-18th-century: 33 was something special, but has been vandalized recently by the removal of glazing bars, which made each of its pointed windows a little Chippendale bookcase. Fishergate School (1893) is the earliest of Demaine and Brierley's large schools; corner pavilions, beautiful brickwork, and a scrolly pedimented door, which seems to have crept in from somewhere else. Northern Command Headquarters (1878), Tudor with a corner tower, was designed by the Command's own architectural staff.

Of the churches of All Saints and St Helen's, Fishergate, nothing remains, and a scrap of wall in Blue Bridge Lane is all that is left of St Andrew's Priory (Gilbertine), founded 1202 and suppressed 1538. Fishergate House is an ambitious design of 1837 by J.B. and W. Atkinson in grey brick, with giant pilasters, an Ionic porch, and balustrades linking the chimney stacks. It has the most imaginative and spatially ingenious of York staircases, much influenced by Soane, with a curved screen of columns at the half landing and plane upon plane of receding arches around the central light well.

Melbourne Street leads E to Cemetery Road, past lozenge-shaped Victorian front gardens and Edward Taylor's Wesleyan church (1877) in rumbustious polychromatic Baroque. York Cemetery is (or should be) one of the glories of the city [48]; poised in a state of admirable decay, between being totally overgrown and cleared away by bureaucratic processes. It was opened in 1837, buildings and layout being designed by J.P. Pritchett. Handsome Walker iron gates and railings are stopped at their extremities by piers with sarcophagus and sphinx. The landscaping merged formal and informal elements: the chapel is at the hub of both; an exquisite Greek revival building, quite without Wilkins's stiffness; Ionic with a portico and engaged porticos at the ends; its condition is an indictment of conservation policy. The monuments are rewarding to study both aesthetically and to the local historian. William Hargrove and Harvey Brook, antiquarians, John Atkinson and William Plows, sculptors, and Henry Cave, engraver, are buried here together with members of the Leeman, Sykes-Rymer, and Terry families. The delightful Gray monument dates from 1837, just before Gothic became serious; the Leetham family monument has not quite settled for Jacobean; the early Roman Catholics have elaborately Gothic table tombs and a Walker iron cross; but the strangest monument is Charles Ellis Hessey (d. 1874) carved recumbent beneath a sheet, Pre-Raphaelite among the briers. On a misty autumn day the place is magical.

The streets w between Fishergate and the river are a strange social and architectural mixture. New Walk Terrace has bow-windowed Regency houses and Dutch-gabled Victorian ones. Beyond The Lighthorseman, a handsome Victorian pub, the Lodge at the corner of Grange Garth is one of York's prettiest houses, with deep projecting eaves and latticed windows. The Grange is grey brick, late-Regency, and a little Gothic house overlooks the river at the end of the lane. Behind the Priory Hotel are medieval 'ruins' and re-erected on the other side of Fishergate is part of John Harper's 1834 front for the Theatre Royal. Villas follow Fulford Road. Behind are working-class streets like Alma Terrace, with a serious, round-arched Victorian Police Station and an Arts and Crafts front to the Wellington, contrasting with Wenlock Terrace, grandly and gloomily Gothic. Fulford Cross was formerly the city boundary.

The Cavalry Barracks were a result of Pitt's building programme of 1792; the original handsome buildings were demolished a few years ago, though the grand Royal Arms in Coadestone has been reused on the excellent new administrative block. The Infantry Barracks, designed by the War Department were added 1877–80. The 'Keep' by the gate has little slit windows spiralling round the staircase towers. The rest of the buildings are neither memorable nor accessible.

Fulford is recorded as Fuleford ('dirty ford') in Domesday Book.

The village starts with outstanding houses. Danesmead (1903) and Ousefield (1899) are both by Brierley, playing a favourite game of bays projecting out between gables projecting up, but where Danesmead is essentially vernacular, Ousefield is designed in the grand manner. Opposite, No. 135 is more relaxed, by Penty and Penty (1903), who also did two pairs of houses just beyond Moorland Road and Langbaraugh, the most Voyseyesque of the group.

St Oswald's Road (right) has pleasant villas and a Gothick cottage, and leads w to Fulford Old Church, a charming building; very small, redundant, boarded up, and in need of a suitable new use. There are Norman windows N of the chancel but most of the others seem plain 17th-century. Tapering 18th-century brick tower. Pretty roof of fishscale tiles by Wade and Cherry of Hornsea. Inside plaster ceilings, a decaying lady mourning over an urn, and two vast benefaction boards taking up most of the N wall of the nave. The concrete path through the pleasant churchyard vies for insensitivity with the nearby pumping station.

The parish church was designed by J.P. Pritchett II in 1868 and restored to the same design after a fire in 1877. Much prickly carved work inside with French overtones, a Salviati mosaic reredos and stained glass by Clayton and Bell, and Hughes.

The Hunt Memorial Homes by Needham Thorpe and White (1954) are a thorough period piece.

Stable Cottage, in Fulford Park, has a delightful Victorian dovecote with a pagoda top. Heslington Lane, with small Regency Houses, leads to East Moor, still open country, though it was bigger when the battle was fought here. The village street has a group of large, attractive houses; Fulford Park, rendered, irregular, Regency to Victorian; the Old House and the White House, with prominent chimney stacks, both Georgian, as is the Old Vicarage, with a handsome and unusual front taken up entirely by two bay windows. In Fenwicks Lane, W, there are excellent cast-iron gates to Fulford Hall, and Delwood Croft is an important Regency House, recently restored, with a grand staircase linking apse-ended drawing rooms. The rest of the village stays pleasantly rural despite unfortunate gaps and bits of infill.

A lane to the right near the end of the village leads to the river. Downstream, Water Fulford Hall, an irregular Georgian house (better seen from the footpath across the fields to Naburn), enjoyed, till recently, an idyllic view over the best riverside scenery near York, to Bishopthorpe in the distance. Now the by-pass bisects the view and traffic trundles noisily along the skyline. However, pedestrians may still enjoy a pleasant walk, under Ove Arup's massive bridge, and will be rewarded with much the best view of Bishop-thorpe Palace. Those with reserves of energy may return to the city by the river, through forgotten, hawthorn-hedged fields of Fulford Ings, with distant glimpses of the Minster, still apparently in the country; round the Yacht Club and past the old church, more fields and then down the New Walk, and John Carr's Pikeing Well (1752), and past a marvellous unfolding medieval skyline, into the city.

The Military buildings are not open. The Old Cemetery is defiantly open at the time of writing. Fulford church is open; the old church is sadly locked and boarded up.

Bishopgate Street is at the SW end of Skeldergate Bridge. The city walls are at their best; the ramparts high, tree-covered, and not too tidy; the iron gates a reminder of the formidable railings that once fortified the fortifications. Opposite, 1830s houses stand above their own green bank and terraced footpath. Those expecting Cherry Hill Lane (left) to provide verdant delights will be disappointed; this cranky industrial alley leads SE to a warren of little streets known collectively as Clementhorpe, the site of St Clement's Nunnery, supposed to have been founded *c.* 1125–35, though the name 'Clementhorpe' is older, probably recalling an earlier parish church. A fragment of precinct wall survives – for the moment – next to new housing. (A worn statue of the Virgin is in the Yorkshire Museum.)

Bishopthorpe Road, straight at first, then curving and climbing briefly, is Victorian and later, Bishopthorpe village having been too far away to promote early linking development. West in Scarcroft Road, St Clement's church stands among late-Victorian stock-brick housing, but a Dudley watercolour in the vestry shows it newly built and still rural. By J.B. and W. Atkinson (1874), it is the grimmest of York's Victorian churches, in red brick, angular Gothic with black bands instead of mouldings, a sharp bell spike at the corner, and an unattractive but impressively scaled interior, red vehemently patterned in black. The E window shows Capronnier at his worst, the choir stalls 'Mousy' Thompson at his best – neither of which is saying much. Fittings and monuments from St Mary, Bishophill Senior; 10th-century tomb slab, several Georgian monuments (Alathea Fairfax, d. 1744; cartouche to Elias Pawson, d. 1715), mayoral boards, a

17th-century altar table, and delightful Georgian bread shelves.

Victorian Bishopthorpe Road ends horribly at Southlands Chapel (1886) by C. Bell, 'free Italian' with twin pyramids and terracotta roses round the window. Rowntree's Park, E towards the river, is a sensible rather than inspired war memorial, designed by Fred Rowntree (1919–21); landscaping coming second best to tennis and bowls; half-timbered memorial lodge, and pond like a dog's bone. At the riverside entrance the very fine early-18th-century gates (of uncertain provenance) were installed in 1954. Ornament is concentrated in panels and then exuberantly along the top. Attribution to Tijou has proved inevitable.

St Chad's, Campleshon Road, further out on the right, is one of Brierley's last works; Gothic conceived in terms of brickwork and concrete roof trusses; no mouldings; huge scale; unfinished; towering arches inside lead to narrow aisles and low arches to an eastern chapel. It is a personal and impressive building with an evident debt to Temple Moore's Middlesbrough churches.

The arcade of John Carr's Racecourse Stand of 1755 has been rebuilt in the Paddock. It was an early commission, important in establishing him with the local gentry.

Terry's dominates the neighbourhood as it dominates the Knavesmire. Five storeys of mullioned and transomed windows beneath an enormous crowning cornice, detached clock tower and offices in Free-Georgian style, it is largely of 1925–30, designed by J.G. Davis and L.E. Wade. It marks an abrupt end to the city, its back to the countryside making much less effort. Knavesmire and the Ouse have here prevented development, so Middlethorpe, just inside the city boundary, was deeply rural till recently. New houses are appearing, old ones are being 'improved' or left to rot, and the sound of traffic on the by-pass is only too audible. Pretty white gates lead to Middlethorpe Manor, which is dull, rendered 18th-century.

Middlethorpe Hall is very grand indeed, the most imposing of the late-17th-century–early-18th-century houses round the city, which include Cumberland House, Myton

279

Hall, and Bell Hall, Naburn. Built *c.* 1699–1701 for Thomas Barlow, it is three-storeyed, brick with stone quoins and bands, with stone surrounds to all the windows elaborated in the centre into a continuous vertical feature topped by the Barlow eagle on each front. The dovecote is earlier than the house. The wings with a Corinthian order on the garden side (and clearly not meant to be seen on the entrance side) are of the mid 18th century, and the porticos were added in the early 19th. The Hall is now a Club. Several fine interiors survive: carved, cantilevered staircase, propped strategically by a Corinthian column; panelled Ionic Dining Room; pretty early-19th-century ballroom ceiling.

The bridge over the by-pass commands a disquieting view over a mile of Knavesmire towards an apparently non-existent city. The Crematorium, by the City Architect's Department (1963), standing in pleasantly landscaped grounds, is excellent outside but desperately antiseptic within. Beyond, parkland and a walled garden lead to Bishopthorpe.

Archbishop Walter de Gray bought the Manor of Thorpe St Andrew in 1241, and built a new house for himself and his successors on the bank of the Ouse. It evidently soon replaced in favour the old Archbishop's Palace by the Minster, and, apart from a short period during the Commonwealth, has been the Archbishops' home ever since. The Palace and grounds form a private residence. They are not open to the general public but are used by a wide variety of groups in the Church and community. However, the Gatehouse and Stables are well seen from the road; the Palace from the river (no landing stage of course), and better still from the opposite towpath (see Fulford, p. 277), whence one has a comprehensive picture of its development.

Archbishop Walter's house was not large, and much of it survives. The lancet windows of the Hall undercroft remain to the river and the chapel, though restored, is largely intact. It makes no show outside, plain bell lancets, gableted buttresses, and a larger gabled projection for a spiral staircase. Inside, continuous wall arcading has windows in alternate bays and is stepped up at the ends to accommodate the E window and Oberammergau carving. The chapel was restored in 1892 when glass by Kempe replaced Peckett glass of 1767. At the end of the 15th century Archbishop Rotherham following the lead of the Abbot of St Mary's (and probably using the same craftsmen) doubled the size of the house, adding a N wing at right angles to the river, in brick with black vitrified patterns, just as at the Abbey. It has been much altered but a fine chimney with corbelled spurs is probably original. Colonel White, who bought the house during the Commonwealth for £525, added the little gabled wings to the forecourt. After the Restoration, Archbishop Frewen (1660–4) rebuilt the Hall with brick rusticated and pilastered façades to the riverside and originally to the forecourt, the most important survivor of this particular provincial style. Inside, the ceiling has heavy beams, leaf trails, and oval panels not yet all Italian. (The grand Doric fireplace is early-18th-century.) Much Archiepiscopal heraldic glass. In the 1760s Archbishop Drummond commissioned a whole series of new works, bringing aesthetic order to this picturesque but hardly unified group of buildings. His architect was Thomas Atkinson, who, apparently feeling the inappositeness of classicism in these surroundings, chose the Gothick style, at which he showed himself delightfully accomplished. Colvin says that Atkinson designed the stables in 1763;* if so their slightly outmoded style, though it may owe its more Baroque touches to subsequent remodelling, must always have been an odd contrast to the rest of the new work. Atkinson's Gatehouse with its long flanking walls is an enchanting piece (probably built largely of material from Cawood Castle). The new Palace front has everything one expects from a Georgian house, symmetry, portico, pediment, and cornice, except that it all happens to be Gothick. Vaulted Gothick entrance hall with niches and ogees leads to the Drawing Room with a delicious confectioner's–Gothic ceiling. Of the series of Archiepiscopal and other portraits ranging from Cardinal Wolsey to the present day, the finest is Kneller's portrait of Archbishop Lamplugh.

* Howard Colvin, *A Biographical Dictionary of British Architects 1600–1840* (1978), p. 74.

Bishopthorpe church (1888–1903) is one of Hodgson Fowler's smoothest and blandest designs, enlivened by recent fittings by G.G. Pace and glass by H. Stammers. In the churchyard is a memorial to Walter Brierley, who designed Bishopthorpe Garth in Sim Balk Lane (W) with long sweeping roofs, low eaves, an attractive Gatehouse to the street, and the remains of a Gertrude Jekyll garden layout.

The village street has plenty of trees and a few cottages pleasantly unimproved. Circumambient roads of semi-detacheds commemorate Archbishops. One nice Georgian farmhouse stands at the corner near the Palace and other pleasant, larger houses line the lane along the edge of the Park, leading to the river and the remains of the old church built by Archbishop Drummond in 1766. The remaining W front is supposed to have been added by Archbishop Harcourt in 1842, which seems an impossibly late date for this enchanting eyecatcher.

☆

St Clement's church is locked, Vicarage tel. 24425; St Chad's church open. There is no public access to Bishopthorpe Palace or its grounds.

The Mount and Clifton and Bootham are the best approaches to York. The Mount is grander, and less unified; has better natural features and has done less with them. However, when its own attractions are supplemented by those of the streets leading from it, it may reasonably claim supremacy. The Mount is only the author's name for it; strictly it comprises Blossom Street (originally Ploxwangate from Ploughman), The Mount proper, over the moraine (but named after the fort or mount that protected this side of the city during the 1644 siege), Mount Vale, Tadcaster Road (by the Knavesmire), and Dringhouses village. It is the ceremonial entrance to the city: the Monarch is usually met by the Lord Mayor at Micklegate Bar, and the Archbishop on his way to his enthronement was met by the Dean and Chapter at St James's Chapel on The Mount. It was along Blossom Street that the garrison departed 'on honourable terms' after the siege.

St Thomas's Hospital stood just outside Micklegate Bar from the 14th century till its removal in 1863 to new white-brick, Dutch-gabled premises near Victoria Bar, having been spared at the reorganization of 1547.

The Bar Convent (The Convent of the Institute of St Mary) was established in 1686, an outcome of the educational work of Mary Ward, whose monument is at Osbaldwick. The present buildings were started in 1766–9 when the Chapel block was built, set well back from the street, the new front block being added in 1786–9: the architect for both was Thomas Atkinson, whose elevation has remarkably generous windows and a centrepiece with door and window treated as an architectural unit under an arch (a favourite device of the architect, who used it again on his house in St

Andrewgate). The little cupola above the clock tower (Henry Hindley clock) can only be seen from further down the street. In 1834 J.B. and W. Atkinson built a courtyard between the earlier blocks and nondescript wings at the back. The Poor School on the corner of Nunnery Lane, with a big Doric portico, was designed by G.T. Andrews, 1844–5. Andrews was responsible for much later work in the building, but not apparently for the railway station roof of the 'Atrium' inside (not added till after 1865) nor its Minton tile floor. The Chapel is upstairs and not impressively approached. It is an exquisite room. Atkinson handled space with marvellous subtlety – his little church at Brandsby is a masterpiece. Here, at the end of a plain arcaded room with a coved ceiling, a domed rotunda on eight Ionic columns is the inside of a building that has no outside, open to the nave, closed by a curved wall immediately behind the altar, the dome decorated with panels like Rococo mirror frames. Everything – like the rotunda just wider than the nave – is slightly unexpected. The altar is partly original. A collection of interesting statuary includes the four Latin Doctors on the reredos and several Baroque groups, all 18th-century, a 17th-century Virgin and Child, and 16th-century wooden Netherlandish panels.

A group of 1830–50 houses follows, some imposingly detailed with stone door and window surrounds. Connoisseurs of pub architecture will enjoy the Lion and the Lamb and the Bay Horse. The Windmill was more exciting when painted with an all-over pattern, like pyramids in relief. The Prudential is decent, and replaced Georgian houses that were better. The Odeon (1937) by Harry Weedon was always the best of York cinemas. In mellowed brick, its cubical design with rounded corners and little spurs will be more admired in a year or two. How long will it be before it is 'listed'? Peter Atkinson Junior lived in South Parade, an excellent terrace of 1825–8 houses with bows and simple doorcases.

Moss Street leads E to Scarcroft Road School (1896), Brierley's masterpiece and one of the grandest of York's buildings [55]. High centre hall-range flanked by teaching-ranges: lower corner wings at right angles, then lower wings still at right angles again, all except the teaching ranges with steep roofs. Turrets run up the corners of the central block to cloak the junction with the wings – because nothing happens quite as expected – and a larger turret tops the whole composition. The 17th-century detailing of the earlier schools has been abandoned. What little historical reference there is, is Gothic. The influence of Robson's London schools is evident, but this is a much grander performance.

East Mount Road is a Victorian version of South Parade, and not so nice. It leads W into the Mount, which starts at Holgate Road. Regency with bizarre touches like The Mount pub (knobbly Victorian) and the cliff-like Abbey Park Hotel (*c.* 1830) with hefty Doric portico. The most pleasing Regency are 92 and 94 with a double porch, and the little terrace of Nos. 100–4. Bricked up beneath 104 is a Roman burial vault. This, the Roman road to Tadcaster, passed through an important cemetery, several of whose monuments are now in the Yorkshire Museum. Nos. 116–32 are of the 1830s and 1840s; 122 ambitious in stone; 130 and 132 with spirally-bandaged columns.

Mount Parade is one of York's delights. Houses of the 1820s and 1840s with big gardens and pretty ironwork; opposite allotments behind a wall is a foreground to the improbable Byzantine vision of the church of English Martyrs. Nothing could be easier or more charming. Cumberland House, otherwise the best of the group, is spoiled by insensitive plumbing.

The Mount continues Regency with a beautifully maintained terrace of 1824. Nunroyd, opposite, has a late-Georgian front with full-height bays. After this the character of the street changes. Houses become bigger, more individual, set back behind large gardens. Villas appear: so do styles – Tudor, Italianate, Arts and Crafts. Italianate predominates in Mill Mount, E. Mill Mount School by J.B. and W. Atkinson (*c.* 1850) was designed as a house. Great restraint and severity are allied to the oddest plan-shape, the two wings at right angles with the porch set diagonally between. The other two, more orthodox villas, are also probably by the Atkinsons. They were certainly responsible for houses in Dalton Terrace and Driffield Terrace, earlier ones in grey brick, still with some semblance of Georgian order, later ones unattractively rendered in Roman cement (some with the remains of spectacular interiors). The Atkinsons must also have designed the agreeable front of The Mount School, a less majestic version of the County Hospital. In the garden, a delightful ogee-domed Summer House of *c.* 1774 is known as 'the Lindley Murray'. It was brought here from the garden of Holgate House (Walk 17), where Murray lived for 39 years. His *Grammar* was written for Esther Tuke's boarding school in Trinity Lane, a forerunner of the present school.

English Martyrs' church (a dedication recalling the proximity of Tyburn) is inter-war Byzantine. Very elaborate brickwork with much use of thin tiles, and a basilican interior, by Williams and Jopling, Hull, 1932.

The Mount continues, downhill now, with assorted villas. Daresbury and the Mount Royale, grey-brick Tudor; several classical ones, then Westmount (1899) by Brierley, whose asymmetrical Tudor porch has a pointed roof. Opposite an old wall with vestiges of windows recalls Mount House, and a 1920s house with curly gables recalls Oliver Hill.

Elm Bank is four-square, grim, grey-brick, of *c.* 1870. Its interiors are among the most important survivals of British Art Nouveau. They were commissioned in 1898 by Sidney Leetham from W.G. and A.J. Penty working in collaboration with George Walton, the Glasgow designer, who worked with C.R. Mackintosh. Walton's work at York has not been thoroughly explored. He is supposed to have had business premises in Stonegate. Though much of his work has been destroyed since the war, much may still be left. The galleried hall is much as Walton left it (though the segmental ceiling is later). Elsewhere there are wriggling friezes in the Bar; ceilings painted with small nervous patterns; a mural much in the style of Walter Crane; a marvellous overmantel in marble, glass and ceramics, and stained glass designed with fronds, tendrils, and little glittering bobbles [53]. So much of this has been recovered by the present owners that one hesitates to complain of the impercipient flock wallpapers whose application has temporarily nullified the good work.

Mount Vale continues small-scale Regency, till the pretty, cross-shaped, bargeboarded Herdsman's Cottage at the end of Knavesmire or Micklegate Stray: largest of the city's strays, on which the Freemen of York had the right among other things to pasture their cattle. They are now held for the benefit and enjoyment of the citizens. Large houses overlook Micklegate Stray from Tadcaster Road. On the other side tiny Victorian terraces are dominated by Terry's factory and the huge, out-of-scale Racecourse Grandstand (Rainger, Roger, and Smithson, 1965), swamping its pretty Victorian predecessor. The aesthetics of racing are apt to be unattractive. Meetings have been held here since 1731.

St George's Place, on the right, was laid out in the 1890s, happily at the exact moment when domestic architecture both locally and nationally had its triumphant resurgence.. After the Harrogate-stone style of No. 2 (George Fletcher, 1897), there are two pairs by G.L Monson (1886): seaside half-timbering with sunflowers on the roof. Penty and Penty designed No. 20 in 1891, showing the beginnings of new sensitivity in excellent stonework detailing; Nos. 16 and 18 (1903) in a Voyseyish idiom, and the Tile House opposite (c.1900) a fine house sadly altered. Bishopbarns was designed in 1905 by Brierley for himself, with a garden by Gertrude Jekyll. Recessed centre between gabled wings round a chequer-cobbled court; the front roof tipped almost vertically to improve the attic rooms. Windows of all shapes and sizes, impeccably controlled. To the garden the roof sweeps and curves down over a loggia between a big gable on one side and a smaller hipped roof on the other. The inventive, varied, and wonderfully satisfying exterior is matched by a comfortable, informal, beautifully detailed interior. It is perhaps the finest house in York of any period [54].

Further along Tadcaster Road, a little patch of paving and some Corporation seats commemorate Tyburn, the place of public execution. The Catholic and Protestant martyrs of the 16th and 17th centuries might be more profitably remembered than rogues and oddities like Dick Turpin and Eugene Aram. Opposite, w, a path past allotments and the Hob Stone (last weathered vestige of a medieval effigy) leads under the railway line to Hob Moor, an unexciting level, surrounded by buildings, lacking a view.

Large houses resume facing Knavesmire; brick with classical references and aberrations, Regency villas (one with tracery in the garden, probably from All Saints', Pavement); the best is No. 310, a beautifully balanced design (1904) by Fred Rowntree, with assorted sash windows in easy-going Lutyens style, and sensitive though regrettable alterations.

Dringhouses village has suffered by the erosion of all but its best buildings. The older houses are Georgian and Regency; the Cross Keys, early-18th-century, nicely remodelled in 1900, the site of a pub here since the 13th century. Walnut Cottage and No. 23, with a pretty openwork porch spanning the garden, flank the gatehouse to Goddards (1926–7), one of Brierley's last houses, away from the road at an angle to the drive, formally Tudor at the front relaxing into vernacular towards the pleasant garden.

Dringhouses has the prettiest of York's Victorian churches: Decorated with no profound ambitions, by Vickers and Hugill, 1847, its interior suggesting Surrey. Its medieval and Georgian predecessors had both been on different sites. Painted texts, and stained glass by Wailes (the E window won a prize at the 1851 Exhibition), Comper (1936), Bewsey (1932), in memory of Mrs Brierley, and Harry Harvey (1960s).

Opposite the latticed-windowed branch library built as the village school in 1852 is the pinfold for the confinement of stray cattle.

☆

The Bar Convent Chapel may be visited by prior arrangement, tel. 29359. English Martyrs' church and Dringhouses church are usually open. Elm Bank is an hotel.

Walk Seventeen
Acomb

A quarter of York's population lives in Acomb, a spreading surburban wedge between the Ouse and London railway line; amply treed though scarcely sylvan, bumping over the moraine on whose back, away from the city, the old village lies submerged in recent growth.

Holgate Road opens inauspiciously W out of Blossom Street, improving after the second bend with Regency and Victorian houses at different levels on a double curve. A steep, setted lane leads up to Mount Parade (see Walk 16) between the jolly, jerky end of 19 Holgate Road and Mount Terrace (1827–8) on top of a bank, where the more imposing end villa was the house of Hargrove the antiquarian and printer.

Holgate Railway Bridge (1911), meccano between gritstone piers, leads to St Paul's church by J.B. and W. Atkinson (1850–1) in lancet style with spindly pinnacles and sharp gables. The unattractively textured stonework arrived early in York and lingered late; unexpectedly pleasant interior with cast-iron columns and gas brackets; later fittings spilling out of the still pre-tractarian chancel. Stained glass by Heaton, Butler, and Bayne (1905), Whitefriars (1937), Stammers (1957). From Watson Street the Minster appears grandly above massed railway buildings. Holgate Road continues with a terrace of 1846–50 with bays and pretty glazing; St Paul's Square is pleasantly Victorian round a green space and the shape of a grand piano; Holgate Hill has large, white barge-boarded villas facing semis high up. Holgate House – with one Georgian doorway apparently superimposed on another – was the home of Lindley Murray from 1785 to 1826.

Poppleton Road forks right past carriage works. Holgate

Road passes uphill terraced streets ending against the sky as though at the seaside, Holgate Methodist church (1910) with inventive brickwork, and Holgate Mill, late-18th-century, lacking its sails, in the middle of a housing estate. West Park, with suspiciously Lutyensian gateposts, has Milburn's Jubilee statue of Queen Victoria, which spent post-war years in a box in the Art Gallery before being exiled here, lacking her nose. Mormon church, an uncomfortable angular design by Peter Nuttall, 1960–1. An entertaining Victorian range fronts Severus Hills, the highest point on this side of the moraine, traditional scene of the funeral of Emperor Septimus Severus, now dotted conspicuously with box-like flats. The next few hundred yards and the blasted village entrance have little aesthetic appeal.

Acomb old village lies along Front Street and round the Green. Front Street keeps one side of a village street, pleasant uneventful 18th- and 19th-century houses; opposite, gaps and new buildings are variously unenjoyable. The school is minor Brierley (1894). No. 68 has a country look (one pretty late-18th-century fireplace). No. 21, the Lodge, is early-18th-century with Regency bows. Acomb House, much the grandest in the village, is early-18th-century with an early-19th-century porch. Excellent panelling downstairs; staircase, approached axially through an arch, leads to the Saloon, whose rococo fireplace with lovely, open twirling pediment contrasts with bucolic Adamesque late-18th-century ceiling.

Gale Farm in Gale Lane improbably has a real fold yard with real hay in barns.

That Acomb Green remains more rural than Clifton Green is a remarkable achievement. A triangular grassy hollow, it is steeply banked round the upper corner, where the war memorial stands among trees, and the church above old cottages. The churchyard, down a long path, is unexpectedly rural with mature trees and excellent early gravestones – the best old churchyard in York. The church is by G.T. Andrews (1831–2), with a chancel of 1851, in the baldest lancet style, sloping buttresses and a ruckled spire apprehensively emerging from a pyramid. Plastered interior with blue and white barrel ceiling of the 1930s, and huge gallery organ apparently about to launch itself down the church. Arms of William IV. Stained glass arms of Charles II (1663), probably the work of Edmund Gyles. Monuments by local sculptors, Atkinson, M. Taylor, Waudby. Taylor's Smith cenotaph is remarkable for the number of people commemorated but buried elsewhere: Croydon, Ceylon, Edinboro', Riegate (sic), and Scarboro'.

Recent ecclesiastical architecture may be studied in Gale Lane and Poppleton Road. Our Lady, Gale Lane (1955), by J.H. Langtry Langton, is brick Byzantine survival, the interior elaborately and incoherently ornamented. James the Deacon church hall by G.G. Pace (1954) is low, unfussy, with just an eyebrow-like dormer for fun. Some distance away in Sheringham Drive, embedded in a housing estate is Pace's later, tougher church of James the Deacon (1970–1). Roses round the walls suggest the locals still find it an odd building. High gable running across, one long slope sweeping low over the vestries interrupted by a shorter, steeper one with a bell turret over the chapel. The plan looks straightforward, but isn't quite. The shape is devised to house an early Pace baldachino from St John's College Old Chapel. Slatted ceiling over bare brick walls. The late-Norman door in the narthex comes from St Maurice's church as do the fittings and glass and 17th-century panels in the side chapel. The foundation stone, a medieval coffin lid, is grandly inscribed '1970'.

Holy Redeemer church (1962–4) in Poppleton Road is the best modern church in York, also designed by G.G. Pace, incorporating as much of the medieval fabric of St Mary, Bishophill Senior, as the fragile nature of the stone would allow, but the setting devised for these ancient elements is wholly free from historical pastiche. Beside the sharp-roofed tower is a porch, beyond it a weekday chapel, and beyond that Pace windows (some under spare bits of parapet from St Martin-le-Grand), and 13th-century doorway and lancets coexist in medieval masonry. The interior, entered by a late-12th-century door, is low but not oppressive, with a ceiling of pyramids, tipped to accommodate a Victorian window (J.B. and W. Atkinson restored St Mary's in 1860). The arcade is very varied; three bays of the late 12th century and the E respond turned into a pier to go with the next three 14th-century bays, then a final 15th-century bay; it is set close to the wall, and opposite are brick piers with simple concrete lintels. Five little parable windows by H. Stammers. Big wrought iron cross incorporating a piece of late-12th-century cross shaft. Other Anglian fragments are in lectern, pulpit, and S wall. The decision to use these in the fabric, rather than leave them as exhibits or commit them to a museum, has proved controversial.

Poppleton Road School (1904), nearer the city, is one of Brierley's best, damaged in 1942 and respectfully rebuilt; a long range with 'wings' at right angles but the same depth, tall arched entrances to the playground, keel-shaped dormers, and a striking chimney.

☆

Acomb churches are now generally locked. St Paul's, Rectory, 100 Acomb Road, tel. 792304; Acomb parish church, Vicarage, 76 The Green, Acomb, tel. 798106; James the Deacon, Vicarage, Thanet Road, Dringhouses, tel. 706047; Holy Redeemer, Vicarage, 108 Boroughbridge Road, York, tel. 798593.

Excursions

Seven main roads meet at York. The A1, 20 miles to the W, makes even the Lake District possible for a day excursion from the city; but these notes are intended for the reader interested in what can be found within a 30–40 mile radius of the city, the suggested excursions arranged clockwise, starting from the N.

North 1

The A19 links York and Thirsk, through flat countryside at first, then touching the edges of the Howardian and Hambleton Hills. Skelton has a perfect 13th-century village church, never extended, closely associated with the Minster transepts in design. Beningbrough Hall, early 18th-century, splendid woodwork, paintings from the National Portrait Gallery. Beyond Easingwold, a Georgian market town, the countryside is rich in Victorian churches: Sessay and Dalton (Morris glass) by Butterfield, who designed a complete village at Baldersby St James; Aldwark, Thirkleby, and Bagby by E.B. Lamb. Coxwold, a beautiful village, is not greatly changed since Laurence Sterne lived there (1760–8). Byland Abbey (Cistercian, founded 1177) is a mile away at the start of hilly countryside. Beyond Thirsk (Perpendicular church), rewarding, small-scale country round Cowesby and Kepwick, and Mount Grace Priory, founded 1398, the most extensive remains of an English Charterhouse.

North 2

The B1363 runs due N to Helmsley. Sutton-on-the-Forest is an overrated village, Stillington better, Crayke and

Brandsby (1767 church, 18th- and early-20th-century houses) better still. Gilling Castle with magnificent Great Chamber of 1575–85 is Junior School for Ampleforth Abbey, where the chapel and much else is by Sir Giles Gilbert Scott. Helmsley is an 'estate town' with Castle and fine Market Place. Rievaulx Abbey and Terrace, both exquisite, are three miles away. North of the Pickering road are charming villages, Appleton-le-Moors, Lastingham, Hutton-le-Hole (all too popular, like Farndale in daffodil time). Bilsdale and Rosedale are better known than Bransdale and Riccal-dale, all deeply pastoral below sober, rolling landscape of North Yorkshire Moors, dotted with tumuli and ancient crosses.

From Pickering (Castle, and medieval wall paintings in church), Whitby is easily reached over the moors, one of the happiest combinations of resort, fishing town, and shrine anywhere. St Mary's church with its Georgian interior is as moving in its way as the Benedictine Abbey ruins. Staithes, Runswick Bay, and Robin Hood's Bay are unexciting villages on their clifftops and breathtaking by the sea.

North-East

Wigginton, Haxby, Huntington, Towthorpe, and Earswick are villages congealed into suburbia. Sherrif Hutton Castle is a Cotmanesque ruin with farm yard and haystacks. The Howardian hills run W to E separated from the Wolds by the Derwent above Kirkham Priory, unspectacular ruins but an excellent place for writing guidebooks. Howsham Hall (Elizabethan) was built from the ruins; Howsham church (1860) is a little masterpiece by G.E. Street. Castle Howard is a national glory. Vanburgh's great Baroque palace overcomes both Palladian attempts to 'bring it into line' and the tragedy of war-time fire; Vanburgh's Temple is uncommonly gentle; Hawksmoor's Mausoleum, the noblest of English Baroque. Malton is a pleasant town of Roman origin, mercifully bypassed. The countryside SE is charming, the Scarborough road duller but with good churches like Street's

East Heslerton and East Knapton by Gibson of Malton, redundant in parkland.

Scarborough is still spectacularly beautiful despite wholesale demolition of the Old Town and massed meretriciousness of the front. Castle and St Mary's half-church – Anne Brontë is buried in the churchyard – separate North-side from South-side, where prim Regency terraces set off Brodrick's self-assertive Grand Hotel. Sitwell associations at Wood End.

East 1

The A166 is partly Roman, crossing the Derwent at Stamford Bridge, site of the battle in 1066. Charming countryside round Bugthorpe and Kirby Underdale, and Thixendale set in ever-bifurcating chalk valleys. The Wolds are dotted with evidences of early history succumbing to agriculture. Wharram Percy village, depopulated *c.* 1500, has been intensively excavated since 1950.

At Fridaythorpe there is a choice for Bridlington. On the northern road (B1251) lies Sledmere, estate village of the Sykes family, which changed the agricultural and ecclesiological face of the Wolds. The village is full of monuments; late-18th-century house; over-exquisite church by Temple Moore: Sir Tatton Sykes was probably the greatest of 19th-century church builders as witnessed by nearby Kirby Grindalythe, West Lutton, Helperthorpe, and Weaverthorpe, near by, all to G.E. Street's designs, and many more. Rudston has the largest monolith in England; Boynton, a charming Georgian church.

On the main road Garton-on-the Wolds has spectacular Sykes–Street–Clayton–and–Bell frescoed interior; Driffield is best around the head of its canal; Burton Agnes is another estate village, church with family monuments, Norman Manor House and Burton Agnes Hall, 1600–10, one of the most perfect of Elizabethan houses, with notable furniture and modern paintings.

Bridlington Old Town is Georgian, dominated by the nave

of the Augustinian Priory, now parochial. By the sea the town cannot compare with Scarborough, but away from their crops of caravans the cliffs of Flamborough, Buckton, and Bempton are superb.

East 2

Towards Beverley the A1079 skirts the Wolds for miles before finally crossing them at Market Weighton. Beyond Pocklington – good church and interesting town plan – Millington Springs is popular and Kilnwick Percy, Warter Priory, and Londesborough provide parkland along the escarpment. Everingham, s if the road, has a magnificent Roman Catholic church of 1836. The older parts of Market Weighton are disappearing fast. The Wolds rise abruptly behind, then fall gently and pleasantly towards Holderness, countryside dominated by the 200-ft-high spire of Pearson's church at South Dalton.

Beverley remains out of sight until the last minute, then has the best approach of any Yorkshire town, across the Westwood and straight into the old town through the North Bar to St Mary's. No town in England has two more glorious churches. The Minster displays continuity of design with flexibility of detail; Early English transepts and chancel; Decorated and Perpendicular nave, and w front, for which, like the Percy Shrine and the NE chapel at St Mary's, no praise can be too high. St Mary's is one of the most lovable and colourful of great parish churches. Most of the best Georgian buildings survive (delightful Market Cross) but the matrix of little houses is being whittled away and brutal road widenings have affected even the best areas.

South-East

Flat countryside as far as Nottinghamshire is good for Ecclesiologists. Norman doorways at Stillingfleet (original ironwork) and Riccall, Anglo-Scandinavian tower at Skipworth. Selby Abbey nave is as much textbook of the development of the Norman style as the chancel is of the perfection of the Decorated. Snaith, Thorne, and Hatfield have other fine medieval churches. Birkin is a complete Norman church. St George's at Doncaster must have been glorious before the fire and Sir G.G. Scott's prickly rebuilding, Paine's Assembly Rooms are a reminder of a fashionable 18th-century centre. But the best churches are along the N side of the Ouse and the Humber estuary: Hemingbrough and Howden with Wressle Castle between, Cottingham, Holy Trinity at Hull, and further east Hedon, Skirlaugh, and, almost at Spurn Point, Patrington. Perhaps only the group between Kings Lynn and Boston can compare with them for splendour.

South-West

Leeds and Bradford, Huddersfield and Halifax, Dewsbury and Wakefield – industrial West Yorkshire – are all too near. The A64 misses Norman churches at Healaugh and Wighill and a Perpendicular one at Bolton Percy, on its way to Tadcaster, famous for beer (and Bramham Park, for its formal gardens). Leeds is still the most rewarding of the larger cities, though its Victorian heritage has been savagely treated. Brodrick's Town Hall crowns what remains. Kirk-'stall Abbey is one of the finest of Cistercian ruins, its site still faintly suggesting former beauty. The glorious Carolean mansion of Temple Newsam and the Norman church at Adel are notable suburban attractions. Wakefield – improbably – has the finest medieval bridge chapel in England. Industry is by no means without nobility; the countryside around is still splendid, especially in Calderdale at Hepton-stall and Hebden Bridge. Haworth, Yorkshire's literary shrine, is a fine tough village under tourist trappings. The Brontës' Parsonage seems to have been a comfortable house.

West

The A59 bypasses Upper Poppleton green, Nether Poppleton church, Nun Monkton Priory, and the pre-Conquest
church at Kirk Hammerton, all just away from the main
road. Harrogate should, in any case, be visited by train, for
the marvellous journey across the viaduct at Knaresborough
– itself one of the pleasantest places to spend a day from
York: castle and church, riverside, and Dropping Well. St
Robert's Chapel carved out of the rock. Harrogate is a spa
town. Had it started a few years earlier it could have been
another Cheltenham. The Royal Hall has enchanting decor.
St Wilfrid's church by Temple Moore is the one great
building; Harlow Car Gardens the Headquarters of the
Northern Horticultural Society; Brimham Rocks is the
ultimate in natural entertainment.

Harewood – Georgian village, great Carr–Adam–Barry
house and medieval monuments in the church – is towards
lower Wharfedale. Otley, Ilkley, and Skipton are dark
gritstone towns in sharp contrast to the glittering limestone
countryside around Malham and Grassington. Bolton Priory
was deservedly a favourite subject for great topographical
painters.

North-West

Aldborough is Isurium Brigantium of the Romans and
much has been excavated. Excellent Museum. The Devil's
Arrows, Boroughbridge, are even older. Newby Hall has
lovely Adam interiors and in the park is one of Burges's
sumptuous churches. Ripon Minster is squat, hunched, with
a Saxon crypt, evidences of late-Norman and Decorated
rebuilding and a nave giving hints of developments in the
Gothic style had not the events of the 1530s overtaken it.
Studley Royal Park has another glorious Burges church, a
great 18th-century garden layout exactly transitional between the formal and informal styles, Fountains Abbey
(Cistercian), the largest of our monastic ruins becoming the

greatest of garden ornaments, sombre, not a building with flights of fancy; the Department of the Environment is now sterilizing it. Down a lane off the A61, Markenfield Hall is a moated and fortified mansion of *c.* 1310, little known, tatty but unspoiled.

Appendix: Some York Architects

York architectural practices tend to be dynastic, making it easier to deal with them chronologically than alphabetically.

John Etty   (*c.* 1634–1708)

A master-carpenter fulsomely described as an architect on his monument in All Saints', North Street. Associated with work at Helmsley, Temple Newsam, Newby. Thoresby describes him as 'Mr. Etty, sen, the architect' with whom 'the celebrated (Grinling) Gibbons wrought at York'.

William Etty   (*c.* 1675–1734)

Son of John; carpenter, carver, and architect. Carved the reredos in St Michael-le-Belfrey. Architect of Holy Trinity church, Leeds. Worked with Vanbrugh at Seaton Delaval and Castle Howard, where he also assisted Hawksmoor on the Mausoleum.

William Thornton   (*c.* 1670–1721)

Carpenter and joiner with architectural connexions; the superb woodwork at Beningbrough is likely to have been designed as well as made by him. Responsible for the marvellous timber frame that winched upright the N transept of Beverley Minster. Monument in St Olave's church.

William Wakefield (d. 1730)

Gentleman architect of Huby associated by Drake with Gilling Castle and Duncombe Park. Did unexecuted designs for the Assembly Rooms, and probably designed the Debtor's Prison. An early disciple of Vanbrugh.

John Carr (1723–1808)

The most successful provincial architect of the 18th century. Worked for Burlington. Set up practice in the 1750s. His Knavesmire Grandstand (1755) quickly established him with the local gentry. His work is competent, professional, lacking the spark of greatness; initially Palladian refreshed with Rococo plasterwork (Fairfax House), his style quickly modified through something more personal (Castlegate House) to accomplished Adamesque of the Assize Courts. Heath Hall, Everingham Hall, Harewood (where as at Wentworth Woodhouse he was estate architect), Denton Park, Farnley Halt, the Buxton Crescent, the Hospital of San Antonio, Oporto, Portugal. Surveyed the fabric of the Minster (1770) and the Bridges of the North Riding (1772–1803). Twice Lord Mayor of York. Built the church in his native Horbury, Wakefield (1791–3), at his own expense and is buried there.

Peter Atkinson, Senior (1735–1805)

Carr's assistant, succeeded to Carr's practice when he retired *c.* 1790, but did not outlive him. Hackness Hall and No. 51 Bootham for Sir R.V.B. Johnstone, Bart. Buried in churchyard of St Mary Bishophill Senior.

Peter Atkinson, Junior (*c.* 1776–1843)

Son of Peter Atkinson, Senior, became a partner in 1801 and continued after his father's death. 1819–27 was in partnership with R.H. Sharp. Several public buildings in the city have been replaced but Ouse Bridge and Foss Bridge remain, more agreeable than dreary Commissioners' churches.

John Bownas Atkinson (1807–74) and William Atkinson (1810/11–86)

Sons of Peter Atkinson, Junior; J.B. Atkinson taken into partnership *c.* 1828 and his brother in 1837. They are underestimated. Their classical work (County Hospital, Mill Mount House, Mount School) is strong and individual, their Gothic church practice much less so. William was probably the classicist and took James Demaine (1842–1911) into partnership in 1877, a shadowy figure at present difficult to assess.

Walter Brierley (1862–1926)

Became a partner after William Atkinson's death. He was an architect of immense skill and versatility; not revolutionary but capable of a functional design where necessary. Eclectic both in approach and sources of inspiration, where Belcher, Lethaby, Ernest Newton, and Robson are more apparent than say Voysey and Baillie-Scott. His best work was done before the First World War; classical pomp followed, lacking Lutyens's witty scholarship. His style can be seen emergent at Fishergate School, fully-fledged at Scarcroft Road School. Ousefield, Danesmead, and work at the Kings Manor play the same design game with entirely different results. One of the three best architects to have practised in the city.

Later partners include H. Rutherford, J.S. Syme, Cecil Leckenby, and the firm continues today as Brierley, Leckenby, Keighley and Groom.

Thomas Atkinson (*c.* 1729–98)

A leading local architect of the late 18th century, not apparently related to the other Atkinsons. Equally skilful at Gothic (Bishopthorpe Palace) and classic design, in which at Brandsby church and the Bar Convent Chapel he showed uncommon subtlety in handling of space. Designed No. 20 St Andrewgate for himself, and died insolvent. Monument in St Saviour's church.

Peter Frederick Robinson (1776–1858) and George Townshend Andrews (1804–55)

Robinson was a London architect with an extensive Northern practice, including the York Gaol, the old Midland Bank, and the De Grey Rooms, in which he worked in partnership with Andrews, who took over the York practice when Robinson moved to Boulogne (for financial reasons) in 1840. Andrews designed numerous railway stations for George Hudson, models of restrained elegance in an immediately recognizable Italianate style. York Old Station and Paragon Station, Hull, are his largest works but many smaller stations (Pocklington, Stamford Bridge, etc.) are thought out with equal care. As so often his Gothic work is less assured.

Rawlins Gould (1822–73)

Took over the practice after Andrew's death, coarsening both classical and Gothic products, conditions not improved by subsequent developments as Gould and Fisher, and Fisher and Hepper.

Charles Watson (*c.* 1770–1836) and James Piggot Pritchett (1789–1868)

Watson practised in York from 1807 and was in partnership with Pritchett from 1813 to 1831. Credit is difficult to apportion. The Friends Meeting House (1816–19) was a joint work. The Assembly Rooms front (1828) is solidly satisfactory, but the Savings Bank (1829) and Cemetery Chapel (1836) are little masterpieces of the Greek Revival. Tudory buildings in the Close are less happy. J.P. Pritchett, Junior (Fulford church) moved the practice to Darlington, where it continued into this century.

John Harper (1809–42)

Died sadly early, of malaria, in Italy. Could manage both the classical (St Leonard's Place) and Gothic (St Peter's School) styles with equal accomplishment. Must share the credit for Everingham church with Agostino Giorgioli.

George Fowler Jones (1819–1911)

Practised in York from the mid 1840s. His Gothic is coarse, occasionally fun; certainly individualistic. Clifton, Heworth, and St Thomas's churches and much restoration work.

William Hey Dykes (1821–60)

A pupil of Kempthorne and Benjamin Ferrey. Restored St Helen's church. Died as a result of falling through the ice when skating on the Ouse.

Walter G. Penty (1853–1902)

Began as a disciple of Alfred Waterhouse (Institute of Arts and Sciences, Clifford Street) with a brick and terra-cotta style fluctuating between Byzantine, Romanesque, and Renaissance. Majestic Leetham's Mill marks a departure of the mid 1890s when his son Arthur Penty became a partner. The new style was influenced by Norman Shaw and Voysey, and directly by George Walton (1867–1933) of Glasgow, who helped with decorations at Elm Bank. The Pentys' other Art Nouveau masterpiece, the Davy Hall, was demolished in the 1950s. Arthur Penty moved to Canada after his father's death.

Edwin Ridsdale Tate   (1861–1922)

Born in York, but spent some years in London before setting up practice here in 1902. An inventive restorer, in the best sense, and a draughtsman of great sensibility. Responsible for two of the strangest buildings in York, Tempest Anderson Hall, and the Anchorage on All Saints' North Street, in shuttered concrete, playing at styles.

George G. Pace   (1915–75)

Started his practice in York in 1946, specializing in ecclesiastical work. Restored Llandaff Cathedral after war damage and became consultant architect to nine other cathedrals, Surveyor of St George's Chapel, Windsor, and to six Dioceses, as well as holding many honorary consultative posts. Extended Comper's 'Beauty by Inclusion' to encompass the modern movement, but his interpretation of that was as individualistic as his extractions from Gothic, Classical, and Vernacular traditions. His University Library, Durham, exquisitely right in its intimidating setting, could not be more different from tough, aggressive William Temple church, Wythenshawe, yet the approach is entirely consistent. A sensitive restorer, he believed in leaving well alone; his design work was never less than profoundly considered and sometimes more than startling. A reserved public image hid a delightful sense of humour.

Two notable Victorian architects were born in the city, Joseph Aloysuis Hansom (1803–82) in Micklegate, and

George Goldie (1828–87) in St Leonard's. Both worked extensively for the Roman Catholics, designing respectively St George's and St Wilfrid's churches in York, though they did not have York practices.

Glossary of Architectural Terms

Abacus   Slab-like, upper part of a capital.

Abutment   Mass of masonry resisting a structural thrust.

Acanthus   Stylized lobed leaf form much used in classical decoration, especially on Corinthian and Composite capitals.

Aedicule   Classical surround to a window or door; from *aedicula*, a small temple.

Ambulatory   A processional way behind a main altar.

Apse   Semicircular or polygonal end to a building or room.

Arabesque   Delicate surface ornament of fronds, flowers, vases, etc.

Arcade   Free standing line of piers and arches.

Arch   Structural device for spanning openings, usually to a curved outline, consisting of wedge-shaped elements called *voussoirs*. Many forms indicative of period. (See fig. 1.)

Architrave   Lowest member of the classical entablature. The moulded frame to an opening.

Ashlar   Evenly worked masonry with squared edges and thin joints.

Atrium   The internal courtyard of a Roman House. A forecourt.

Attic   The space within a roof. Part of a classical design above the main cornice.

Aumbry   Cupboard to house sacred vessels.

Bailey   The open court or courts of a castle (inner and outer bailey).

Ball Flower   Early-14th-century ornament of a ball set inside a three-lobed globe.

Baluster   Small pillar of moulded and swelling outline to support a parapet.

Barbican   Defensive outwork to a gate consisting of parallel walls linked by an outer arch.

Bargeboards   Boards, often decorative, set against gable ends to protect structural elements behind.

Baroque   Style originating in Rome in the 17th century; a reaction against classicism; though the vocabulary remained the same its use was much freer and more emotional.

Basilica   An aisled hall, essentially Roman or Early Christian.

Bastion   Projecting defensive tower on the line of a wall.

Battlement (*crenellation*)   Indented parapet, originally defensive but frequently purely decorative. The low parts are *embrasures*, the high parts are *merlons*.

Bay A compartment, usually repeated, defined by principal structural elements.

Beakhead Formalized bird's head with prominent beak. Norman.

Berm Level ground between defensive wall and ditch.

Billet Norman ornament of small cylindrical elements.

Black-and-White See *Timber Framing*.

Blind Arcade Small-scale arcade used decoratively on a wall face.

Block Capital Norman capital; cubical, the underside rounded and tapered to column shape.

Bond The arrangement of brickwork in a wall.

  Stretchers are bricks laid with long side showing.

  Headers are bricks laid with short end showing.

  Stretcher Bond is laid with all stretchers.

  English Bond is laid with alternate courses of stretchers and headers.

  Flemish Bond is laid with stretchers and headers alternating in a course.

Boss Carved, projecting block at the intersections of vaulting ribs, etc.

Bow Window Curved projecting window. Late Georgian, Regency, and, alas, modern.

Box Pew High panelled church pew with a door.

Bressumer Horizontal beam to support a projecting upper storey.

Broach Spire Octagonal spire drawn out of lower pyramidal form.

Buttress Projecting masonry or brickwork support to a wall. Angle buttresses meet at the corner. Clasping buttresses enclose the corner like a turret. Diagonal buttresses are set at an angle to the corner. Flying buttresses are half arches set against buttresses especially to support high stone vaults.

Cable Mould Cord-like Norman ornament.

Campanile Detached bell tower.

Canopy Projecting feature protecting an opening, statue, etc., often richly ornamented.

Capital The upper termination of a column or pier.

Cartouche Acanthus, cherubs, flowers, etc., composed to frame an inscription or coat of arms.

Caryatid Female figure supporting an entablature.

Chamfer The most basic of mouldings where the angle between two planes at right angles is cut away at 45°.

Chancel The eastern arm of a church.

Chantry Chapel endowed for saying Mass for the soul of the founder etc.

Chevet Fully developed apsidal end to a church with ambulatory and radiating chapels.

Chevron Norman zigzag ornament, capable of great variety.

Choir The place where service was sung, loosely applied as the eastern arm of the church, cf. chancel.

Clerestory   The upper stage of a building pierced by windows.

Coadestone   Late-18th-century, early-19th-century artificial stone of great durability.

Coffering   Repeated square or polygonal panels sunk in the face of a ceiling or vault.

Colonnade   Range of columns supporting an entablature.

Console   Classical bracket of complex outline like a drawn-out volute.

Corbel   Projecting block supporting a structural or decorative feature.

Corbel Table   Range of corbels along the upper part of a wall.

Cornice   The uppermost, projecting section of a classical entablature. Any projecting crowning feature running horizontally.

Cove   Prominent concave surface between wall and ceiling.

Crocket   Regularly spaced leaf-shaped knobs. Gothic, on gables, pinnacles, etc.

Crypt   Underground or semi-underground stage of a church – usually below the eastern arm – or of a secular building.

Cupola   Domed turret, popular on stable blocks.

Cusp   The pointed element formed between the foils of a foiled opening.

Dado   Panelling along the lower part of a wall.

Dagger   Symmetrical, cusped tracery element pointed at both ends.

Decorated   English architecture of the last quarter of the 13th century and first half of the 14th century.

Diapering   Repeated surface patterning of square or lozenge shapes, foliated.

Dogtooth   Universal Early English ornament of pyramidal star shapes.

Dormer   Window within a roof slope with its own roof above.

Dutch Gable   A gable of curved outline crowned by a pediment, loosely used of all curving gables.

Early English   English architecture of the first three-quarters of the 13th century.

Embrasure   Small defensive window, widely splayed inside. The openings in battlements.

Encaustic Tiles   Glazed earthenware tiles, patterned.

Engaged Column   Half or more of a column attached to a wall face.

Entablature   Horizontal structural element in classical architecture, spanning between columns. Comprises architrave, frieze, and cornice.

Feretory   Chapel behind the high altar to house the chief relics.

Finial   Foliated top ornament of a canopy or pinnacle.

Flamboyant   Late French Gothic with flamelike and waving forms.

Fleche   Tall spirelet of light construction set on a roof ridge.

Flushwork   East Anglian decoration of stone tracery and panels inset with cut flint.

Fluting   The vertical channels on a classical column, usually 24 in number.

Foil   Lobe of a cusped form; hence *Trefoil, Quatrefoil*, etc.

Foliated   Leafed.

Fresco   Painting on wet plaster.

Frieze   Central section of a classical entablature, between architrave and cornice.

Gable   The flat end of a pitched roof.

Galilee   Western chapel or porch.

Gardérobe   A medieval lavatory.

Gargoyle   Horizontal waterspout often carved with great fancy.

Gazebo   Look-out tower or summerhouse.

Geometrical   English architecture of late 13th, early 14th centuries with tracery formed of circles and other simple geometrical forms.

Gibbs Surround   Early-18th-century door and window treatment where orthodox classical elements are alternated with large stone blocks.

Grisaille   Painting in shades of grey.

Groin   The intersection of two vaulting surfaces, without ribs.

Grotesque   Fanciful ornament.

Hagioscope   Squint, an internal window allowing a view from one part of a building to another.

Half-timbering   See *Timber Framing*.

Herringbone   Anglian and Early Norman masonry; small stones set on a slope reversing direction with each course.

Hood Mould or *Label*   Weathering moulding over a window.

Hypocaust   Hollow floor on short pillars for hot-air central heating.

Impost   Horizontal band or moulding on which an arch rests.

Jetty   The overhang of the upper floors of a timber-framed house.

Keep or *Donjon*   The most strongly fortified tower of a castle, usually with extensive living accommodation.

Keystone   The apex of an arch.

Lacing Course   Horizontal band bonding together the face and core of a wall, may be large stones or bricks.

Lancet   Narrow, sharply pointed openings characteristic of Early English style.

Lantern   Open, traceried tower or turret.

Light   The individual glazed areas of a window.

Linenfold   Tudor panelling carved with a representation of linen in vertical folds.

Lintel   Horizontal member spanning an opening.

Loggia   Covered colonnade or arcade open on one or more sides.

Glossary of Architectural Terms

Long and Short Work Anglian system of quoining with stone posts alternating with flat slates.

Louvre Roof opening to let out smoke from a central hearth. Infilling of belfry windows with inclined slabs for sound transmission.

Lozenge Diamond shape.

Lychgate Roofed churchyard gate for the reception of a coffin.

Machicolation Military. Deeply projecting parapet on brackets. Designed for dropping missiles on attackers below.

Mannerism· Highly intellectual style in 16th-century Italy involving subtle reinterpretation of classical themes, often with very disturbing results.

Mansard Roof Roof with a double slope, admitting an extra storey.

Mathematical Tiles Interlocking tiles applied to timber framing to give an appearance of brickwork.

Mezzanine An intermediate storey.

Misericord Tip-up seat with carved bracket beneath to provide support during long services. Also called a *miserere.*

Modillion Bracket repeated beneath the main projecting element of an Ionic or Corinthian cornice.

Mouldings Narrow flat or curved bands designed to catch the light. The Gothic and classical styles each had its characteristic repertoire of profiles, the classical ones being minutely governed by rules of proportion. (See fig. 2.)

Motte and Bailey Earliest form of Norman Castle with a mount and bailey, both moated and defended by timber pallisades.

Mouchette Cusped tracery element with asymmetrical curving outline.

Mullion Vertical member between window lights.

Nailhead Late-12th-century, early-13th-century ornament of small pyramids.

Newel The main structural vertical of a staircase.

Newel Stair A spiral staircase round a central newel, usually stone.

Nodding Ogee Ogee arch projecting in three dimensions.

Norman English Romanesque style, mid 11th, late 12th century.

Order Concentric layers of an arch, especially Norman.

Orders Backbone of classical architecture, originating in Greece, adapted by the Romans and revived during the Renaissance. Five principal orders: *Tuscan, Doric, Ionic, Corinthian, Composite* (see fig. 3). Capable of infinite variation. The subject is vast.

Oriel Window Window projecting from an upper storey.

Palladian Architecture following the rules, though seldom the inspiration of Andrea Palladio.

Palladian Window Popular 18th-century motif of a three-light

311

window with a tall arched central light between lower rectangular lights.

Parapet   Low wall surrounding a roof.

Pargeting   External ornamental plasterwork.

Patera   Small circular classical ornament.

Pedestal   Block supporting classical statue or column.

Pediment   Low gable end to a classical temple with horizontal and raking cornices. Essential to the vocabulary of 18th-century windows and doors. Segmental pediments were common, and they sometimes took on fanciful shapes. *Broken pediments* have a gap in the horizontal cornice. *Open pediments* have a gap between the two raking cornices.

Pendant   Boss or vaulting form elongated downwards.

Pendentive   The device for converting a square or polygonal plan shape to a circular one to take a dome: consisting of sections of a hemisphere struck from the largest diameter.

Perpendicular   English Gothic from the mid 14th to early 16th century, characterized by vertical lines. A wholly English creation in startling contrast to French Flamboyant.

Piano Nobile   The principal, usually first floor of a classical house.

Pier   The support for an arcade.

Pilaster   Shallow sections of classical columns applied to wall face, or broad, flat, Norman buttresses.

Pinnacle   Upper termination of Gothic buttresses, parapets, and towers, of tapering crocketed outline. May be structural in providing additional weight to resist a thrust, or purely decorative.

Piscina   Stone basin for washing Sacred vessels.

Podium   The stepped base of a classical building.

Poppyhead   Foliated finial to bench ends.

Portico   Classical feature based on a temple front.

Postern   Small gateway.

Presbytery   The part of a church where the altar is placed.

Pulpitum   Stone screen separating choir from nave.

Quoins   Dressed angle stones of a building.

Rendering   The plastering of an external wall.

Reredos   Screen with canopies, images etc. behind an altar.

Respond   Half column or other termination of an arcade against a wall.

Rococo   Late, lighter phase of Baroque; mid 18th century.

Romanesque   Norman style of the late 11th, early 12th century, characterized by round-headed arches.

Rood   Cross or crucifix generally placed at the entrance to the chancel above a screen with gallery approached by staircases, known respectively as rood screen, rood loft, and rood stairs.

Roofs   Common rafters were the basis of all traditional roof construction. Single-framed roofs had only these transverse elements, often with collars, ties and struts, but not tied together longitudinally. Double-framed roofs introduce trusses at intervals supporting purlins, which in turn support the common rafters, allowing more economical construction and greater spans. (See fig. 4.)

Rose Window   A traceried circular window.

Rotunda   A circular building usually domed.

Rustication   Rock-faced stonework used particularly on quoins and on the lower storeys of classical buildings.

Saddleback   Short gabled roof over a church tower.

Sanctuary   Area round an altar.

Sash Window   Georgian and after. Window designed in two planes, which slide in front of one another, either vertically or horizontally.

Scagliola   Imitation marble.

Scalloped Capital   Block capital with conical elements on the under surface.

Screen   Timber or stone partition used in both domestic and ecclesiastical work.

Screens Passage   Passage between kitchen and hall in medieval planning.

Sedilia   Seats for priests on south of chancel.

Soffit   Underside of an arch or horizontal member.

Solar   Medieval living room, almost always upstairs.

Sounding Board   Flat canopy over a pulpit.

Spandrel   The flat area between two arches.

Spire   Pyramidal or conical tower termination. The junction with tower capable of endless variety. (See *Broach Spire*.)

Springing   The level at which the curve of an arch starts.

Stanchion   Upright steel member.

Stiff Leaf   Lobed conventional foliage of Early English capitals.

Storey Posts   The main posts in a timber-framed wall.

Stoup   Stone bowl for holy water near church door.

Strapwork   Elizabethan and Jacobean ornament of flat interlacing bands.

Stretcher   See *Bond*.

String Course   Projecting horizontal moulding or band on the surface of a wall.

Stucco   Plaster.

Studs   Subsidiary verticals in a timber-framed wall.

Swag   Carved decoration based on suspended cloth.

Terracotta   Unglazed, burnt clay used for decorative elements.

Tessellated Pavements   Flooring made of tesserae, small pieces of marble, stone, brick, or glass set in cement to form patterns, figures, etc.; Roman.

Three-decker Pulpit   Pulpit, reading desk, and clerk's desk on descending levels.

Timber Framing   Also known as *half-timbering* and *black-and-white*. Structural system of wooden beams, posts, struts, etc., often involving one or more overhanging storeys. The spaces between the frame are filled with lath and plaster or brickwork.

Tomb Chest   Medieval box-shaped tomb, often with supporting effigies and richly decorated.

Tracery   The stone framework of a Gothic window, developed from the coupling of lancets and the piercing of the space between their heads to windows of great size and elaboration designed to show off the products of the stained-glass artist. Plate tracery, the earliest form, is cut out of flat slabs. Bar tracery is formed of moulded or chamfered sections common both to straight mullions and curved tracery elements. Tracery designs were also much used as a wall decoration. (See fig. 5.)

Transept   The cross arm of a church.

Transom   A horizontal member in window tracery.

Tribune   Large gallery at triforium (q.v.) level.

Triforium   Central horizontal subdivision in Romanesque or Early Gothic church above the arcade and below the clerestory.

Tympanum   Panel, carved or traceried, between the springing line and an arch.

Undercroft   Underground or semi-underground room below more important building.

Vault   Stone vaulting was one of the great ambitions of the medieval architect.

    Barrel Vault. Early Romanesque, continuous semicircular section on side walls.

    Groin or *Cross Vault*. Intersecting barrel vaults concentrating thrust.

    Rib Vault. With introduction of pointed arch. The ribs built first as permanent shuttering then the *webs* or spaces between filled in.

    Quadripartite Vault. Each bay divided into four quarter vaults.

    Sexpartite Vault. Double bays transversely divided so that each has six parts.

    Tierceron Vault. Additional ribs from springing to ridge, from early 13th century.

    Lierne Vault.   Has more ribs joining the tiercerons etc. to form star patterns etc., from end of 13th century.

    Fan Vault.   Ribs fanning out from springing, all the same length and curvature. Ribs and panels no longer formed of separate stones, from mid 14th century.

Vaulting Shaft   Wall shaft to support a vault.

Venetian Window   Wide-arched opening between two lower rectangular ones. Popular 18th-century motif from Palladio.

Volute   Spiral scroll of Ionic capital (also used in Corinthian and Composite).

Waggon Roof   Roof with closely set curved braces.

Wainscot   Panelled wall linings and partitions.

Waterleaf Capital   Late-12th-century flat leaves turned in at the top corners.

Wealden House   Timber-framed hall between two jettied wings, the eaves running across at the outer line leaving deep cove over recessed centre.

Weatherboarding   Overlapping horizontal boards to weatherproof exterior.

ARCHES

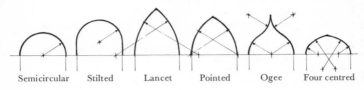

Semicircular Stilted Lancet Pointed Ogee Four centred

Fig. 1

MOULDINGS

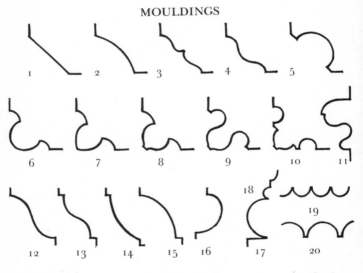

1 Chamfer	8 Filletted roll	14 Ovolo
2 Hollow chamfer	9 Filletted roll between hollows	15 Cavetto
3 Double ogee		16 Scotia
4 Wave mould	10 Triple Filletted Roll	17 Torus
5 Hollow	11 Scroll Mould	18 Astragal
6 Roll	12 Cyma	19 Reeding
7 Keeled roll	13 Cyma reversa	20 Fluting

Fig. 2

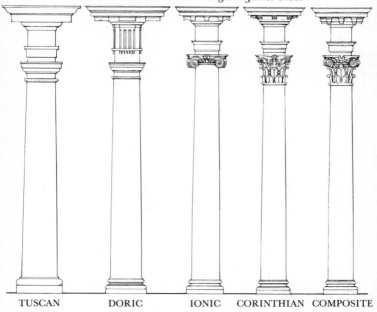

Roman orders based on the designs of James Gibbs

TUSCAN   DORIC   IONIC   CORINTHIAN   COMPOSITE

Fig. 3

ROOFS

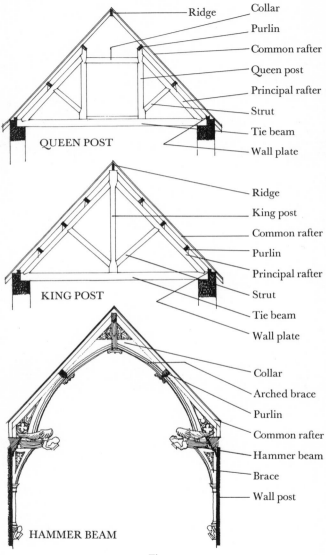

QUEEN POST

- Ridge
- Collar
- Purlin
- Common rafter
- Queen post
- Principal rafter
- Strut
- Tie beam
- Wall plate

KING POST

- Ridge
- King post
- Common rafter
- Purlin
- Principal rafter
- Strut
- Tie beam
- Wall plate

HAMMER BEAM

- Collar
- Arched brace
- Purlin
- Common rafter
- Hammer beam
- Brace
- Wall post

Fig. 4

TRACERY

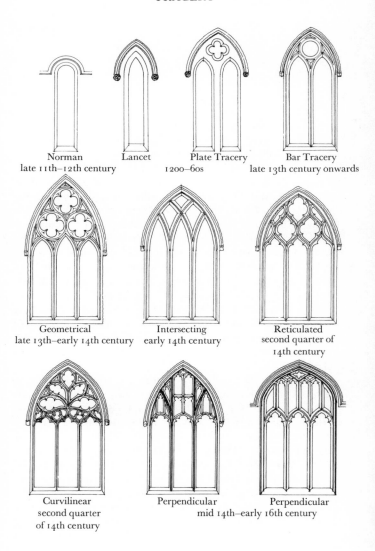

Norman
late 11th–12th century

Lancet

Plate Tracery
1200–60s

Bar Tracery
late 13th century onwards

Geometrical
late 13th–early 14th century

Intersecting
early 14th century

Reticulated
second quarter of
14th century

Curvilinear
second quarter
of 14th century

Perpendicular
mid 14th–early 16th century

Perpendicular

Fig. 5

Further Reading

The first great history and description of the city and Minster, still in many ways the best, is Francis Drake's *Eboracum* (1736, facsimile reprint 1978). Sir Thomas Widdrington's *Analecta Eboracensia* (*c.* 1660) was not published until 1897, and Thomas Gent's rather strange productions, *Ancient and Modern History of the Famous City of York* (1730) and his book on the *Great Eastern Window* (1757), cannot seriously compete. Drake was republished in various diminished forms and remained the basis of most subsequent histories. Useful additional information is provided by Hargrove's *History of York* (1818) and Sheahan and Whellan's *History and Topography of the City of York* (1855 and 1857), Davies's *Walks through the City of York* (1880), sadly a fragmentary work, George Benson's three volumes *An Account of the City and County of the City of York* (1911–25, reprinted 1968) and C.B. Knight's *History of the City of York* (1944).

The best modern scholarly history is *A History of Yorkshire, The City of York*, edited by P.M. Tillott (*Victoria County History*, 1961). *The Noble City of York*, edited A. Stacpoole (1972), has a series of articles, at best excellent, but very variable in quality. What should be a definitive account of all significant buildings before 1850 is in progress as *An Inventory of Historical Monuments in the City of York* (Royal Commission on Historical Monuments), four volumes to date (1962–75); another is promised soon. These are bulky volumes, not easy to follow, certainly not handy to carry about. They are also curiously uninformative on, not to say unobservant of, architectural values. Readers who prefer to start with shorter introductory reading are referred to the excellent *Portrait of York* by R. Willis (1972) and *York* by John

Harvey (1975). Patrick Nuttgens' *York (City Buildings Series,* 1970) is a superbly illustrated account of York's architecture, and Sir Nikolaus Pevsner's *Yorkshire: York and the East Riding* (Penguin *Buildings of England* series, 1970) is a scholarly catalogue of the most important buildings. Two enjoyable collections of early photographs are R. Willis, *York As It Was* (1973) and R. and T. Willis, *York Past and Present* (1975).

Everything published on the Minster is out-of-date, even *A History of York Minster,* editors G.E. Aylmer and R. Cant (1977), another volume minimizing the artistic importance of its subject; a series of scholarly articles on various aspects of the Minster fabric and history, sharing with the present work an interesting line in omissions. The Royal Commission volume and the account of the excavations are still being prepared. The finds during the excavations were so remarkable as to invalidate all previous theories on the Minster's early history. However, there is still much to be said for the series of classic works of the early and mid 19th century, not least the superb quality of their illustrations. *Gothic Ornaments of York Minster,* Joseph Halfpenny (1795), *Twelve Perspective Views of the Metropolitical Church at York,* Charles Wild (1809), *The History and Antiquities of the Metropolitical Church at York,* John Britton (1819), with exquisite engravings; but most magnificent is *The History of the Metropolitan Church of St Peter, York,* by John Browne (1847). G.A. Poole and J.W. Hugall's *Historical and Descriptive Guide to York Cathedral* (1850) rounds the series off rather less memorably; Dean Purey Cust's *Walks round York Minster* has interesting information on the monuments. J. Raine's *The Fabric Rolls of York Minster* (1859) provoked Browne's *Defence* of his own great book (1863), a nice comment on the controversies raised by architectural history in the 19th century. Clutton Brock's volume on the Minster in *Bell's Cathedral* series has opinions that we need not share today, but at least it has them. Dean Addleshaw's work on Minster artists between 1590 and 1960 (1962, republished in *Journal of Architectural Historians of Great Britain,* 1967) is an invaluable piece of research.

Works on stained glass are almost as out of date as those on the Minster, thanks to Dean Milner White's ministrations. Benson's *Ancient and Painted Glass of the Minster and Churches of the City of York* (1915), J.A. Knowles's *The York School of Glass Painting* (1936), and Chancellor Harrison's *The Painted Glass of York* (1927) should certainly be consulted, together with the *Reports* of the Friends of York Minster. The most recent, though not quite comprehensive account of the Minster windows, is in *A History of York Minster*.

J. Halfpenny's *Fragmenta Vetusta* (1807) and H. Cave's *Antiquities of York* (1813) both record much of interest and beauty that has vanished. *The Churches of York*, by Monkhouse and Bedford (*c.* 1845), is a beautifully illustrated record of their condition before Victorian restoration. J. Morris's *Little Guide to York* (1924) is still a sound guide to the churches. *Some Account of the Ancient and Present State of the Abbey of St Mary, York* (1829) by C. Wellbeloved has excellent illustrations of the newly-excavated site before the building of the Yorkshire Museum.

On the defences, T.P. Cooper's two books are still essential reading, *York: The Story of its Walls and Castles* (1904) and *The History of York Castle* (1911). Both Cooper and George Benson produced many learned articles on aspects of the city's history and Benson's two articles in *Burdekins Old Moore's Almanac* for 1930 and 1931 are still the most informative available on the city's Victorian architects.

Detailed accounts of special periods include *Soldier and Civilian in Roman Yorkshire*, edited R.M. Butler (1971); *Viking Age York and the North*, edited R.A. Hall (1978); A. Raine, *Mediaeval York* (1955), a topographical account rather than a history; D.M. Palliser, *Tudor York* (1980); L.P. Wenham, *The Great and Close Siege of York* (1970); and A. Armstrong, *Stability and Change in an English County Town: A Social Study of York 1801–1851* (1974). Publication of the Minster excavations is still awaited, but several fascicules have already appeared in *The Archaeology of York*, a series of reports by the York Archaeological Trust edited by P.V. Addyman. The text of the miracle plays was published by L.T. Smith as *York Plays* (1885, reprinted 1963), and modernized by J.S. Purvis as *The York Cycle of Mystery Plays*

(1957). The literature on street-names is summarized in *York Historian*, vol. 2 (1978), pp. 2–16, and contemporary descriptions are reprinted in *York As They Saw it*, by D. and M. Palliser (1979). As to what might yet be, Lord Esher's *York* (1968) should certainly be studied.

The Corporation's archives will have moved to a new home behind the City Art Gallery by the time this book is published. The City Library includes an excellent York History Room with a fine collection of books and periodicals open to the public. The Minster Library in Dean's Park includes both a fine collection of printed material on the city and the archives of the Minster Dean and Chapter. The Borthwick Institute of Historical Research in St Anthony's Hall houses the archives of the archbishops and other ecclesiastical records of the city and of the whole Northern Province, including most of the city's parish registers. These three record offices are open to the public, but a prior appointment is advised. There are also smaller collections of archives still in the custody of the Companies of Merchant Adventurers and Merchant Taylors.

Index